Library of
Davidson College

SPENSER,
RONSARD, AND DU BELLAY

A RENAISSANCE COMPARISON

Spenser, Ronsard, and Du Bellay

A RENAISSANCE COMPARISON

BY ALFRED W. SATTERTHWAITE

KENNIKAT PRESS
Port Washington, N. Y./London

SPENSER, RONSARD, AND DU BELLAY

Copyright © 1960 by Princeton University Press
Reissued in 1972 by Kennikat Press by arrangement
Library of Congress Catalog Card No: 75-153279
ISBN 0-8046-1582-9

Manufactured by Taylor Publishing Company   Dallas, Texas

FOR
Mary S. Kurtz

PREFACE

EDMUND SPENSER is the first great poet of the English Renaissance. It has been recognized for a long time that his theory of poetry, and his poetry itself, owes some kind of debt to the work of the French poets of the Pléiade, principally to Joachim du Bellay and Pierre de Ronsard. Comparisons of these three poets have been made in the past, but they have usually consisted of a simple juxtaposition of analogous passages, placed side by side without critical analysis, or of a broad and general demonstration that all three poets subscribed to certain theories that are referred to as Renaissance clichés.

Among the three there are differences as well as likenesses, and these differences are as important to a full understanding of the poets as are the similarities. Furthermore, within the similarities themselves there are significant variations in the manner of statement that are sufficient to alter, if not the meaning itself, at least the tone.

It is the purpose of this study to set certain poems of Spenser beside certain other poems by Du Bellay and by Ronsard, not merely with a view to pointing out the resemblances, but in order to examine both the nature and extent of the likeness, and to demonstrate the discrepancies in tone that separate the poets. The common use by Renaissance poets of literary clichés that were current at the time is almost without significance, while the nuances in the quality of the use, on the other hand, show the originality of the poets and constitute a personal signature upon the common idea.

The Introduction first describes very generally the Renaissance framework into which the poets were born, and the first chapter places each poet more precisely against his own particular background. The differences that appear ini-

PREFACE

tially in the education of the poets, in their development during their formative years, will be seen to have an enduring consistency throughout their lives and careers. The second chapter establishes a tentative connection between Spenser and Du Bellay, and in an Appendix makes a detailed analysis of Spenser's early translations from the French poet, with a view to questioning his authorship of certain translated sonnets.

In the third chapter the relationships between the English movement to write quantitative verse and the Pléiade experiments in *vers mesurés* is examined in some detail, especially as it pertains to the three poets under consideration. The fourth chapter is a comparison of the attitudes of the poets to their Muses and to contemporary literature. The fifth compares and contrasts their ideas of time and of mutability; and the sixth considers their moral, or amoral, views of literature and of life itself.

At this point the chief likenesses and divergences have emerged, it is hoped, with some degree of clarity. The three chapters that follow (seven through nine) deal with the attitudes of all three poets toward the Platonic and neo-Platonic theories that were a part of the inherited culture of all educated men in the second half of the sixteenth century; and with the final religious orientation of the three, their vision of the world in the mirror of eternity.

Spenser and Ronsard are almost polar contrasts to each other, in spite of their many superficial likenesses; Du Bellay stands somewhere between them, linked in certain respects to both, but also separate and wholly individual. Finally, the relationship of each of these poets to the others, and to the Renaissance in his own country is seen not only to be particular and peculiar for each poet, but also to be typical of the development of the European Renaissance as a whole. In the Conclusion the dual nature of the Renaissance, which has been adumbrated in the Introduction, is further

PREFACE

defined, and is shown to be reflected in the work and in the lives of the three poets under discussion.

I owe particular and emphatic thanks to Professors Douglas Bush, Harry Levin, and Reuben Brower, under whose direction this book in its original form was written as a doctoral dissertation. Thanks also are due to Professor Cedric Whitman, whose knowledge of the classics was often helpful and always inspiring; and to Mrs. Firman Houghton, who read the original manuscript with patient kindness and who succeeded as I never could in leavening some of the pedantry.

I wish to express my gratitude to the Haverford College Research Fund for its generous grant in aid of publication.

I appreciate the courtesy of the editors of *Comparative Literature* and of the *Philological Quarterly* for their permission to reprint portions of the book which they have already published.

My greatest debt, however, is to my wife, not so much for her intrepid typing, as for the unfailing encouragement which made the book possible at all.

Haverford College   ALFRED W. SATTERTHWAITE

CONTENTS

PREFACE	vii
INTRODUCTION	3
I. THE YOUNG POETS	12
II. THE EARLY TRANSLATIONS FROM DU BELLAY	25
III. THEORY OF POETRY	37
IV. THE COMPLAINTS OF THE MUSES	66
V. THE CONQUEST OF TIME	93
VI. THE MORAL VISION OF THE WORLD	113
VII. PLATONISM IN SPENSER	133
VIII. PLATONISM IN DU BELLAY AND RONSARD	171
IX. DEVOTIONAL VERSE IN THE THREE POETS	201
CONCLUSION	240
APPENDICES	255
INDEX	275

SPENSER,
RONSARD, AND DU BELLAY
A RENAISSANCE COMPARISON

INTRODUCTION

A COMPARISON of Edmund Spenser, Joachim du Bellay, and Pierre de Ronsard is inevitably an essay on the Renaissance. In all the confusion of radical disagreement among scholars concerning the dates of the Renaissance, there is general accord in admitting that the second half of the sixteenth century in both France and England falls into this period. When it began, and when (or whether) it ended, is a more complex question about which many books have been—and will be—written.

Since Jacob Burckhardt in the nineteenth century—and certainly not for the first time—set up the Renaissance as a concept of cultural history, with national, social, religious, and psychological implications, there has been a host of denials, reversals, and qualifications of his thesis. It is not the purpose of this study to venture a definition of the Renaissance; that would be a foolhardy act of "surquedry," Spenser's word for the Greek *hubris*. It is, however, a significant part of my purpose to examine Spenser, Ronsard, and Du Bellay against the background of their received ideas, their inherited culture, as it is seen in their work. This culture is mainly classical, but, unlike the classical culture of the Middle Ages, it is Renaissance, and distinguishably so.

The meaning of the word Renaissance as it pertains to poetry in the period and in the two countries with which this book deals should become clearer in terms of the entire book. An attempt will be made in the conclusion to draw together the various threads of discussion, of comparison, and of investigation. For the time being, the broad lines of Renaissance and Reformation development may be indicated in a general fashion, to serve as guideposts to the final chapter.

The Renaissance was, among other things, a revival of

INTRODUCTION

classical learning. Humanism was the literary study of classical ideas of man. It goes without saying that these Greek and Roman ideas were non-Christian. They were pagan and were expressed in a variety of sources bound together by no single tradition, wholly free and eclectic. These sources could be studied in relation to Christianity, or by themselves, or in some tempered compromise between these extremes. By themselves the classics are purely humanistic in the sense that they deal chiefly with man as a terrestrial being. Wholly merged with Christian doctrine, as in Richard Hooker's *Of the Laws of Ecclesiastical Polity* (1594-1600), the classics are converted, or perhaps diverted, to a purpose that is predominantly Christian, and the result is called Christian humanism. But there are many stopping-places between the extremes.

There was a tendency in the pursuit of pure humanism to ignore religion, to find in the study of man for his own sake an end in itself. Men who devoted a major part of their time to a reading of the pagan classics, while they found no body of doctrine that was an acceptable substitute for organized Christianity, nevertheless tended to develop the *nonchalance du salut*[1] of which Pascal was later to accuse Montaigne. They did not become pagans, but they did move in the direction of a general skepticism. The degree of their skepticism is always difficult to ascertain since there was a reluctance on the part of all authors at this time to express views that might provoke a suspicion of unbelief. In addition, as Léon Brunschvicg has observed, the non-religious thinkers of the Renaissance did not dominate their material as they did in the next century.[2] They were not sure, themselves, of their own skepticism.

[1] The difficulty of translating the French word "nonchalance" is signalized by its adoption into English. The whole phrase "nonchalance du salut" may be adequately rendered as "a lukewarm attitude toward salvation."
[2] Léon Brunschvicg, *Le Progrès de la Conscience dans la Philosophie Occidentale* (Paris, 1927), I, 120.

INTRODUCTION

The Christian humanists, on the other hand, read the classics in the light of orthodox Christian doctrine. They preempted the classics to the use of Christianity, as Augustine had done with Plato, as Aquinas had done with Aristotle, and as Dante had done with Virgil according to the mediaeval interpretation of the fourth eclogue. But they were nevertheless men of the Renaissance in the sense that they were serious and devoted students of the recently rediscovered classics.

Two outstanding examples of Christian humanists before the Reformation are Erasmus, on the continent, and his friend Thomas More in England. More may stand as a link between the Middle Ages and the Renaissance, having as it were his soul in one and his heart in the other. For the tradition of Christian humanism is essentially continuous from the mediaeval to the Renaissance because it added the classical to the Christian, unlike the exclusively humanist tradition, which, as it took its inception in the revival of classical learning, tended to ignore or subtract the Christian and thus create a chasm between the Middle Ages and the Renaissance. To the humanist in the sixteenth century, Christianity sometimes became a formality, as the meaning of the classics claimed a position in the center of his thought. But for the Christian humanist the classics filled Christianity itself with a greater significance and wider validity.

The execution of Thomas More is not only the gesture of a new social world; it also marks, ironically, both the triumph of the Reformation in England and the temporary reprieve of Christian humanism. The Christian humanists, and More among them, had striven hard for a reconciliation within the Catholic Church. Luther and Henry VIII destroyed the conciliatory work of Colet and More. Calvin and Bèze in France destroyed the work of Bishop Briçonnet of Meaux and his circle of reforming Catholics. A breach was made between Catholic Christianity and other forms of Christian worship which came to be called Protestant.

INTRODUCTION

This split seemed at first to have nothing to do either with humanism or Christian humanism, since up to the time of the Reformation all humanists were not only Christians but also Catholics. Its causes and its effects were in a realm divorced from the scholarly pursuit of learning. The breach, however, was a blow from which Christian humanism on the continent never recovered, and, in England, Renaissance Christian humanism received no more than a liberal extension of time.

While the Reformation had other and more important causes than the nonchalance toward Christianity that humanist studies had generated, this nonchalance was a contributory factor. The Catholic Church, entrenched in a position of power throughout Europe, refused to recognize that the growing movement toward reform "was essentially a return to a purer morality, to a more primitive and inspired form of religion."[3] It could have provided this inspiration itself. In this sense, the movement was anti-humanist; it desired the real substance of Christianity, unembellished by learned doctrinal accretions.

While humanistic studies had distracted some scholars from Christian doctrine and from the Scriptures, it had sent others back to the Greek of the New Testament. Colet reexamined the Pauline teaching in its original language, as a Christian and as a humanist. Like Erasmus and like so many Catholic humanists before the Reformation, Colet looked for a reformation within the Church. These men wanted to reckon with the agitations from within, and prevent a schism. They were unsuccessful.

The breach, when it came, did not seriously affect the pure humanists. If anything, it improved their position, in spite of the stringent measures of the Counterreformation. Christianity had lost its universality: there was no longer one Church, but many churches. After the Reformation,

[3] Lilian Winstanley, "Spenser and Puritanism," *MLQ* 3 (1900), p. 6.

INTRODUCTION

if any scholar suspected that Christianity was an outworn formality, a way of life sanctioned not so much by God as by custom, he was likely to find substantiation for this opinion in the divisions of the Church and in the growing futility of the Church's repressive measures. Christian humanism was almost worn out, and became as difficult for Catholics as skeptical humanism became easy, until in the seventeenth century Jansenism arose within the Church as a native-born heresy along Augustinian lines that paralleled the original new interpretations of St. Paul by Colet a hundred and fifty years before.

Meanwhile, in England, after the Catholic interlude in the fifties, the Protestant Church struggled afresh to formulate a basis for separate existence. The entire atmosphere was far from nonchalant. Christianity and Christian doctrines were burning questions of the day. English translations of the Bible and Cranmer's *Prayerbook* were available in print. The skepticism of the continental humanists had very little place in a world in which the very bases of Christian belief were a matter for the examination of everyone who could read and think.

In this atmosphere Edmund Spenser grew to manhood and, growing, could reconcile his religious beliefs with his humanistic studies, as More and Colet had done in England before him. He could deplore contemporary Catholics, but a careful reading of the *Fowre Hymnes* reveals that he could also understand Dante as if very little except time stood between him and the Italian Catholic poet.

Ronsard and Du Bellay inherited the new Catholic dispensation of the Council of Trent which in Ronsard's lifetime had to fight for its existence. They also inherited the old tradition of humanistic studies that had made some fifteenth century Italians nonchalant about their salvation. Du Bellay died young, at thirty-eight, and seems never to have leaned seriously toward humanistic skepticism. Ronsard

INTRODUCTION

lived a long and productive life as a humanist poet. The reader will determine for himself whether Ronsard was a Christian humanist, as Spenser certainly was; or whether Ronsard may be said to represent an element in the Renaissance that had begun to separate itself from traditional Christianity and, without knowing it, to pave the way toward the march of modern science in the next century.

This book will have to give a meaning to these generalities through the medium of detailed comparisons. Douglas Bush maintains that Spenser stands on an eminence near the end of the English tradition of Christian humanism which began on the continent, came to England very late in the fifteenth century, and ended with Milton.[4] Certainly Spenser's admiration for the learned Catholic poet Chaucer is significant, and his religious connection with Colet is obvious. Spenser is a near ancestor of Milton, who owed him so much and admitted the debt so freely in *Areopagitica*. He is likewise a progenitor of such men as Swift and Samuel Johnson, who owed a great debt to the same tradition and who, though they were not men of the temporal Renaissance, were nevertheless Christian humanists in a tradition that has not been entirely lost even today.[5]

Du Bellay, on the other hand, Catholic though he was, and without any conscious Protestant sympathies, may be said to trace his own religious conscience to a man such as Briçonnet of Meaux, who, while he was not as radical as Luther and Calvin, was a liberal Catholic and an agitator for the spirit and not the letter of Christianity. Du Bellay is the spiritual ancestor of Pascal and perhaps of Racine in the following century: men who infused a new passion into their religious beliefs, humanists who were less nonchalant than he because their time and their temperament not only permitted but required both heat and passion.

[4] *The Renaissance and English Humanism* (Toronto, 1939), *passim*.
[5] See the later work of T. S. Eliot, *passim*.

INTRODUCTION

Ronsard, differing from both Du Bellay and Spenser, may be said to have Rabelais as progenitor both of his devout humanism and his gay Latin wit, in spite of the glaring superficial differences between the two men. His contemporary, Michel de Montaigne, is his spiritual brother. As a scholar, his liberated humanism, somewhat like that of Montaigne, leads to Descartes. All three were believing Christians, but the quality of their Christian belief leads along a devious but certain route to scientific positivism.

Modern scholarship has happily made it unnecessary to produce an elaborate excuse for comparing the two chief poets of the Pléiade[6] with Edmund Spenser. This has been done by such men as Sidney Lee, Louis S. Friedland, Jefferson B. Fletcher, and W. L. Renwick. The encouragement of Merritt Hughes to a study of the "general influence" on Spenser of the Pléiade, which has "never been seriously recognized,"[7] has been taken to heart, as has R. E. Neil Dodge's caveat against over-enthusiastic source-hunting.[8] It is W. L. Renwick—whose book on Spenser was published in 1925,[9] as if in answer to Merritt Hughes' plea—who has been a model and a source of constant inspiration in the

---

[6] Membership in the Pléiade varied during the thirty odd years of its existence, but from the time of its inception Ronsard remained the acknowledged leader, and in the perspective of four hundred years Du Bellay has been recognized as a poet second only to Ronsard. The traditional seven members were Dorat, Ronsard, Du Bellay, Baïf, Belleau, Tyard, and Jodelle. To this group one might adjoin others, especially Jacques Peletier du Mans, Guillaume des Autels, and Jean de la Peruse. The membership fluctuated because at best the Pléiade was never more than a loosely knit group, an inconstant poetic constellation. See Henri Chamard, *Histoire de la Pléiade* (Paris, 1940), I, 1-6, and *passim*. For a view of the Pléiade as a somewhat more formal and more academic organization, see Frances A. Yates, *The French Academies of the Sixteenth Century* (London, 1947), Chapter II.

[7] Merritt Y. Hughes, "Spenser and the Greek Pastoral Triad," SP 20 (1923), p. 197.

[8] R. E. Neil Dodge, "A Sermon on Source-Hunting," MP 9 (1911), pp. 211-223.

[9] W. L. Renwick, *Edmund Spenser, An Essay in Renaissance Poetry* (London, 1925).

INTRODUCTION

writing of this study. His small book deals broadly with the whole question of the Pléiade influence on Spenser, and comprises within its limited scope much material of primary significance. Certain aspects of the relationship of Spenser to Ronsard and to Du Bellay, however, are passed over, and certain other comparisons are not drawn with full distinctness. These will be exploited in the following chapters with a view to discerning the main lines of likeness and difference not only among the three poets, but between the two Renaissances they reflect and that in turn derive their own character from the work of these poets as much as from any other literary men of their time.

The whole body of Spenser's work will not be considered directly. The *Faerie Queene* may have certain analogies with Ronsard's *Françiade* and with other works of Ronsard and Du Bellay, in the text as well as in the introductory material, but a pursuit of these analogies is futile in view of the total discrepancy between the two epics.[10] The moral or didactic quality of Spenser's work may be seen as clearly, and more conveniently, elsewhere. The debt of the *Amoretti* to French Petrarchism is a subject more appropriate to a consideration of Petrarchism as a whole, including of course Petrarch himself, and Desportes as well as Ronsard and Du Bellay. Certain other of Spenser's poems are heavily laden with elements of the local and the temporary, and as such are of more concern to an historian than to a critic of literature.

My subject then is Spenser, who almost alone was the standard bearer of English poetry during that long period of preparation that culminated in the burst of the Elizabethan drama; and his relationship to Ronsard, his contemporary and counterpart in the French Renaissance, whose career he paradoxically parallels, but whom he never mentions; and

---

[10] For a discussion of this subject, see E. M. W. Tillyard, *The English Epic and its Background* (London, 1954), Part III, Chapter VI.

INTRODUCTION

Du Bellay, who died when Spenser was eight years old, but who left upon him the imprint of an intimate spiritual affinity.

The method is comparison of poems, and passages from poems, in which there is either a significant analogy in the treatment or an equally significant divergence. This may be seen with special lucidity in passages which deal with the same received material, but with differences in treatment, in approach or in tone, that constitute the originality of the poet. The anonymous author of a brilliant though somewhat patriotic article called "The Pléiade and the Elizabethans," writes: "Originality . . . becomes not the idea itself, but the personal attitude towards the idea, so that the same idea might give birth to as many original poems as there were individuals to write them."[11]

This study, thus, is one of originality more than of influences, or plagiarisms, or of borrowings. The writer of the above-mentioned article goes on to point out that the distinction between the English and the French may well be measured in their treatment of the subjects of mutability, love, and religion. These subjects will be explored in some detail and the differences, as the Edinburgh author suggests, will constitute not only the originality of the poets but the divergence that is inevitable between a Renaissance predominantly Catholic and French, and one Protestant and English. In the broadest sense, the comparative study of these poets should illuminate the cleavage within the European Renaissance itself, the inevitable result of a studious reexamination of man as man, in conflict with the enduring but less durable study of man as wayfaring pilgrim.

Let us look first into the educational backgrounds of the three poets, as a preliminary to a more thorough consideration of their gradual maturation.

[11] "The Pléiade and the Elizabethans," *The Edinburgh Review or Critical Journal*, 205 (1907), p. 366.

I · THE YOUNG POETS

𝒜N introductory sketch of the backgrounds of the three poets will serve to establish the early relationships of each to his cultural heritage. In spite of the fact that documentation is scanty in all cases, and that opinion varies sometimes to the point of contradiction, the main lines of development are nevertheless clear. It is interesting to find that even in the sixteenth century the child was apparently father to the man, that the tendencies of adolescence and young manhood all point, whether piously or impiously, to the characteristics of the mature man. Each poet was cast upon the literary world—or, one might perhaps better say, dropped into the contemporary literary void—by a preceptor who became famous in his own right; and each in the long run more than justified his master.

Born in 1524, Pierre de Ronsard grew up in the Vendômois countryside until he entered the service of Charles d'Orléans in 1537 as a page. He was a bookish young man, but was destined for service at court as a gentleman of the minor nobility. He visited Scotland in 1537, and Germany in 1540, as a member of an ambassadorial entourage in which, though an *écuyer*, he served as secretary to the ambassador, Lazare de Baïf. At the end of 1540, however, he became ill and was forced by circumstance to abandon a career which would have led to the sword rather than the pen. Three years later, at Le Mans, he entered minor orders in the Church, the conventional alternative to a more active career. His illness impaired his hearing, which continued throughout his life to become increasingly deficient, though he was never totally deaf.

At Le Mans, Ronsard met Jacques Peletier du Mans, who encouraged him to write poetry. The following year, after the death of his father, he went to Paris, and at the invitation of Lazare de Baïf he came to live with Baïf's young son, Jean-Antoine, at the "riche maison des Fosses-Saint-Victor."[1] Here he stayed to study with the young Baïf, who was only a little more than half his age but who was far ahead of him in humanist learning. Their tutor was Jean Dorat.

There is some question whether Ronsard met Du Bellay for the first time at Poitiers in 1545, or whether the first encounter took place in Le Mans in 1543, or in Paris at some questionable date. In any case, there seems to be no doubt that Peletier and Dorat gave both Ronsard and Du Bellay their initial impulse toward poetry and humanist study. Whichever one has precedence, it was Dorat who continued to teach and inspire Ronsard for five more years, until 1549-1550, and Du Bellay for a shorter time, perhaps one year.

In 1547 Lazare de Baïf died, and Jean Dorat became the head of the collège de Coqueret in Paris. Ronsard and Jean-Antoine de Baïf entered the college as boarders. Two years later they were joined by Joachim du Bellay. Whether Ronsard had met Du Bellay before this time (1549) through the offices of Peletier is unknown, but it is presumed that Peletier, if he had not actually brought them together either in Paris, Le Mans, or Poitiers, had at least spoken to each of the other. The only certainty is that they became fellow boarders under Dorat's tutelage. Even the year that Du Bellay arrived is in question, though the preponderant evidence points to 1549.

Very little is known of Joachim du Bellay previous to his arrival at the collège de Coqueret in Paris. Born in 1522 of parents well past the prime of life, he was a younger member of the senior branch of the famous Du Bellay family which included in its junior branch Rabelais' patron, Guillaume du Bellay, Seigneur de Langey, and Cardinal Jean du Bellay, whom Joachim was later to serve in Rome.

[1] Henri Chamard, *Histoire de la Pléiade*, I, 85.

Our knowledge of his youth is extremely obscure. Both his parents died before he was nine and Joachim fell to the negligent care of his elder brother. In 1545, when he was twenty-three, he was sent to the University at Poitiers to study law. But he probably met Jacques Peletier in Le Mans in 1543 at the funeral of the Seigneur de Langey, and he was probably taken into minor orders at approximately the same time, becoming a cleric but not a priest. It is very likely that he studied canon law and that his personal interests turned slowly toward poetry. At any rate, Peletier is apparently responsible for the eventual arrival of Du Bellay at the collège de Coqueret, where Ronsard and Baïf had been for some years in residence. Peletier is thus said to have prepared the future Pléiade group, perhaps without knowing it.

Dorat's teaching, both in the household of Lazare de Baïf and after 1547 in the collège de Coqueret, was oriented preponderantly toward the culture of Greece. Rome came second, Italy next, and mediaeval France last of all.[2] It was significant, however, that French was present at all in the curriculum. Dorat was an enthusiastic, omnivorous, and undiscriminating reader. According to contemporary sources he translated Hesiod, Aeschylus, Musaeus, Pindar, Orpheus, Callimachus, and Lycophron into French. He taught chiefly Homer in Greek and was both famous and infamous for his intemperate symbolic interpretations of the text as a moral allegory. This training affected Ronsard's early verse, in which mythological allusions are profuse. Furthermore, Ronsard never entirely shook off a tendency to find meanings in pagan myth which, though they had a plausible, superficial analogy with Christianity and though they were to some extent sanctioned by mediaeval Christian practice, at the same time contained such a strong infusion of pagan-

[2] Mathieu Augé-Chiquet, *La Vie, Les Idees et L'Oeuvre de Jean-Antoine de Baïf* (Paris, 1909), pp. 32-37.

ism that it is sometimes difficult to discover exactly where the real sympathies of the poet lay.

Among Greek writers after Homer, Dorat especially stressed Sophocles and Demosthenes; among the Romans, Virgil, Horace, and Cicero. He consistently taught that Greek culture as a whole was superior to Roman, and he urged that, as the Romans had profited from the Greeks, so the French should profit from the splendid blossoming of the Italian Renaissance. He thought that "on pouvait espérer pour la France un épanouissement analogue à celui qu'avait connu jadis, dans l'ordre littéraire, le Rome de César et d'Auguste."[3] As much as any other single factor, perhaps this enthusiasm on Dorat's part led to the realization of his hope, in Du Bellay and especially in Ronsard.

At the collège de Coqueret the students worked hard. Claude Binet, an acquaintance of Ronsard's and a younger contemporary, writes that Ronsard was "accoustumé à veiller tard, estudioit jusques à deux heures apres minuit, et se couchant resveilloit Baïf, qui se levoit, et prenoit la chandelle, et ne laissoit refroider la place."[4] Though the veracity of Binet's circumstantial description has been challenged, and though this statement may represent a romantic view of the youth of a famous poet, it is probably fair to assume that such intense avidity for learning was close to the spirit that Dorat maintained in Lazare de Baïf's house and at Coqueret. Binet repeatedly refers to Dorat as either "la source de tous noz poetes," or as "la source de la fontaine qui a abreuvé tous nos poetes des eaux Pieriennes."[5] And he is far from alone in his praise for the great Hellenist.

Dorat was acquiring an international reputation, and soon students were flocking to him from all parts of Europe.

[3] Henri Chamard, *Histoire de la Pléiade*, I, 104-105.
[4] Claude Binet, *Discours de la vie de Pierre de Ronsard*, critical edition, ed. Helene M. Evers (Philadelphia, 1905), p. 49.
[5] *Ibid.*, pp. 42 and 47.

THE YOUNG POETS

Meanwhile, Ronsard, Du Bellay, and Baïf lived a "vie de cénobites, entrecoupée de promenades à la campagne."[6] Perhaps the most typical of these early excursions, the prototype of the later crypto-pagan picnics held by the Pléiade, was that to Arceuil in 1549, a "folastrissime" outing of the young Brigade,[7] including Ronsard, Du Bellay, and Baïf, at which much wine was drunk and much poetry recited. Participation in these picnics was later held against Ronsard by Huguenot pamphleteers, who grossly exaggerated the pagan meaning of the ceremonies, just as some hundred years later Catholic writers were to exaggerate and misinterpret the causes of Milton's blindness. The facts as we know them make it impossible to deny that these rural celebrations were based on Dorat's knowledge of ancient Greek rites, but the facts also make it clear that all the participants were perfectly good Renaissance Catholics. While the later Huguenot accusation of arrant paganism was absurd, the recent interpretation of these picnics as evidence of a mystical representation of Christianity seems to err in the opposite direction.[8] One may conclude that the

[6] Augé-Chiquet, *De Baïf*, p. 41.

[7] "Brigade" was the title assumed by Dorat's pupils, who were later to take the more dignified and symbolic title of "Pléiade."

[8] The "pagan" meaning of these celebrations has been seriously questioned by Frances A. Yates in *The French Academies of the Sixteenth Century*. She points out that "when one remembers the satyrs at Vincennes and the pagan-Christian synthesis of imagery in the debates of the Palace Academy, one realizes that the Huguenots had probably been right in thinking that Ronsard's Dionysian enthusiasm was more than a literary pose. It was a part of this whole poetical Counter Reformation, a part of the effort to counteract the rationalizations of the Reformers by insisting on the mystical aspect of religion" (p. 190). It seems hardly likely that the facts that are known today concerning the picnics of the Brigade will support such a theory as that quoted above. A solidly contradictory view is taken by Morris Bishop in his *Ronsard, Prince of Poets* (New York, 1940), which, though it is not ostensibly a work of such thoroughgoing scholarship as that of Frances Yates, contains a description of the affair at Arceuil in 1553 (pp. 64-66) and a full account of the earlier expedition in July 1549 (pp. 64-71). Bishop apparently believes that these picnics were pagan, but innocently so. For a further discussion of similar influences on Ronsard, see below, Chapter IX.

truth is likely to lie between these extremes; that the celebrants were scholars and poets and Catholics, but that they were drunk; and that in their drunkenness their scholarship remained active, their poetry enthusiastic, and their Catholicism dormant, though dormant only temporarily.

The young scholars, as nascent poets, were intoxicated with their classical studies: Ronsard and Baïf with the glory of Greece, Du Bellay more especially with the grandeur of Rome. Chamard says that Dorat "faisait passer dans l'âme de ceux qui l'écoutaient l'ardeur passionée qui brulait la sienne."[9] Ronsard was youthfully and foolishly graecophile; from the Greek classics he acquired a pedantry, a capacity for mythological flights; and a moral laxity from both the Greeks and from contemporary neo-Latin poetry. These continued to affect him for the rest of his life. Du Bellay, the late offspring of elderly parents, the child who had been so much alone in the world, and who came late to the Greek studies in which Ronsard and Baïf were already so proficient, never went as deeply into classical Greek as did the others; and his more somber temperament very soon showed him the hollowness that lay behind the external grandeur of the Eternal City.

All three, however, participated wholeheartedly in the intense work and the less frequent but equally intense play of the collège de Coqueret. In Ronsard's future poetry there were to be thirty-seven references to his college days under Jean Dorat,[10] all of them warm with enthusiastic gratitude to his teacher. Du Bellay was to make much less of Dorat, the Hellenist par excellence, and to address his most enthusiastic thanks to Ronsard himself, for whom, apparently, he acquired at this time an admiration that nothing in the future could diminish. Du Bellay thus placed himself at

[9] *Histoire de la Pléiade*, I, 125-126.
[10] *Oeuvres Completes de Pierre de Ronsard*, ed. Paul Laumonier, 8 vols. (Paris, 1914-1919), "Index," VIII, 375.

the mercy of the junior poet, who was more proud, more selfish, more learned, and, finally, more talented than he. Baïf went on to become a pedant, fabulously productive of a prodigious variety of verse, some of which will be discussed below and all of which is inferior to the work of his two friends, who reached humanism later than he but who did not subjugate their talents to its sheer ponderosity.

Ronsard, the gay and brilliant lover of the divinity of Greek literature, and of the bawdiness of neo-Latin verse; Du Bellay, the older, somber student of both Greece and Rome; and Baïf, the pedestrian scholar from his early youth to his old age—all for a few golden years mingled in the electric atmosphere of Dorat's presence. Henri Chamard writes that they were all "des hommes de la Renaissance, intensément, éperdument, par leur amour de la nature et de la vie."[11] He goes on to say, several pages later, in words which apply more aptly to Ronsard than to the others: "Plains d'ésperance et d'enthousiasme, ils aspiraient à realizer par l'union de la science et de l'art, leur rêve juvénile de gloire, en s'appuyant sur cette force, qui rend tous les efforts légers: la joie de vivre." They left the collège de Coqueret sometime in 1549-1550. Ronsard and Du Bellay published books almost immediately and continued to publish almost every year for the rest of their lives. Dorat's dreams of a French *éclosion* like the Italian were in process of being translated into fact.

Within a few years of Ronsard's and Du Bellay's first publications, Edmund Spenser was born, so much more obscurely than either of the Frenchmen that the date of his birth is only conjectural (1552)[12] and his father's Christian name is still uncertain. Unlike the French poets, he was born in urban surroundings, insofar as London was

[11] *Histoire de la Pléiade,* I, 124.
[12] Alexander C. Judson, *The Life of Edmund Spenser* (Baltimore, 1945), p. 1.

urban in those days of gardens, trees, and river-travel. Spenser's father is presumed to have been a merchant, and hence not a gentleman; yet he is also presumed to have been related to the Spensers of Wormleighton and Althorp, and hence above the bourgeoisie which were merely in trade.

A year after the conjectural date of his birth, Queen Mary initiated in England her short and bloody reign, which is memorialized by Foxe's *Book of Martyrs* and which strengthened the tendency toward Puritanism in which Spenser was to share. In the same year Richard Chancellor sailed the White Sea to Russia and was entertained in Moscow. It was a new and dynamic world. The young Spenser attended the Merchant Taylor's School, which was founded in 1561 with Richard Mulcaster as headmaster: this is one of the few early matters of documentary fact.[13] But whether he was at this day-school from the year of its inception is an open question, since only the time of his departure from the school is recorded.

Richard Mulcaster, like Jean Dorat, is a literary figure in his own right. He was about thirty years old when he took over the headmastership of the new school, and he continued in this position for twenty-five more years. Spenser's most recent biographer refers to Mulcaster's influence as "wholesome and stimulating."[14] As a teacher and as a writer he showed "a love of order, system, thoroughness. . . ."[15] It sounds as if Mulcaster were merely a conventional, competent teacher, in a tradition that has endured until the present day. He was not. Far more than this, he was a quiet, meticulous, decorous, brilliant revolutionary. His views on education and on language were far ahead of his time. As much as Dorat, he was a humanist of the Renaissance,

---

[13] *Ibid.*, p. 13.
[14] *Ibid.*, p. 15. It should be pointed out that in all the praise I have read of Jean Dorat, no one has ventured to call his influence wholesome, although there is general agreement that it was stimulating.
[15] *Ibid.*, p. 16.

though as an Englishman he was not one to encourage study after midnight, or to stage a *déjuner sur l'herbe* in the suburbs of London.

The curriculum at the Merchant Taylor's School was based, as was traditional, on the Greek and Roman classics. But, like the new teachers of the Renaissance, Mulcaster believed too in physical training, in the development of the whole man. He was also in favor of education for women, though of course not on a coeducational basis; he recognized as did Castiglione and Montaigne and later Spenser himself that women are made of the same stuff as men and are full of potentialities beyond the merely sexual. His ideas of education are thus more liberal than was usual in his time.

But it is in his attitude toward language and literature that Mulcaster departs clearly from the tradition of purist humanism that had characterized such English educators as Cheke and Ascham.[16] A detailed comparison of the relationship of Mulcaster's radical linguistic theories to those of Du Bellay and Ronsard has been made by W. L. Renwick, who writes: "Spenser, then, was educated under a principal master who held views on the nature of language and on the necessity for labour, freedom, and boldness in the improvement of the mother tongue which were in sharp conflict with those of the most famous educationists of his day, and which were those identified with the Pléiade, and especially with the *Deffence et Illustration* of Du Bellay. It was under this tutelage that he translated the *Songe ou Vision* from Du Bellay's *Antiquitez de Rome* . . . the inference that thus early he became acquainted with the prose as well as with the poetical work of Du Bellay is at least possible."[17]

It was not only the matter of his linguistic theories that Mulcaster borrowed from Du Bellay; he also borrowed the

[16] W. L. Renwick, "Mulcaster and Du Bellay," MLR 17 (1922), *passim*.
[17] *Ibid.*, p. 287.

manner, the forthright exhortations, the pithy, categorical statements of the value of the vernacular, "that our hole tung was weined long ago, as having all her tethe."[18] Mulcaster was perhaps less of a scholar than Jean Dorat, and certainly less of a Hellenist; but, less omnivorous, he was more discriminating. His greatest enthusiasm was not for the classics, as was Dorat's, but for the vulgar tongue, as was Du Bellay's. The words of his *First Part of the Elementarie* (1582) ring with a vibrant patriotism and a profound confidence in the future of the language, as did the *Deffence* thirty-three years earlier, a confidence that was to find its justification in Spenser, as Du Bellay found his in Ronsard. If the words of the classroom matched those in the book he was so long in writing, Spenser must have been enthralled and inspired to hear such stirring rhetoric as: "For is it not in dede a meruellous bondage, to becom seruants to one tung for learning sake, the most of our time, with losse of most time, whereas we maie haue the verie same treasur in our own tung, with the gain of most time? our own bearing the ioyfull title of our libertie and fredom, the *Latin* tung remembring vs, of our thraldom & bondage? I loue *Rome*, but *London* better, I fauor *Italie*, but England more, I honor the Latin, but I worship the *English*."[19]

Spenser, of course, went on to Cambridge University in 1569 as a sizar, as he had been a scholarship student at the Merchant Taylor's School. He needed the formal education for future preferment, unlike Du Bellay and Ronsard, who were better born and who could look to the Church as well as to the aristocracy for patronage.

At Cambridge Spenser met Gabriel Harvey, found himself in the midst of the Cartwright-Whitgift controversy, and studied Plato in the original;[20] it is thought probable

[18] *Mulcaster's Elementarie*, ed. E. T. Campagnac (Oxford, 1925), p. 89.
[19] Ibid., p. 269.
[20] James Jackson Higginson, *Spenser's Shepherd's Calender in relation to Contemporary Affairs* (New York, 1912), p. 263.

that he acquired his theory of poetic ἐνθουσιασμὸς ultimately from the *Ion*.[21] But his first divine inspiration must have come from his teacher, Richard Mulcaster, in a non-Platonic sense, as a stimulus toward the *illustration* of his own vernacular, which then stood in great need of such a poet as he was to become. Colin's tribute to Wrenock in the December eclogue of *The Shepheardes Calender* is thought to be Spenser's acknowledgment to Mulcaster; he writes:

> And for I was in thilke same looser yeares,
> (Whether the Muse so wrought me from my birth,
> Or I tomuch beleeued my shepherd peres)
> Somedele ybent to song and musicks mirth.
>   A good olde shephearde, Wrenock was his name,
>   Made me by arte more cunning in the same.
>
> Fro thence I durst in derring doe compare
> With shepheards swayne, what euer fedde in field;
> And if that *Hobbinol* right iudgement bare,
> To *Pan* his owne selfe pype I neede not yield.
>   For if the flocking Nymphes did folow *Pan,*
>   The wiser Muses after *Colin* ran.
>
> But ah such pryde at length was ill repayde. . . .
>
> (Lines 37-49)

The lines are not directly autobiographical, and one must allow for the fiction, but it is interesting to note that the fictitious pride meets a fictitious fall. The "derring doe" brings to mind the *Faerie Queene,* and in the light of this evocation the self-esteem does not seem to overflow into "surquedrie." There is a certain significant chastity in leaving the nymphs to Pan, and claiming only the "wiser Muses." Out of a temperate ἐνθουσιασμὸς a new poet is taking form, grave and moral.

[21] *Ibid.*

One sees this most clearly in contrast to Ronsard's tributes to Dorat. In his "Hynne de l'Autonne" from *Le Second Livre des Hynnes* he writes:

> Disciple de Dorat, qui long temps fut mon maistre,
> M'apprit la Poesie, et me monstra comment
> On doit feindre et cacher les fables proprement,
> Et à bien desguiser la verité des choses
> D'un fabuleux manteau, dont elles sont encloses.[22]

The straightforward acknowledgment is filled with occult implications. Something more than "arte" has been learned: a *mystique*, in line with Dorat's symbolic interpretations of Homer and Pindar. But more typically perhaps, Ronsard, in "A Jan Dorat" (1550), while he is still close in time to his early instructor, uses the expression:

> Sucer le laict savoureus
> De te feconde mammelle![23]

Such a symbolic reference to a man who has served as preceptor is said by Gustave Cohen to be quite usual in the French Renaissance.[24] Ronsard goes on to say in the same ode:

> Si j'ai du bruit, il n'est mien,
> Je le confesse estre tien,
> Dont la science hautaine
> Tout alteré me treuva,
> Et bien jeune m'abreuva
> De l'une et l'autre fontaine.

The thanks are decorous in their confession of indebtedness. But the reference to the two fountains, even if they refer to Greece and Rome, has implications in its doubling

---

[22] Ronsard, *Oeuvres Complètes*, ed. Gustave Cohen (Paris, 1950), II, 241.
[23] *Ibid.*, p. 693.
[24] *Ibid.*, "Notes," p. 1111. Cohen, interestingly enough, cites Rabelais as an example of another Renaissance writer who uses similar imagery.

of the earlier "feconde mammelle." Ronsard thinks in images that come naturally from his classical education and from his amorous disposition. The "orgeuil" that Gustave Cohen finds at the end of this short ode is as much a part of Ronsard's temperament as is the humble acknowledgment of the fall of pride at the end of the quotation from the December eclogue of Spenser's.

While one can very easily make too much of a careful arrangement of quotations such as the above, nevertheless, if the quotations be typical, as I believe they are, they may then be considered at least to foreshadow, in the early work of the two poets, a contrast which will become more clear as this study progresses: a contrast in their early work between a gravity that is moral, earnest, and chaste even in its enthusiasms, and an enthusiasm that is neither chaste nor humble, but gay and amoral. The following chapters will attempt to elucidate and substantiate this comparison, and to establish the position of Spenser both in relation to Du Bellay, and to Du Bellay's more famous compatriot, Pierre de Ronsard.

II · THE EARLY TRANSLATIONS FROM DU BELLAY

It is now generally agreed that Spenser's first published work consisted of translations from the French which appeared in a book entitled A *Theatre wherein be represented as wel the miseries & calamities that follow the voluptuous Worldlings, As also the greate ioyes and plesures which the faithfull do enjoy* . . . , published in London in 1569. According to the title page, this book was "Deuised by S. Iohn vander Noodt," and, according to the lengthy dedicatory epistle, the precise date of writing was 25 May 1569.

The book consisted of two sections of verse, the first entitled *Epigrams*; and the second *Sonets*, containing emblematic woodcuts on the page opposite each verse unit except the first of the "Sonets"; and of a far longer prose section which constitutes the main body of the book, and is said, at the beginning, to be "Translated out of French into Englishe by Theodore Roest." The prose need not concern us because it clearly does not concern Spenser.

The *Epigrams* and the *Sonets* were translated from a French edition of the same book, *Le Theatre*, which was published in London 28 October 1568, that is, almost exactly seven months before the English version. The French edition itself was preceded by a Flemish edition published in London 18 September 1568, which again does not concern us except for the sake of the background of the book. No translator is named clearly for the English version of the *Epigrams* and the *Sonets*. But because there appear in the edition of Spenser's *Complaints* published in 1591 a reproduction with minor alterations of the *Epigrams*, under the new title *The Visions of Petrarch*, and a reproduction with major alterations of the *Sonets*, under the new title *The Visions of Bellay*, it has long been assumed that the originals in Van der Noot's A *Theatre* were probably the work of Spenser.[1]

The association of the *Epigrams* drawn ultimately from Petrarch, and of the *Sonets* drawn from the *Songe* appended to Du Bellay's *Antiquitez de Rome*, is particularly appropriate.[2] Their connection is natural, for, as Henri Chamard has pointed out, the Du Bellay sonnets are of Petrarchan inspiration,[3] and, not only this, but follow Petrarch's text with some measure of general similitude in the opening lines of both the *Songe* and the *Canzone*, as well as more specifically in lines 37-49 of the *Canzone* and "Sonnet XII" of Du Bellay (which is the tenth in Van der Noot's A *Theatre*). Petrarch's poem, however, has been subjected to a multiplicity of interpretations, only one of which has any relationship to the more easily attainable interpretation of Du Bellay's *Songe*.

How the job of translator for Van der Noot ever reached Spenser we shall probably never know. Whether it came to him quite fortuitously or whether, as has been suggested,[4] it reached him through the good offices of his teacher Richard Mulcaster, in any case that it came to him at all was a significant and a felicitous circumstance. It brought him a text, on the whole, of better than mediocre quality on which he wrought almost no improvement and which he occa-

---

[1] See Appendix 1 for a discussion of Spenser's authorship of this translation.

[2] That Van der Noot was an intelligent if somewhat perfervid man, and a talented poet in his own language is quite clear, even though the sonnets he wrote in French are crabbed, halting, and cast in a language that in Paris had been superseded by a smoother and more fluent poetic diction under the influence of members of the Pléiade. For further information about Van der Noot, see August Vermeylen, *Leven en werken van jonker Jan van der Noot* (Antwerp, 1899), and a complete new comparative edition of his work, *Het Bosken en Het Theatre*, ed. Dr. W. A. P. Smit (Amsterdam, 1953), reviewed with praise by Louis S. Friedland in *Comparative Literature* VII (1955).

[3] *Histoire de la Pléiade*, II, 45.

[4] Elizabeth Jelliffe Macintire, "French Influence on the Beginnings of English Classicism," PMLA 26 (Sept. 1911), p. 514.

sionally debased; but the subject matter of Du Bellay's poems, and the mood of melancholy that they express, make a signal beginning for a literary career which was to end on a related note. Thus Spenser's first known occupation with poetry concerned ideas—mutability and worldly vanity—which were to become for him a preoccupation and which were to pursue if not actually haunt him throughout his lifetime.

Henri Chamard writes of Du Bellay, "Poète *antiquaire*, il eut le premier des modernes, le sentiment des ruines . . . et condensa ses emotions en quelques sonnets que traversa le frisson mysterieux du passé."[5] Without claiming Spenser as the first modern Englishman to feel this "shiver," one may apply Chamard's statement to Spenser with equal truth. And he felt it, unlike Du Bellay, and Du Bellay's nearest predecessor in this respect, Petrarch, without the necessity of a journey to Rome. It was such things as Du Bellay's *Songe* and his *Antiquitez de Rome*, among others, that made the past so vivid to this Londoner who presumably never visited the continent.

Du Bellay, as well as being the first poet since Petrarch to write of the ruins of Rome, was also an innovator in another respect: he was the first to use the sonnet form for a subject other than Love. Chamard says: "Dans ce forme du sonnet, que tous, et lui-même avec eux, n'avaient employée qu'à chanter l'amour, il coule le premier une matière toute neuve, qui va l'élargir et le transformer, et dont il tire les éléments du lugubre spectacle étalé sous ses yeux."[6]

It is not to be regretted that this departure had no effect on Spenser, for Spenser was always magnificently able to invent and master his own verse forms. But, young as he was, he must have been aware that Du Bellay was staking new ground, was being "Petrarchan" in a sense in which

[5] *Histoire de la Pléiade*, II, 350.
[6] *Ibid.*, pp. 46-47.

the word was not and is not generally understood, and this awareness must have acted as one encouragement in the program of experimentation that he was to devise and to carry out.

The form of Du Bellay's sonnets in the *Songe* follows that of the *Antiquitez*: there is an alternation of sonnets written in alexandrines, and in decasyllabic lines; the former are the even numbers, the latter the odd. This represents a transitional phase in Du Bellay's development. The sonnets in his *L'Olive*, published in the same year as his *Deffence et Illustration de la Langue Françoyse* (1549), had been entirely in decasyllabic lines; those to appear in his *Regrets*, published in 1558 but written after the *Antiquitez*, were to be entirely in alexandrines. All the sonnets are built on five rhymes, on the continental system, as against the seven of the conventional English system. It can readily be seen why Spenser, in translating, made no effort to reproduce the rhyme scheme of the original, either in 1569, when he was seventeen years old, or indeed, in the 1591 revision in the *Complaints*, where the sonnets are rhymed, but not according to the originals.

The quality of the sonnets in the *Songe* is somewhat inferior to that of those in the *Antiquitez* proper. Chamard writes of them, "C'est une vision apocalyptique, pittoresque et brillante, mais d'un brillant trop artificiel."[7] This artificiality is of course reflected in the translation, which is un-Elizabethan in its literalness, but it is enhanced and exaggerated by the emblems which appear opposite the English text. In almost every case these illustrations depict simultaneously the construction and the destruction described in each sonnet. In the fourth, for instance, the triumphal arch occupies two-thirds of the picture, and its ruins "with sodaine falling broken all to dust" occupy the remaining third. This addition of woodcuts in the English version, reiterat-

[7] *Ibid.*, p. 45.

ing with crude simultaneity the message of the words, gives the English an air of constructed propaganda, which apparently is just what Van der Noot intended, while the French, artificial though it may sound as a whole, still has the mien of literature.

Another excellent French critic, V.-L. Saulnier, writes of the *Songe*, "Monotones, inéluctables, c'est le flux suivi du reflux," and goes on to compare it unfavorably with the *Antiquitez* itself: "Plus ample, élaboré, avec un art parfait, se presente la vision romaine dans les trente-deux sonnets" (of the *Antiquitez*).[8] It is certainly true that neither individually, nor as a whole, are the sonnets of the *Songe* up to the high standard of the *Antiquitez*; they have something of the air of an exercise, they are not as deeply felt. This too emerges in Spenser's translation, and must not be attributed to Spenser as a fault; he is, after all, translating a series of artificial set-pieces. There is a monotonous sameness in the *Songe*, ineluctable only in the sense that a continued slight variation on a theme may seem to be ineluctable if it never stops. Happily, it does stop, and leaves the impression of a well-made artifact, a well-wrought tomb such as that described in Du Bellay's third sonnet (also the third in the translation), which is not destroyed in the end, as it is in the poem, but which turns out to be a cenotaph, empty of the more ample and more intense meaning that vibrates in the sonnets of the *Antiquitez*, and especially the *Regrets*.

V.-L. Saulnier terminates his discussion of the *Songe* with the following statement: "Et quand le *Songe* formule d'avance sa conclusion, tout n'est que vanité, nous ne sommes pas sorti de l'*Ecclésiaste*. Reste ce pont cruel, d'un Testament a l'autre: accomplir faut les Ecritures . . . des mots de fatalité comme ceux-la pourraient bien servir d'exergue."[9]

[8] Du Bellay, L'Homme et L'Oeuvre (Paris, 1951), p. 75.
[9] Ibid., pp. 79-80.

This provides a thematic contrast between the first work, the work of another, to which Spenser laid his hand, and his own attitude toward the vanity of worldly things. For if we may assume Spenser's spiritual development to have been consistent, and may look ahead to the mature Spenser, placing him alongside the mature Du Bellay, it will be seen that in Spenser's attitude toward sublunary vanity there is a preponderance of confidence in the immutable divine, a spirit which is evidenced only once, in the sonnets of Du Bellay's *Songe*. The last lines of the first sonnet read:

> Voy comme tout n'est rien que vanité,
> Lors cognoissant la mondaine inconstance,
> Puis que Dieu seul au temps fait resistance,
> N'espere rien qu'en la divinité.

Spenser translates the final lines, changing the negative form to the positive, substituting the word "confidence" for Du Bellay's verb "hope" and the word "God" for the more vague "divinité," as if somehow he foresaw the respite from Change described in his own final stanzas in the *Faerie Queene* (VII, viii, 1-2):

> Sith onely God surmountes the force of tyme,
> In God alone do stay my confidence.

The vague word "divinité," of course, is required in the French for the sake of the rhyme, and perhaps also to avoid a repetition of the word "Dieu" in the preceding line. Spenser's repetition of the word "God" in the last two lines not only is required by the metre but may also proceed partly from the naïveté of a budding poet, or on the other hand may reflect a less pessimistic view than that expressed by Du Bellay.

Certainly Spenser's translation fulfills a reasonable standard of literalness; it says substantially the same thing as the French, but there seems to be a difference in *tone*. It is not intended that the comparison of these quotations should do more than suggest a slight contrast. But it is clear that a completely literal pentameter translation of the French might read: "For nothing hope except in God alone . . ." and that such a negative rendering was perfectly available to the translator, who shows throughout a talent for literalness unusual in Elizabethan times. Furthermore, it may not be without significance that this line remains unaltered in the 1591 rhymed revision of this sonnet. It is a tonic difference in a very small way indicative of the contrast between the religious atmosphere on the Continent at this time and that in England. For Du Bellay wrote out of a disgust for and a disappointment with the Catholic hierarchy in Rome, though he was a good Catholic; and Spenser even in his youth wrote out of a militant and unwavering Protestant faith. I do not mean to imply that Du Bellay lacked faith, merely that the faith he possessed was influenced by historical factors that existed in Rome and did not exist in Spenser's England, and that it lacked the positive militancy one sees so frequently in Spenser's work.

That Spenser's translations are in blank verse is an indication not only of his youth, haste, and inexperience but also of how far the development of English poetry was running behind that of French poetry at this time. The form of Du Bellay's sonnets is thoroughly finished and polished. He licked them into shape, and did not rush to publish them, in true Horatian fashion. The form of Spenser's is tentative and undeveloped, sometimes even awkward. Yet Jefferson B. Fletcher points out that these translations are "the first printed exception to the fossilized 'heroic verse' universally current in Elizabethan poetry before Spenser," and goes on to say that "in this blank verse alone is to be found the same nicely calculated variety in the feet and in the caesura which obtains in the *Shepheardes Calender*."[10]

Harold Stein disagrees with this: "The exigencies of translation may partly account for the curious freedom in the

[10] "Spenser and the Theatre of Worldlings," MLN 13 (1898), p. 414.

position of the caesura found by J. B. Fletcher. It is exceedingly doubtful that the freedom should be interpreted as evidence of metrical inventiveness and poetic genius, as Professor Fletcher argues."[11] In view of the fact of Spenser's skill and inventiveness not long afterward, in the *Shepheardes Calender*, it would seem to remain an open question who has the better of this argument.

Stein says further, "Indeed though the verse is at times excellent, it is never good blank verse. It fails consistently to exploit the possibilities that blank verse offers." He goes on to suggest that Spenser was not experimenting at all in the blank verse form, but was simply saving time by ignoring the formalities of Du Bellay's sonnets, and he adds that if Spenser had been experimenting, as he is supposed to have done, according to the conventional theory: "In fact we would be confronted with the situation of an author in what would normally be his imitative period writing in a form which had not yet achieved any kind of solid recognition. What is more, it would mean that the young translator was repudiating the poetic principles of the author whose work he was translating."[12]

The first part of this statement attempts to repudiate the experimentation theory, but the second part, which presumably refers to the lack of rhyme, would hardly amount to a general repudiation of Du Bellay's poetic principles. One of these principles, in fact—the use of archaisms—is specifically put into operation in these translations, but whether self-consciously and as such, it is impossible to say. Veré L. Rubel points out in a painstaking study of Spenser's poetic diction that, "Already in the first form of the sonnets [from Du Bellay] Spenser is showing his early interest in poetic

---

[11] *Studies in Spenser's Complaints* (New York, 1934), p. 132, n. 13. Stein's, I believe, is the fullest account in print of the *form* of Spenser's earliest translations, though he does not himself profess that it is complete (*Studies*, p. 141).

[12] *Ibid.*, p. 137.

archaisms, such as *grisly, leames, welkin, whilome,* and *yshrouded;* in rabbated past participles, such as *astonned* and *erect;* in *y*-adjectives: *creekie, scaly, sunny;* in compounds of adverb and verb: *outbrast, outgushing, overcast.* . . . The most interesting word in these early endeavors appears in the last line of Du Bellay's "Sonet" Number VIII: *croked* applied to *shore,* for it implies that the young poet, like others of his time, was going to school to *Tottel's Miscellany,* and getting suggestions for his later daring adaptations of borrowings from Latin, Italian, or French."[13]

It has been stated by Bruce Robert McElderry, Jr., in a scholarly yet spirited defense of Spenser's poetic diction,[14] that the use of archaism and neologism in Spenser has been greatly exaggerated, even in reference to the *Shepheardes Calender.* Since the sonnets we are discussing constitute the only work of Spenser that is known to precede the *Shepheardes Calender,* the present moderate use may be taken as representative, and this early use both of archaisms and of innovations may have been the result of contact with Mulcaster, or may well have resulted from a youthful reading of Du Bellay's *Deffence,* or from both; it is impossible to say. At any rate, their use seems to represent some theory of poetic diction; it comes very close to Du Bellay's exhortation in the *Deffence:* ". . . enchasser, ainsi qu'une pierre precieuse & rare, quelques motz antiques en ton poëme, à l'exemple de Virgile . . . Ne doute point que le moderé usaige de telz vocables ne donne grande majesté tant au vers comme à la prose: ainsi que font les reliques des sainctz aux croix & autres sacrez joyaux dediez aux temples."[15] This perhaps gives a romantic sanctification to the use of rare old words.

Thus Spenser's rejection of the rhymed sonnet form does

[13] *Poetic Diction in the English Renaissance, from Skelton through Spenser* (New York, 1941), p. 222.
[14] "Archaism and Innovation in Spenser's Poetic Diction," PMLA 47 (1932), pp. 144-170.
[15] *Deffence,* ed. Henri Chamard (Paris, 1948), pp. 142-143.

not seem to be a repudiation of Du Bellay and, as I have indicated, the use of archaisms seems the contrary of a rejection, whether self-consciously in accordance with the *Deffence*, or unwittingly. Stein, however, not only thinks that the use of blank verse was "in all probability . . . accidental" but that it is likely that the *Sonets* "do not represent the product of a critical theory at all."[16] This statement seems to go too far into unknown territory.

For as well as demonstrating at least the embryo of a theory concerning the use of archaisms, the first eleven sonnets from Du Bellay also contain several examples of lines which have a recognizably Spenserian ring, which adumbrate the poet's mature style. Such for example is:

> Let me no more see faire thing under heauen,
> Sith I haue seene so faire a thing as this,
> With sodaine falling broken all to dust.[17]

This is one of the few cases in which Spenser's translation achieves and possibly exceeds the mellifluousness of the original French, and it is all the more remarkable that in this case he is dealing with alexandrines, which are more difficult to contain in an English pentameter.[18]

Another example is the third line from the eighth sonnet from Du Bellay:

> Did tuen hir plaint to falling rivers sound,

and a final example, lines 7-8 of the tenth sonnet:

> There was to heare a noise alluring slepe
> Of many accordes more swete than Mermaids song,

a softly sibillant series of words, artistically reproducing the alliteration of the French original, and marked with the stamp of the nascent master. The eighth line of this sonnet,

---

[16] *Studies*, pp. 141 and 139.   [17] Sonnet 4, lines 12-14.
[18] So that the reader may judge for himself, I give Du Bellay's lines:
   Las je ne veux plus voir rie de beau soubz les cieux
   Puis qu'un oeuvre si beau j'ay veu deuat mes yeux
   D'une soudaine cheute estre reduict en poudre.

in fact, remained unaltered in the 1591 edition of the *Complaints*; apparently it satisfied the mature poet.

But Spenser was far from always at his best in these sonnets. Sometimes he writes like the schoolboy he was rather than like the poet he will be, as in the following example from the first line of the fourth sonnet recently quoted for its excellent terminal lines:

> I saw raisde up on pillers of Iuorie,

a prosy beginning; and a poetic ending. Or the last three lines in the eleventh sonnet, which are almost as awkward as so many of the lines in the sonnets from the Apocalypse:[19]

> I saw the heauens warre against hir tho,
> And seing hir stricken fall with clap of thunder,
> With so great noyse I start in sodaine wonder.

An adventitious rhyme, and a thoroughgoing debasement of the original French, which reads,

> Le ciel encor je luy voy guerroyer:
> Puis tout a coup je la voy foudroyer
> Et du grand bruyt en sursault je m'esveille.

But such pedestrian verse is rare in Spenser, even in these early efforts. On the whole, the high level of mediocrity attained in these blank verse translations is remarkable, in view of the youth of the poet and the lack of the development of blank verse in his contemporaries and predecessors. That the poet himself did not consider many of the lines unworthy is evidenced by his retention of them in the revisions published twenty-one years later.[20]

It is an interesting though perhaps an insoluble problem to consider what elements in these early sonnets remained sufficiently attractive to the mature Spenser to permit his revising them and including the revisions in the 1591 edition

---

[19] For a discussion of these four sonnets, see Appendix I.
[20] These revisions of 1591 will not be discussed here since their chief importance is in respect to the development of Spenser's sonnet technique rather than to his relationship with the Pléiade.

of the *Complaints*. I have pointed out that the general theme of the series—worldly vanity and mutability—was one that concerned Spenser throughout his lifetime. Thus the lesson or moral of these sonnets remained significant for him. It should be added that each sonnet is a melancholy exemplum, a small allegory of the vanity of human endeavor. Furthermore, some of the details of these allegorical descriptions bear an obvious likeness to the more extended descriptions in *The Faerie Queene* of the House of Pride (I, iii), the House of Holiness (I, x), and the House of Busyrane (III, xi), to cite only the most immediate examples. The desolate river nymph in Sonet VIII is a Spenserian figure, as is the nocturnal monster in VII, both in the text of the sonnet and in the woodcut emblem, and the satyrs' attempted ravishment of the nymphs beside the clear fountain in Sonet x recalls both the Bowre of Blisse (II, xii) and the story of Hellenore and the satyrs in III, x. Without succumbing to anything more Freudian than Wordsworth's theory that the child is father to the man, it seems reasonable to assume that the poet who was to become England's greatest allegorist should retain an affection and a sympathy for the first allegories to which it is known that he put his nascent literary talent.

Thus we have seen Spenser in his earliest known association with French literature, proving himself an apt but inexperienced student of Du Bellay; doing an act of minor injustice to the elder poet, in his translation, but concurring implicitly in one of the elder poet's theories. In the following chapter I shall point out in general Spenser's connection with the poetic theory of the Pléiade, and his more specific involvement with the English movement that favored the use of quantitative measures in vernacular verse, which has significant parallels with a similar movement among the members of the Pléiade.

III · THEORY OF POETRY

RENAISSANCE literary theories in both France and England were almost entirely received from the classics, and from Italian commentators or expositors of the classics. The general movement was from Italy to France in the first half of the century, and from both continental countries to England throughout the second half. The nature and extent of these foreign influences in both France and England has been exhaustively studied, in general and in particular. The position of Ronsard and Du Bellay in relation to the doctrines of Aristotle, Plato, and Horace has been defined and clarified, as well as the nature and origin of their theories concerning the exploitation of French, the vulgar tongue. England had the good fortune to inherit not only from the classics and from the Italian Renaissance, but also from the Pléiade, thus receiving the richest legacy by an accident of history and geography.

Spenser's share in this legacy was very large; its size and the use he made of it are the measure of his contribution to the development of English poetry, a contribution that can hardly be exaggerated. His own expressions of literary theories, unfortunately, are scattered; *The English Poet*, a treatise that he apparently wrote in the seventies, before the publication of *The Shepheardes Calender*, has been lost. His critical opinions, therefore, must be gathered from a variety of sources in his work, and must be deduced from the nature of the work itself. This has been well and frequently done. The assembled body of opinion has been related to the literary theories of the Pléiade, which are more readily available, in a more cohesive and organized form. It would be a futile and repetitious exercise to review at any length the vast compilation of careful comparison that has been accomplished in this field.[1]

What has not been thoroughly discussed, however, is the relationship between French experiments in *vers mesurés* and the English quantitative verse movement that both

[1] The primary sources for an understanding of Du Bellay's theory of literature are, of course, his prefaces, and especially his *Deffence et Illustration de la Langue Françoyse* (1549). His poetry itself is a mine of critical theory, see for example "Sonnet CXCII" of *Les Regrets*, A Olivier de Magni (*Oeuvres*, ed. Henri Chamard [Paris, 1912-1948], v, 58-69), *Contre Les Pétraquistes* (v, 69-77), A Bertran Bergier (v, 117-123), A Pierre de Ronsard (v, 360-365), *Discovrs av Roy svr la Poesie* (vi, 159-166).

For Ronsard's literary theories, see especially his prefaces, and the *Abregé de l'Art Poétique François* (1565) (*Oeuvres*, ed. Gustave Cohen [Paris, 1950], II, 971-1034). The expressions of critical beliefs in his verse are more extensive and more explicit than Du Bellay's: see, for example: Ode X, A Michel de L'Hospital (I, 386-406), Ode XXVI (I, 464-465), A Henry III, Roy de France (I, 787-795), Au Roy Charles IX (I, 821-825), Elegie XXV (II, 118-121), *Hynne de l'Autonne* (II, 239-250), *La Lyre* (II, 321-331), *Discours Contre Fortune* (II, 399-409), *Discours, a Jean Morel, Ambrunois* (II, 449-452), *Response aux Injures et Calomnies* (II, 595-621), *Encores au Lecteur* (II, 647), *Epistre a Charles, Cardinal de Lorraine* (II, 855-862), Elegie (from the Theatre of Jacques Grévin) (II, 920-924).

Secondary material based on these sources, among others, is plentiful. The best expositions and analyses may be found in Henri Chamard's *Histoire de la Pléiade* (4 vols.; Paris, 1939), in Robert J. Clements' *Critical Theory and Practice of the Pléiade* (Cambridge, Mass., 1942), and in Frances A. Yates's *The French Academies of the Sixteenth Century* (London, 1947).

Spenser's expressions of literary theory may be found chiefly in the Spenser-Harvey correspondence, the "October" eclogue of *The Shepheardes Calender*, *The Teares of the Muses*, *The Ruines of Time*, *Colin Clovts Come Home Again*, the *Fowre Hymnes*, and in the letter to Raleigh that prefaces *The Faerie Queene*. Secondary material is available throughout the commentary on these in the Spenser Variorum. B. E. C. Davis' book, *Edmund Spenser, A Critical Study* (Cambridge, 1933), devotes most of Chapters III, VI, and VIII to general questions of literary theory.

For comparisons of Spenser and the Pléiade poets, especially Du Bellay and Ronsard, see W. L. Renwick, *Edmund Spenser, An Essay on Renaissance Poetry* (London, 1949), a classic of broad, comparative criticism; and Louis S. Friedland, "Spenser's Early Poems" (Ph.D. dissertation, New York University, 1912), especially Chapters 4-5, which contain a meticulous analysis of the likenesses and differences between Spenser's literary theory and practice and that of the Pléiade.

paralleled and followed it.[2] Louis S. Friedland deals summarily with Spenser's part in the English experiments, and mentions the French only in passing; W. L. Renwick treats the subject very generally, but with almost all his emphasis on Spenser's development of metrical skill.[3]

These two movements are a small paradigm of Renaissance concomitance, an example in which one may see as it were in miniature a reflection of the larger developments which made their way from the Continent in the sixteenth century. As in the case of other literary influences at this time, it cannot definitely be established that the French knew the Italian movement, or the English the French. The links are putative. All three countries were more or less in the throes of literary creativity in a comparatively new medium, the vernacular, and all three had before them the example of the quantitative measures of Greece and Rome. The idea of imposing the rules of classical prosody upon the native language may have grown up spontaneously in France and England as it did in Italy on two occasions. But it seems quite probable that the links which do exist are evidence of direct influence or stimulus, though this cannot be proved.

Ronsard and Du Bellay were both to some extent involved in the French movement, though the standard-bearer was Jean-Antoine de Baïf, their former fellow-student at the collège de Coqueret and later a fellow-member of the Pléiade.

[2] The double meaning of *vers mesurés* in sixteenth century France is defined by Paul-Marie Masson, quoted in Frances A. Yates's *The French Academies of the Sixteenth Century* (London, 1947), p. 51, fn. 1; the distinction is between *vers mesurés à la lyre*, which throughout a given poem have the absolute regularity necessary for a setting to music, and *vers mesurés à l'antique*, "which are, theoretically, unrhymed, and which reproduce the metrical combinations of the ancients by observing the prosodic qualities of the syllables." It is, of course, in the latter sense that there is a parallel to the English quantitative verse movement, which sought, chiefly, to reproduce the prosodic quantities of the classical hexameter.

[3] "Spenser's Early Poems," pp. 104-108, and *Edmund Spenser*, pp. 103-116.

In England, Spenser participated briefly in the experiments which had been initiated before he was born and were to continue for a few years after his death. The presumed link between France and Italy is Baïf; between England and France, Sidney.[4] Before considering the place of the particular poets in the movements, I shall sketch as concisely as possible the general course of the developments which constitute a background against which the poets may be better understood, compared, and contrasted.

The use of classical metres in a modern language began in Italy with Leon Battista Alberti and Leonardo Dati in Florence in 1441, the former writing hexameters for a competition, the latter a Sapphic Ode. This incident was isolated even in Italy, and bore no fruit. In the following century another Tuscan, Claudio Tolomei, published an anthology of quantitative verse, with a long preamble of rules (1539).[5] This book contains an ingenious combination of ancient prescriptions imposed upon modern pronunciation.[6] It was the opinion of Joel Elias Spingarn that Baïf might have acquired his first knowledge of the Italian use of quantity from this book, but Mathieu Augé-Chiquet believes that Baïf's ideas were spontaneous.[7] In any case, Baïf took up quantitative verse as a serious life work which was to occupy him from the sixties until his death just before the turn of the century.

A little before Baïf's investigations of the adaptability of

[4] J. E. Spingarn, *A History of Literary Criticism in the Renaissance*, pp. 224, 300.

[5] *Versi e regole della nuova poesia toscana* (Rome, 1539).

[6] Mathieu Augé-Chiquet, *La Vie, Les Idées et L'Oeuvre de Jean-Antoine de Baïf* (Paris, 1909), p. 328. I shall be indebted throughout my general discussion of Baïf to this painstaking, detailed study of a minor member of the Pléiade, and to the monumental work of Frances A. Yates, referred to above.

[7] It may be observed, parenthetically, that there is a general tendency on the part of French critics to find a minimum of foreign influence on French literature, and a maximum of influences by French writers on other literatures.

French to classical quantity, another Frenchman had worked on the same project. Jacques de la Taille, the brother of the dramatist, a young man who died in 1562 at the age of twenty, left a manuscript entitled *La Maniere de faire des vers en françois comme en grec et en latin*, which was published by his brother in 1573.[8] De la Taille's system was fairly complete. The author apparently had the confident disposition that often accompanies youthfulness; he thought that French would be as receptive to classical measures as Latin or Greek had been, if only one worked out the system with labor and diligence. His aim was to free French poetry from its slavery to Italy. This liberation ultimately took place, of course, but for other reasons.

The aim of Baïf was to cement the union between music and poetry, that is, to produce measured lines of verse that would conform exactly to a measured phrase of music.[9] The difficulty, of course, was that while music is susceptible to mathematical analysis because it has measurable and unchanging values, language is not, because it is a living, mutable thing, subject to local and temporal variations. Both Ronsard and Du Bellay as poets dreamed of a poetry that

[8] J. E. Spingarn asserts that de la Taille's work was independent of that of Baïf, and vice versa (*A History of Literary Criticism in the Renaissance*, p. 224).
[9] That the ultimate aim, or final cause, of Baïf's prolonged experimentation with *vers mesurés* was not artistic, but religious, deserves to be pointed out, but is not our primary concern in this context. Frances A. Yates, in *The French Academies of the Sixteenth Century*, discusses this aspect of Baïf's mission at some length. She writes that "these artistic labours are undertaken, not for art's sake alone, but for certain effects which are expected of them. These melodies in the antique manner are believed to have the power of refining and purifying the minds of the auditors, and, through this purification, of initiating them into higher states of knowledge. The projected reformation in music is thus related to moral and religious reformation . . ." (p. 36), and "the effects of the measured poetry and music could be understood, not only literally as the power believed to be generated by the kind of music used by the ancients and which the academicians were trying to revive, but also more widely as the results of an education, 'musical' in the Platonic sense, and based on long discipline in the moral and intellectual virtues . . ." (p. 60).

might approximate music, and both achieved some kind of approximation in their best work. But Baïf did not merely dream. As a pedant, he set about to reduce language to a system of mathematically estimable values.

The spelling of French in the sixteenth century was as chaotic as that of English during the same period, and was a great hurdle to the standardization of pronunciation and to the ascertaining of the values of syllables. Baïf therefore constructed a system of phonetic spelling, which was defined in two treatises, *De la pronunciation francoise*, and *De l'art metric ou de la facon de composer en vers*. Both these have been lost, but Augé-Chiquet has reconstituted the latter by an analysis of Baïf's *vers mesurés*.[10] Baïf began to use this system himself in 1567 in the surviving manuscript of his *Psaumes*.[11] His phonetic principles may be illustrated by saying that he used "l'egzakte ékriture konform' ω parler an tŏs lez élémans d'iselui, létre pŏr son ŏ voéiel ŏ konsonant."[12]

Once spelling was reduced to phonetics, an attempt could be made to impose classical metres on the French language. This Baïf did; his manuscript list of Greek metres for use in French survives. In it there are fifty-seven variations on ten basic metres, such as iambic, trochaic, dactylic, anapaestic, and choriambic. In a certain sense the "docte" Baïf had succeeded. In 1570 Charles IX patented an *Academie de Musique et de Poësie* with Baïf and the musician Thibault de Courville jointly in charge.

[10] *De Baïf*, pp. 347-355. Frances A. Yates states that Augé-Chiquet's table of rules is not reliable in detail (*French Academies*, p. 53, fn. 1). She asserts that a better discussion of this subject is to be found in an unpublished thesis by D. P. Walker on *Vers et Musique Mesurés à l'antique* (1940), "a copy of which is deposited in the Bodleian Library . . ." (p. 52, fn. 1).

[11] Frances A. Yates emphasizes the religious aspect of this translation of the *Psalms* into quantitative *vers mesurés*. Four different translations exist in autograph manuscript in the *Bibliothèque Nationale*, one completed in 1569, one in 1573, one in 1586, and the last in 1587.

[12] *De Baïf*, pp. 347-355. (L'exacte ecriture conform' au parler en tous les elements d'iselui, lettre pour son ou voyelle ou consonant.)

THEORY OF POETRY

Baïf continued to write poems in almost all the fifty-seven metres, and in 1574 published his *Etrénes de poézie fransoeze*. The reception of this book on the part of the princes "qui dirigent une nation" was decorously benevolent, since they did not understand what they read; Baïf's fellow poets, however, although not actually hostile, "faisaient à sa tentative un aceuil plus réservé."[13] But the publication of this book, together with that of Jacques de la Taille's treatise the previous year, created a stir in Parisian literary circles.

Upon the death of Charles IX (1574), who had been so kind to the members of the Pléiade, Baïf's *Academie* was liquidated, and at the same time the French *vers mesurés* movement waned also, as far as the public was concerned; but it lived on in Baïf, who was never convinced of its basic futility.[14]

Baïf had made a double error. The French language proved fundamentally recalcitrant. The Greek metres conflicted with the natural though slight stress in the rhythm of a line of French verse. The scrupulous application especially of iambs and trochees to the French language resulted in a violation of either the classical metre or of French pronunciation. Secondarily, Baïf was guilty of a tactical error in publishing his *Etrénes* without any musical accompaniment. He thus deprived these quantitative poems of any popularity they might have enjoyed through singing, and deprived them also of the understanding that singing might have contributed to the verse.

His most serious error, according to Augé-Chiquet, is that he let the humanist run away with the musician; and "l'humaniste a tendu le cou au joug 'gregois' . . . le 'docte' Baïf a été victime de sa science."[15] It might be said further that

[13] Chamard, *Histoire*, IV, 371.
[14] Frances A. Yates observes with some warmth that the Palace Academy created under Henry III after the death of Charles IX "does not 'supplant' Baïf's Academy," but that the Palace Academy is an extension of Baïf's rather than a replacement, that it is in fact "an additional sign of royal favour for the academic movement . . ." (*French Academies*, p. 31).
[15] *De Baïf*, pp. 366-367.

THEORY OF POETRY

though poetry may aspire to the condition of music, language will not lend itself to an arbitrary superimposition of musical rules. Such imposition stifles inspiration. Not even great music is made according to mechanical laws, nor can it in the final analysis be reduced to such laws. This the poets knew, but not the "docte" Baïf.[16]

Thus *vers mesurés* may be said to have scored a certain *succès d'estime* in France with the publication of De la Taille's treatise and Baïf's poems in the early seventies of the sixteenth century. While the news of this small éclat would inevitably travel more slowly and less strikingly than such news as that of St. Bartholomew on August 24, 1572, it is nevertheless far from impossible that Baïf's experiments might have reached court and university circles in England during this decade. This must be borne in mind when one comes to a consideration of the Spenser-Harvey correspondence which was devised in the late seventies and which is the first published exposition of English quantitative theory.

Let us now consider the relationship of Du Bellay and Ronsard to this French movement, which, slight though it be, is significant. In the lively atmosphere of the collège de Coqueret in 1549, the idea of *vers mesurés* inevitably crossed Du Bellay's mind. But coming late to the Hellenistic studies with which Ronsard and Baïf were already thoroughly impregnated, Du Bellay considered the imposition of clas-

---

[16] The futility of the artistic or poetic aspect of Baïf's work is more than compensated by the intense religious motivation, according to Frances A. Yates, who writes that "the 'music' of the French realm is corrupted by the songs of the heretics; by providing Catholics with songs of greater power—songs which they are to sing in their ordinary walks and ways as the Huguenots sing theirs—Baïf hopes to effect through the power of Music and Poetry rightly married together a Counter Reformation in which religious discords shall be harmonized and the 'music' of France shall be once more that of a united Catholic country . . ." (*French Academies*, p. 71). From the perspective of the present time, prejudiced as it inevitably must be, in one way or another, this aspiration itself, real as Frances Yates demonstrates it to have been, seems not wholly free from futility.

sical metres upon the French language only in the vaguest and most wishful terms. He writes in the *Deffence*: "Qui eust gardé notz ancestres de varier toutes les parties declinables, d'allonger une syllabe & accourcir l'autre, & en faire des piedz ou des mains? Et qui gardera notz successeurs d'observer telles choses, si quelques scavans & non moins ingenieux de cest aage entreprennent de les reduyre en art?"[17]

Here with his usual enthusiasm and the slight degree of levity that characterizes this manifesto, Du Bellay envisions a time when the art of learned poets in the vulgar tongue will have produced not only feet but hands in the vernacular. The statement reflects the mood of the Brigade. That the first sentence is taken from Sperone Speroni's Italian treatise[18]—as is so much of Du Bellay's *Deffence*—is significant only in that the second sentence directly contradicts the meaning of the Italian. Speroni is denying the possibility of measured verse in the vulgar tongue, Du Bellay is asserting it. Henri Chamard points out that this expression is evidence that "l'idée des vers métriques ou mesurés . . . hantait les jeunes humanistes du collège de Coqueret."[19] Baïf was to bring this dream to a certain degree of reality, but neither he nor Du Bellay knew at this time that something more than the "scavans" and the "ingenieux" was needed.

Generally speaking, however, Du Bellay's advocacy of *vers mesurés* in the *Deffence* is weak and ambiguous. In one of the many apostrophes to the reader, he writes: "Adopte moy aussi en la famille Françoyse ces coulans & mignars hendecasyllabes, à l'exemple d'un Catulle, d'un Pontan & d'un Second: ce que tu pouras faire, si non en quantité, pour le moins en nombre de syllabes."[20] Here it

---

[17] *Deffence*, ed. Henri Chamard (Paris, 1948), pp. 51-52.
[18] See *Dialogo delle Lingue* in Pierre Villey, *Les Sources Italiennes de la Deffence et illustration de la langue francoyse de Joachim Du Bellay* (Paris, 1908).
[19] *Deffence*, p. 52, n. 2.
[20] *Ibid.*, pp. 124-125.

THEORY OF POETRY

would seem that little hope was held that poets in the vulgar tongue could achieve the quantitative music that was available even to neo-Latin poets. Du Bellay is willing to settle for the old system of syllabic count but with a new variety in the numbers of syllables. He believed, at least for the time being, that syllabic count plus rhyme was sufficient for the "illustration de la langue françoyse," and it seems highly likely that this conservatism in his first consideration of the matter would have remained unchanged even had he lived to see Baïf's experiments. He writes that, "Quand à la rythme [this word should be translated "rhyme"], je suy' bien d'opinion qu'elle soit riche, pour ce qu'elle nous est ce qu'est la quantité aux Grecz & Latins."[21]

This would seem to be a strong stand for rhyme as an adequate equivalent for classical quantity, but Du Bellay goes on to say that if the rhyme is not natural and native, "il vaudroit beaucoup mieux ne rymer point, mais faire des vers libres."[22] He admits the possibility of blank verse, but with certain restrictions: "Mais tout ainsi que les peintres et statuaires mettent plus grand' industrie à faire beaux & bien proportionez les corps qui sont nuds, que les autres: aussi faudroit-il bien que ces vers non rymez feussent bien charnuz & nerveuz, afin de compenser par ce moyen le default de la rythme."[23]

Henri Chamard points out that blank verse, even when "charnuz" and "nerveuz," has never succeeded in French and that Du Bellay and Ronsard seemed to realize this, since in all their works there are only two efforts in unrhymed verse.[24]

[21] *Ibid.*, p. 144. For a full discussion of "rich" rhyme, see Chamard, *Histoire*, IV, 122-128.
[22] *Ibid.*, p. 147.
[23] *Ibid.*
[24] *Ibid.*, n. 5. The Ronsard poem in blank verse is *Ode XII, sur la Naissance de Francois, Dauphin de France* (*Oeuvres*, ed. Cohen, I, 503). Du Bellay's is "Sonnet CXIV" of *L'Olive* (*Oeuvres*, ed. Chamard, I, 123).

It seems, therefore, that for all the vibrant enthusiasm, the liberal speculation, the surcharged imagination, and the untrammelled wishful thinking that probably went into the lucubrations of the Brigade, Du Bellay was unwilling, at least in print, to go beyond the most tentative suggestions for classical measures and for blank verse. Perhaps this was because he was less steeped in the classics than either Ronsard or Baïf, because he was more of a Latinist than a Hellenist, and because he could take refuge in Latin poetry of his own.[25] Or perhaps he was a temperamental mean between the religiously pedantic Baïf and the overenthusiastic Ronsard.

For Ronsard was not only more audacious than Du Bellay; he was also more practical than Baïf. Besides his single poem in blank verse, he wrote only two others, both of them short, in *vers mesurés*. The poems are from *Le Cinquiesme Livre des Odes* (1552): one is called "Ode Sapphique," the other "Vers Sapphiques." An example from each will indicate how much concession Ronsard was willing to give to quantity:

> Mon traistre penser me nourrist de souci;
> L'esprit y consent et la raison aussi.
> Long temps en mon mal vivre ne puis ainsi,
>   La mort vaudroit mieux.[26]

And, from "Vers Sapphiques:"

> Plus ne veux ouyr ces mots delicieux:
> Ma vie, mon sang, ma chere ame, mes yeux;
> C'est pour les Amans à qui le sang plus chaud
>   Au coeur ne defaut.[27]

In the first place, rhyme has not been abandoned. The Greek metre has been imposed on a rhymed line, which

---

[25] See his *Poemata*, 1558.   [26] *Oeuvres*, ed. Cohen, I, 648.
[27] *Ibid.*, p. 649.

would seem to be the ultimate in embellishment and in the wedding of Renaissance to classic. The first two lines of the "Ode," however, are the best in either stanza, and they are passable because they read like an ordinary rhymed hendecasyllabic couplet. The third line in the "Ode" breaks down in the second half because the rhythm does not follow the sense; the second half limps. In the next stanza, the initial line has the normal hendecasyllabic cadence, but the second is halting. In the final line, the poet is forced by the exigencies of the metre ($-\smile--/-\smile\smile-/\smile-$ x, hendécasyllabique sapphique)[28] into an awkward negative statement. As a whole, neither stanza is good, neither has the musical quality that usually inhabits Ronsard's lines. Rhythm, sense, and logic are violated by the tyranny of Greek metre. It is easy to understand why these poems were an early experiment, and why the poet did not go further in this direction. He could write much better poems so much more easily according to the conventional cadences of the French language.[29]

This is not to deny that Ronsard experimented. On the contrary, his experiments are more broad and more comprehensive than those of Baïf. His imitation of the classic was not only thematic in his odes and hymns; it was also metric, and with as much precision as was consonant with the rhythms of his native language. Unlike Baïf, he did not seek entirely new effects, which, as it turned out, could not be achieved. He sought to vary and modulate rhythms that were conventionally based, adding a contrapuntal play that did not violate the basic pattern but enhanced it. During the course of his life he forged the alexandrine into an instrument of varied and subtle power—and then failed to use it

[28] Augé-Chiquet, *De Baïf*, p. 358.
[29] It is an academic irony that in the year following Ronsard's death the requiem mass that was said for him was composed by Jacques Maudit in "musique mesurée à l'antique" (Frances A. Yates, *French Academies*, p. 177).

himself in his *Françiade*, because of external pressures exerted by the royal family. But he left it a fit vehicle for the magnificence of Corneille, and for the passionate undertones of Racine. The great dramatists used the line after their own fashion, but they found it developed, tried, and proved.

Ronsard was initially more concerned with the possibility of *vers mesurés* in French than was Du Bellay. In the *Advertisement au Lecteur* of 1550, he speculated about the use of dactyls and spondees in French.[30] Then, as we have seen above, he tried out classical measures. And, finally, he was immensely interested from the beginning of his career to the end in the auditory or musical quality of poetry. In his *Abbregé de l'Art Poetique François* (1565), which with characteristic *outrecuidance* he claimed to have tossed off in three hour's work, he places a great deal of stress on the connection of poetry with music. He writes: ". . . tu feras tes vers masculins et foeminins tant qu'il te sera possible, pour estre plus propres à la musique et accord des instrumens, en faveur desquels il semble que la Poësie soit née, car la Poësie sans les instrumens, ou sans la grace d'une seule ou plusieurs voix, n'est nullement agreable, non plus que les instrumens sans estre animez de la melodie d'une plaisante voix."[31]

His concern is with the sound of the words, a sound which has a melody of its own, just as music itself does. He thinks of the two in such close connection that he can consider quite naturally the reverse of our modern idea that words are a mere accompaniment to music. For Ronsard music may be an accompaniment to words, and it may be the words that animate the music, which is not pleasing without them.

The auditory test was the only certain and final proof for

[30] *Oeuvres*, ed. Cohen, II, 976.
[31] *Ibid.*, p. 999.

verse. Ronsard insists on this several times in the *Abbregé*. The poet is urged to keep "tousjours une certaine mesure consultée par ton oreille,[32] laquelle est certain juge de la structure des vers. . . ."[33] He recommends in addition: "Je te veux aussi bien advertir de hautement prononcer tes vers en ta chambre, quand tu les feras, ou plus-tost les chanter, quelque voix que puisses avoir, car cela est bien une des principalles parties que tu dois le plus curieusement observer."[34] This insistence on reading aloud, or on singing, is perhaps the most important aspect of Ronsard's theory of poetry. As he grew older it helped to cure him of his early bookishness, of his tendency toward *livresque* verse; it kept his poetry an active, living thing; it brought the fruits of his humanistic studies into the mouths of all who could sing, even the illiterate Vendômois peasants who sang his songs and his sonnets. He never forgot, except in the *Françiade* and in some other examples of his forced court poetry, the close linkage between music and poetry that originally led him to publish his sonnets of 1552 with airs specially composed for them by four musicians, Certon, Goudimel, Janequin, and Muret. His awareness of this connection, however, was on a creative level, intuitive and inspired, far different from the level of mechanical pedantry on which Baïf practiced so long, with such religious ardor, and with such ultimate futility.

[32] This statement is remarkably similar to that of George Gascoigne in *Certayne Notes of Instruction* (1575): "I will next advise you that you hold the iust measure wherwith you begin your verse." (*Elizabethan Critical Essays*, ed. G. Gregory Smith [London, 1950], p. 49.)

[33] *Oeuvres*, ed. Cohen, II, 1009.

[34] *Ibid.*, p. 1008. It is interesting to note that these words are written by a poet whose best lines have few rivals in the history of French verse, yet who was almost totally deaf, and indeed who originally chose the career of poet because his deafness disabled him for a more active life in court affairs. One should add that this reflection is even more curious in view of Du Bellay's deafness, which became total during his lifetime. Thus the two most melodious poets of the Pléiade, or for that matter of France in the sixteenth century, were more or less physically deaf, but certainly aware, as Beethoven was later, of the musical value of their creations.

THEORY OF POETRY

Du Bellay stands between the two, holding back from Baïf's singleminded pursuit up a blind alley, experimenting in many new stanzaic forms, as did Ronsard, and with lines of many various lengths, but never achieving the broad and full success that usually was Ronsard's lot, except in his own peculiarly personal melancholy mode in which he was never surpassed. It was Du Bellay's fate to cry out for new genres in the *Deffence,* to initiate them in his own work, and then to have Ronsard exploit them, carry them off, and win the laurels for himself.

This rivalry was a tonic to the development of French poetry in the fifteen-fifties: Du Bellay's first sonnet sequence induced a series of sequences from Ronsard; Du Bellay's small collection of odes was followed by five books of odes from Ronsard, together with the assertion that he was the first French poet to "Pindarize," which is true if one may call his approximate imitations Pindaric. Ronsard stole Du Bellay's imitation of the classical hymn; Ronsard preempted his political discourses and continued to develop them for twenty years after Du Bellay's death. Almost every new minor genre that Du Bellay first illustrated, Ronsard used and developed and then added new creations of his own, imitating the classics or giving a new turn to a classical genre such as the elegy or the eclogue. Du Bellay was certainly the lesser poet, but one thing Ronsard could never copy: the sad, grave music of melancholy, of exile not only from France, in *Les Regrets,* but as it were from the world itself in *Les Antiquitez de Rome.* Ronsard could not get away from his world, nor did he wish to do so; he remained in it, writing and experimenting with overflowing enthusiasm, a Faustus of French poetry.[35]

Sainte-Beuve has written that "toute idée de pratiquer les

[35] See Chamard's *Histoire,* IV, 93-116, for a complete and careful breakdown of the metrical and stanzaic forms used by both Ronsard and Du Bellay. A similar schematic breakdown for Spenser's work may be found in Louis S. Friedland's "Spenser's Early Poems," pp. 114-119.

vers métriques ne peut être qu'un caprice, un jeu d'esprit."[36] This sentence probably sums up Ronsard's view of the matter; it certainly is a severe judgment on Baïf's earnest persistence; and, though it was obviously not written with Spenser in mind, it comes very close to defining what was probably his view of the English movement.

Spenser's excursion into quantitative verse was apparently of brief duration (1579-1580), but it resulted in the first public mention of the English movement to introduce classical measures into vernacular verse.[37] Before we discuss the well-known Spenser-Harvey correspondence, however, it will be best to survey as briefly as possible the English movement in order to set it beside the French.

The first known example of quantitative verse to appear in England was the famous quotation in Ascham's *Scholemaster* (1570), from Master (later Bishop) Watson's translation of the *Odyssey*. These lines, which probably date from the forties, are still unrivalled for pedantic pedestrianism. Ascham himself was the first to speak out generally in favor of classical measures: "But now, when men know the difference, and haue the examples, both of the best, and of the worst, surelie, to follow rather the *Gothes* in Ryming, than the *Greekes* in trew versifying, were euen to eate ackornes with swyne, when we may freely eate wheate bread emonges men."[38] This pithy remark indicates an impatience with the slow course of poetic development that is akin to Du Bellay's in the *Deffence*.[39]

During the seventies Thomas Drant and Gabriel Harvey began their experiments. Virtually nothing is recorded about Drant, except that he was known to Harvey and to Sir Philip

[36] Quoted in Mathieu Augé-Chiquet, *De Baïf*, p. 425.
[37] R. B. McKerrow, "The Use of So-called Classical Metres in Elizabethan Verse," *MLQ* 4 (1901), p. 178.
[38] Roger Ascham, *The Scholemaster*, in *Elizabethan Critical Essays*, ed. G. Gregory Smith, I, 30.
[39] The resemblance between Du Bellay and Roger Ascham, however, goes no further than this.

Sidney. Along with Sidney, Edward Dyer enters the scene in the latter part of the decade; and at the same time Spenser becomes involved. This group was once thought to constitute a sort of English Pléiade, a counterpart of the French group, until the idea of an organized "Areopagus" was definitively blasted by Howard Maynadier in 1909.[40] In any case, there seems to have been a loose association in the group, particularly in respect to quantitative verse. Exactly what it was can only be surmised from the Spenser-Harvey correspondence, and Maynadier has demonstrated the danger of surmising too much.

Two general schools may be distinguished within this movement: those who wished arbitrarily to enforce quantity upon English verse by the imposition of the rules of classical prosody, a procedure which required the alteration of both spelling and pronunciation; and those who held back from such a radical method. The latter wished rather to determine quantity by customary pronunciation. This more liberal school seemed aware, if only subconsciously, of the importance of accent or stress in English verse; it moved gradually toward the idea of accentuated verse based on classical rhythms. Broadly, Drant stands for the first school, and his name has been made into an ignominious verb, "to drant"; Harvey stands for the second, always more liberal than Drant, and never as liberal or inspired as Spenser.[41]

R. B. McKerrow writes of Harvey and Spenser, "I do not think they had any precise idea of what they were after."[42]

[40] G. H. Maynadier, "The Areopagus of Sidney and Spenser," MLR 4 (1909), pp. 289-301.
[41] This distinction between Drant and Harvey will hold only in the widest sense. C. L. Hendrickson has recently pointed out that the old sharp differentiation propounded by McKerrow, Spingarn, and Saintsbury—that Drant stood for quantity and Harvey for accent—is false. He asserts that the coincidence of accent and quantity in Harvey's published quantitative verse is fortuitous, and states that "the verses which admit of pronunciation like the modern accentual hexameter are as carefully constructed in quantity as those in which accent and ictus conflict in the Latin manner ("Elizabethan Quantitative Hexameters," Ph.Q. 28 [1949], pp. 251-252).
[42] "The Use of So-called Classical Metres," MLQ 4 (1901), p. 177.

They shared with their fellow experimenters a strong feeling of dissatisfaction with contemporary poetry. Their classical education led them to envy the stability and the homogeneity that they found in Latin, and they inferred quite naturally that if classical metres could be borrowed and used properly, "new harmonies worthy of noble themes"[43] might emerge in English. Like their French counterparts, they had to try out the classical metres in order to discover the recalcitrant quality of their own language. And English, with its strong Anglo-Saxon stress, proved even more stubborn than French. For though both are analytical rather than synthetic languages, and in this respect differ radically from Greek and Latin, English is even less susceptible to alterations in word-order than is the more fully inflected French. Thus the disarrangement of normal word-order that is required by the exigencies of classical metres is more obtrusive in English than in French, and results more frequently in awkwardness or in obscurity.[44]

After 1580 Spenser never again abandoned rhyme in his published work. His two excursions into blank verse are thus confined to the brief examples of quantitative poems quoted in the correspondence with Harvey, and to the blank verse of his early translations from Du Bellay, the so-called "sonets," which were published in Jan Van der Noot's A *Theatre for Worldlings* . . . in 1569.[45] Harvey, on the other hand,

[43] *Ibid.*, p. 174.
[44] The normal French system of counting syllables in verse is clearly more adequate to classical quantity than is the stress-count in English verse, although neither is fully adequate. Catherine Ing, in demonstrating the unsuitability of Spenser's lyric poetry for musical accompaniment, because of its lack of perfect syllabic regularity, underlines this point by implication. She states in addition, and most importantly, that Spenser's lay to Eliza in "Aprill" of *The Shepheardes Calender*, "is most musical, but its music is its own, and leaves no place for the music of an air." (*Elizabethan Lyrics* [London, 1951], p. 213). It need hardly be added that the music of an air is quantitative, while Spenser's music, one might say, is verbal, or poetic.
[45] That these translations were later revised and cast into Spenser's usual sonnet form is a mute attestation to Spenser's fundamental respect for rhyme.

did not leave hexameters so easily; his last mention of classical metres is in the 1590's.

Meanwhile, Richard Stanyhurst published his translation of four books of the *Aeneid* in 1582 along with a prefatory discussion of prosody. McKerrow points out that Stanyhurst's hexameters scan according to the usual English accentual method, in their final two feet, with much greater frequency than do those of either Sidney or Harvey.[46] The movement seems thus to be turning at least slightly in the direction of what one might call natural English scansion. In 1586, William Webbe's *Discourse of English Poetrie* was published. Webbe's critical opinions at this time are anachronistic; he looks backward to Drant; he is "in accordance with the earliest experimenters"[47] who desired a rigid application of classical rules. The following year Abraham Fraunce's *The Lamentations of Amyntas* came out, and was so popular in spite of its classical hexameters that it went through several editions up to 1596.[48] Thus Fraunce was the most successful of the classicizing poets; and, though he left no theory, one may explain his success by noting that normal accent coincides with long syllables in his work far more frequently than in any other Elizabethan hexametrist.

Two years later, in 1589, *The Arte of English Poesie* appeared, written, apparently, by George Puttenham, who "practically returns to the idea that the meter of English verses should be accentual."[49] With this, the whole movement seems almost to have come full circle; but McKerrow points out that in the nineties there were two further publi-

---

[46] R. B. McKerrow, "Classical Metres II," *MLQ* 5 (1902), p. 7. G. L. Hendrickson, quoted above, would probably regard this identification as fortuitous.

[47] *Ibid.*, p. 8.

[48] The popular pastoral subject of this translation from Tasso probably did a great deal to overcome the form of the verse.

[49] *Spenser's Prose Works*, ed. Rudolf Gottfried (Baltimore, 1949), "Appendix I c.," p. 480.

cations in hexameters, in 1595 and 1599.[50] The final manifesto for classical measures, as is well-known, was Thomas Campion's *Observations in the Art of English Poesie* (1602), which elicited Samuel Daniel's reply, *A Defence of Ryme*, in the following year, a reply of such eloquence and cogency that it constitutes not merely an epitaph on post-classical experimentation but a cornerstone for future literary criticism.

Thus, the most active period of English experimentation is the years 1579-1589, when Spenser, Harvey, Sidney, Dyer, Fraunce, and Webbe all either wrote in or about classical metres, and in most cases also published. The culmination of the French movement has been seen to have occurred in 1574 with the publication of Baïf's *Etrénes*.

It is known that Sidney visited France during this period.[51] No one knows whether Drant travelled or, indeed, where he lived. It has been established on documentary evidence that Sidney's friend Edward Dyer was in close communication with the English ambassador to France at this time, Sir Amias Paulet.[52] It seems possible, therefore, that direct infection may have taken place. This matter, however, is one of indifference when one considers that English humanists as early as Bishop Watson and Roger Ascham had generated the idea of classical, unrhymed verse, perhaps quite spontaneously. It was an idea that was bound to occur in the Renaissance in any country in which there was a surge of literary activity in the vernacular. As soon as a generation of new poets arrived and developed with the self-conscious intention of exploiting their native tongue to the full, inevitably, as educated men, they thought to pillage the metres

---

[50] "Classical Metres II," *MLQ* 5 (1902), p. 10. The reference is to Francis Sabie, *Pans Pipe* (1595), and the anonymous *The First Booke of the Preservation of King Henry the vij . . .* (1599).

[51] See W. L. Renwick, *Edmund Spenser*, p. 104.

[52] See Ralph M. Sargent, *At the Court of Queen Elizabeth, The Life and Lyrics of Sir Edward Dyer* (Oxford, 1935), pp. 49ff.

as well as the matter and the themes of classical literature. French influence, therefore, probably did no more than bring native tendencies to a head.

English experiments moved generally in the direction of hexameters because English humanism at this time was oriented predominantly in Latin literature, and the Latin uses of Greek hexameters were most familiar to Englishmen. Had the English poets been educated by Dorat, they might have become involved in the labyrinthine complexities of Baïf's Greek metres instead of the more simple and straightforward hexameters. But in both cases the language refused to be shackled. Drant nevertheless laid down rules, as did Baïf: Harvey, like Baïf, persisted for a long time in entertaining thoughts of the feasibility of quantitative verse, but, unlike Baïf, he did not insist on a crippling application of rules. Webbe is a caricature of Baïf: a private tutor of no great learning, he is said to have written his book only to curry favor with his master.[53] His "Saphick" travesty on Spenser's lay to Eliza in "Aprill" of *The Shepheardes Calender* is a blood-curdling example of the danger of a little knowledge.[54]

All the English experimenters may be said to represent some aspect of the French martyr to *vers mesurés*, except that one aspect which most distinguishes the French movement from the English: Baïf's profound Hellenic scholarship, his complete persistence, and his willingness to build systematically from the ground up, to remake the language for the metre. No English poet was so fanatical, and the movement itself did not die with the passing of a man, but with the arrival of common sense in Puttenham and Daniel, and by attrition. Curiously, at the very end Campion produced some unrhymed songs that refuse to be scanned by

[53] R. B. McKerrow, "Classical Meters II," *MLQ* 5 (1902), p. 8.
[54] William Webbe, *A Discourse of English Poetrie*, in *Elizabethan Critical Essays*, ed. G. Gregory Smith, I, 286-290.

the normal English system of accent, and yet have the light and gentle, almost eerie quality of disembodied melody.[55]

Spenser, nearly thirty years after Ronsard, profited by his own quantitative verse experiments in very much the same manner as the French poet. One can imagine his arguing the question with the more rigid, more learned, but less inspired Harvey, very much as Ronsard probably argued with Baïf. But for both, this *jeu d'esprit* turned out to be a far more profitable venture than either could have suspected, or perhaps than either knew. For even the most self-conscious poet is unlikely, at the height of his mature powers, to trace the generation of these powers in part at least to the broadening influence of what must have appeared at the time to be merely a youthful indiscretion.

We have observed that when Spenser came to his period of experimentation with classical metres, there were two advocates of radical change behind him in time: Ascham, who was specific only in his uncompromising hatred of rhyme, and Drant, who was seeking to overthrow English prosody by the force or violence of rigid rules. In the more immediate past George Gascoigne had published *Certayne Notes of Instruction* (1575), which reflected a liberal point of view in its strong advocacy of custom and usage. Gascoigne wanted a "natural *Emphasis* or sound" in words as they were "commonly pronounced or vsed."[56] Not only this, but he wanted "all sentences in their mother phrase and Proper *Idioma*" as well.[57] Such requirements would make the "dranting" of verses impossible, and the view expressed in 1580 by Spenser and Harvey in their correspondence seems to be a compromise between Drant's rules and Gascoigne's common sense. It is interesting to note that Gas-

[55] See *A Pageant of Elizabethan Poetry*, arranged by Arthur Symons (London, 1906), *passim*, and Catherine Ing, *Elizabethan Lyrics*.
[56] *Elizabethan Critical Essays*, ed. G. Gregory Smith, I, 49.
[57] *Ibid.*, p. 53.

coigne's short treatise is influenced in other respects by the critical pronouncements of Ronsard and Du Bellay, according to G. Gregory Smith;[58] it may be that here too Gascoigne is profiting from the experience of Ronsard's rejection of *vers mesurés* in the radical fashion of Baïf.

Let us examine the nature of Spenser's experiment. His correspondence with Harvey appeared in the second half of 1580, in a quarto volume containing two separate parts, a group of *Three Proper* letters, followed by *Two Other* ones.[59] Spenser wrote the first and the fourth; the others are much longer, and are by Harvey. Spenser states in the fourth letter[60] that Sidney and Dyer have had long practice of writing quantitative verse, have set up a "Scnate" or "ἀρείω πάγῳ" and have "drawen" Spenser into their faction. He says that he is "of late, more in love wyth ... Englishe Versifying than with Rhyming." This letter contains a poem in "Iambickes" called *Iambicum Trimetrum,* twenty-one lines long, of which the first three are:

> Vnhappie Verse, the witnesse of my unhappie state,
> Make thy selfe fluttring wings of thy fast flying
> Thought, and fly forth unto my Loue, wheresoeuer
>   she be . . .

The poem proceeds with its wretched classic measure, entirely barren of the natural cadences of the English language.[61] The almost immediate and complete abandonment

---

[58] *Ibid.*, "Introduction," p. lxxxix.

[59] *Three Proper and Wittie, familiar Letters* . . . (London, 1580), and *Two Other very commendable Letters* . . . (London, 1580).

[60] This letter was actually written first, but the discrepancy between the published order and the real order is not important here since all the letters were written in a period of less than six months. See *The Works of Edmund Spenser, A Variorum Edition,* ed. Edwin Greenlaw, Charles Grosvenor Osgood, Frederick Morgan Padelford, Ray Heffner, Vol. ix, *The Prose Works,* ed. Rudolf Gottfried (Baltimore, 1949), p. 1.

[61] Herbert D. Rix writes that these lines and the rest of the poem not only keep the hexameter measure, but "are equally perfect from the point of view of rhetoric." He adds that the poem "of course has no poetic

of this kind of verse is an indication of the value Spenser must have set on it. This, and the following, from the first letter, represent the total of quantitative verse that Spenser was willing to publish:

> See yee the blindefoulded pretie God, that feathered Archer,
> Of Louers Miseries which maketh his bloodie Game?

and so on for two more lines. And the following "couplet" which Spenser "translated *ex tempore* in bed . . . in Westminster":

> That which I eate, did I ioy, and that which I greedily gorged,
> As for those many goodly matters leaft I for others.

The first quatrain and the second two lines, along with the *Iambicum Trimetrum*, are a fair sampling of Spenser's work in this field. Harvey carped at them with petty, pedantic criticisms in which one suspects some degree of earnestness; Spenser seems rather to have tossed them off as a joke. Compared with the rest of his work, these poems occupy a position analogous to that of Ronsard's "Ode Sapphique" and his "Vers Sapphique." Neither poet was willing for long to force his genius into an artificial classic mold. Both had the intuition, and the practical capacity, to turn the classic forms to the use and not the abuse of the vernacular. The tone of the following passage will give some indication of Spenser's seriousness in this correspondence with Harvey: "I would hartily wish, you would either send me the Rules and Precepts of Arte, which you obserue in Quantities, or else followe mine, that M. *Philip Sidney* deuised, but en-

---

value whatever." (*Rhetoric in Spenser's Poetry* [State College, Pennsylvania, 1940], pp. 63-64.)

larged with *M. Sidney's* own iudgement, and augmented with my Obseruations, that we might both accorde and agree in one: lest we ouerthrowe one another, and be ouerthrowen of the rest."[62]

The final sentence seems to contain a degree of levity. If the matter was not entirely a joke, at least it had some of the elements of an academic game, a game in which, however, Spenser's poetic intuition was probably more useful than Harvey's scholarship. For in the first of the *Three proper wittie familiar Letters* . . . Spenser exclaims, "For, why a Gods name may not we, as else the Greekes, haue the kingdome of oure owne Language, and measure our Accentes by the sounde, reseruing the Quantitie to the Verse. . . ." In this statement G. L. Hendrickson acutely points out that "a true solution fell from Spenser's innocent lips, in an outburst of vexation at the whole perplexing business with which he was toying halfheartedly."[63] Spenser seemed to know, if one may assume that he understood what he was writing, that as in Latin verse there is no necessary correlation of accent and quantity, so also if quantitative verse in English was to be in any way successful, the poet must reserve "normal accents for speech or pronunciation, quantity for the construction of the verse." Thus it is probable that Spenser understood intuitively the true nature of quantitative verse, though he could not practice it in English. Harvey, on the other hand, practiced the classical quantitative system as well as the English language would permit, but made no theoretical statement as perceptive as Spenser's.

The paucity of examples shows that Spenser "dranted" few verses of which he was unashamed. Harvey too, even at this time, was unwilling to subscribe fully to Drant's rules. In the third letter of the series he exclaims: "Else neuer

[62] *Prose Works*, IX, 16.
[63] "Elizabethan Quantitative Hexameters," *Ph.Q.* 28 (1949), p. 251.

heard I any that durst presume so much ouer the Englishe (excepting a few suche stammerers as haue not the masterie of their owne tongues) as to alter the quantitie of any one sillable, otherwise than oure common speache and general receyued Custome woulde beare them oute."[64]

He continues a few pages later in the same conservative vein: "It is not, either Position, or Dipthong or Diastole, or anye like Grammar Schoole Deuice that doeth or can indeed either make long or short, or encrease, or diminish the number of sillables, but onely the common allowed and receiued PROSODYE, taken vp by an vniuersal consent of all, and continued by a generall vse and Custome of all."[65] By PROSODYE Harvey means accent. Thus one finds him in accord with Spenser in respect to measuring "Accentes by the sounde," but unlike Spenser in his lack of theoretical understanding of the English quantitative system as a whole. So, in spite of his continuing interest in quantitative verse, dating presumably at least from the early seventies, and certainly continuing until 1592, Harvey was no fanatic. Like Baïf, he wanted "ONE AND THE SAME ORTHOGRAPHIE," and was ready to alter spelling in favor of a clearer representation of quantity,[66] but he was loathe to tamper with accented pronunciation. He hoped that quantity would eliminate the "counterfeit and base ylfauored Copper" of rhyme, and substitute a "pure and fine Goulde."[67] This, of course, it was never to do.

After his brief involvement with hexameters, Spenser declared his freedom from such restrictions, as all his future work demonstrates. He achieved a mastery of the line that few English poets have exceeded, and a mastery of the stanza and inter-stanzaic play that few have equalled.[68] W. L. Ren-

[64] *Elizabethan Critical Essays*, I, 117.
[65] *Ibid.*, p. 121.   [66] *Ibid.*, pp. 102-103.   [67] *Ibid.*, p. 101.
[68] A contrary view has been expressed by the late Theodore Spencer, who has written that Sidney was a better hexametrist than Spenser— which is probably quite true—and that Sidney's poetic accomplishment,

wick writes that Spenser learned from Minturno and from Gascoigne that a poet should strive for "the reconciliation of metrical pattern and rhythm which is dictated by the nature of the language."[69] It might be added that he learned this also from his classical experiments, just as Ronsard had learned the same kind of reconciliation from his own. Probably neither realized explicitly that his vernacular tongue was analytic, and not synthetic like Latin or Greek; and each discovered this, but not with discouragement, for each was full of talent and enthusiasm and ready to move forward within the limitations set by language. The experiments in quantitative metres and in *vers mesurés* were a significant means to this discovery.

Renwick points out further that "it is a striking fact—or a profound problem—that the revival of English verse coincides with the great age of English music." The same is true in France: this is why Ronsard asks the poet to sing his verses, if possible, and this is why Ronsard's early sonnets were published with music of their own, and why much of his later work was set to music. Renwick insists that as an educated man, Spenser must have known music well;[70] the same is true of Ronsard, deaf though he was. Perhaps it is

---

what he did as a whole for English poetry in the seventies and early eighties, "has been somewhat overshadowed by the more ambitious and apparently [sic] more professional work of Spenser . . ." ("The Poetry of Sir Philip Sidney," ELH 12 [1945], p. 277).

[69] *Edmund Spenser*, p. 109. In regard to the nature of the English language, Catherine Ing points out significantly that "English syllables have not in natural speech any consistent relation to each other in quantity (*Elizabethan Lyrics*, p. 195). Her conclusion is based on measurements of the length of vowel sounds in hundredths of a second, made by E. A. Sonnenschein (*What is Rhythm?* [Oxford, 1925], Appendix II); she writes, "we speak and hear syllables of almost every possible variation of quantity between the obvious longs and the obvious shorts. Such variable material cannot provide a basis for recognizable structure." Thus the nature of the language itself is seen to deny the possibility of stringent quantitative measurement in English verse.

[70] *Ibid.*, p. 110.

even more true of Ronsard because it was from France and Italy that the new music came to England.

The important thing about sixteenth century music and its relationship to poetry is that the music was polyphonic, full of contrapuntal variety. It taught that many voices can play upon a basic melody, and by analogy that there is an area of free invention within the bounds of a basic rhymed iambic pentameter or an alexandrine couplet. Renwick has expressed this musical parallel in a fine metaphor: "that the metre is an implied or silent ground bass over which the poet plays a descant."[71] This speaks for Ronsard as well as for Spenser. This, and one other factor, is the key to Ronsard's and Spenser's capacity to write many long poems that contain such varied music, varied but all consistently based in a single metre. It is the key also to Racine's long speeches and to Milton's *Paradise Lost*.

The additional factor is the measurable pause, which also derived from musical practice: the varying caesura, the line-ending, and the denial of pause, enjambment. The consummate skill with which both Ronsard and Spenser manipulate the ebb and flow of their mature verse, while it is in one sense a mark of unfathomable genius, is also the sign that a long road of trial and error led to this final result. The youthful experimentation with quantitative measures was an important milestone along this road.

Writing about the problem of language and diction, W. L. Renwick says that "Spenser worked on precisely the same lines as Ronsard and Du Bellay."[72] The statement holds also

[71] *Ibid.*, p. 112. See Frances A. Yates's *The French Academies* for an excellent discussion of the relationship of poetry to music in France, especially Chapter III; and Catherine Ing's *Elizabethan Lyrics* for a discussion of the same relationship in England, especially her chapter on Campion. One should mention further that what is referred to as the new contrapuntal quality in French and English verse refers to the vernacular languages, and does not take account of similar qualities in mediaeval Latin verse, which is beyond the scope of this essay.

[72] "The Critical Origins of Spenser's Diction," *MLR* 17 (1922), p. 15.

for Ronsard and Spenser in their classical experiments. Both were moved initially by the same pressures: a disgust with contemporary verse, its paucity, its emptiness and its lack of cadence, and a further distaste for their recent predecessors. Both were young and enthusiastic. The education of both took place in a world in which music was a common part of everyday life. Each grew up in an atmosphere of classical study, Spenser's leaning toward Latin, Ronsard's toward Greek; and this difference may be seen in the fact that Spenser's surviving quantitative verse is in hexameters, Ronsard's in sapphics. In both cases the vernacular offered a new world, ready for conquest.

So far, however, the situation is common to many Englishmen and Frenchmen besides Spenser and Ronsard. What they brought to this common background that ultimately distinguished them from everyone else was a dynamic talent that could envision, pursue, and grasp a goal to which the others were blind. Spenser was constantly distracted by poverty, by public affairs, by melancholy. Ronsard was at first the slave of his own enthusiasms, later the slave of an unappreciative court for which he had to write countless lines of flattery, and always somewhat the slave of his passions. The two are perpetually in disaccord about everything in this life that is considered of high value, with the single exception of poetry. But as poets each possessed a divine gift and was possessed by it, and each earned the name of prince in his own land.

IV · THE COMPLAINTS OF THE MUSES

On the poetry of the Pléiade and in that of the English Renaissance the ancient Greek muses were accustomed to descend either singly or in a body to inspire the poet, to preside over the poem, to be apostrophized whether thankfully or hortatorily, or to be inveighed against, or, finally, to act as literary critics, separating the author from contemporary poetasters.

Spenser's *The Teares of the Muses* (1579-1590?)[1] is a formal complaint against the abuse to which the gifts of the Muses have been subjected. In the poem this general theme is examined at some length and with much repetition by the Muses themselves, who analyze the causes for the absence of truly poetic works and the causes for the presence of bad verse. The Muses, presumably on Spenser's behalf, make a thoroughly damning diagnosis of contemporary literary illness; and their prognosis is despondent if not actually despairing, in spite of the paradoxical statements of Polyhymnia at the end of the poem, which sound almost like a palinode.

It is an open question, however, whether the literary pessimism expressed in the poem is the result of a thoughtful and considered opinion of contemporary poetry, or whether it is merely the expression of a mood, real at the time, but ephemeral in its nature. Harold Stein maintains that "the

[1] The date of composition of the poem has not yet been settled with any degree of certainty. Renwick writes, "If we can date this poem about 1579-80—I have suggested some reasons why we should, and I can find none why we should not . . ." (*Complaints*, p. 205). But in making an analogy between lines 339-354 in Spenser's poem, and Ronsard's *Dialogue entre les Muses Deslogées et Ronsard* on p. 212, Renwick fails to note that Ronsard's poem appeared in 1584, *after* the date he assigns to Spenser's poem. Harold Stein assigns *The Teares of the Muses* on "slight but positive evidence" to 1589 or 1590 (*Studies*, p. 48). If nothing else, these discrepant dates may be taken as limits.

poem is a conventional set piece, not a personal analysis."[2] In this he is certainly correct, as one can clearly see both in the content and in the careful structure of the poem.[3] As a set piece, *The Teares of the Muses* is squarely in a tradition established in France by the Pléiade in the decades immediately preceding the composition of Spenser's poem. Thus such a mood expressed in a set piece may well be as firmly grounded in the French tradition of the Muses' lament, so often sung by Du Bellay and by Ronsard, as it is in a critical estimate of English poetry at the time of composition.

A moody poem, in the form of a manifesto or a plaint or a propagandistic pamphlet, carefully wrought and fully elaborated in order to document its statements by elusive reference and drive home its general argument by reiteration of the chief points, Spenser's poem has striking connections with the work of Du Bellay and Ronsard. This has not escaped previous critics, of course, and the Variorum Edition of Spenser's *Works* is lightly strewn with analogous passages from the work of the two French poets.

But the French analogies have not been examined in their contexts, nor indeed has the text of an entire French poem been examined in relation to Spenser's poem. Previous analogies have been confined to a few single expressions of similar ideas, many of which were commonplace in the Renaissance. It is clear that such analogies were more widespread in the French poets than has been explicitly remarked; and it is probable that a pursuit of them will elucidate some of the major contrasts between Spenser and his French seniors, as well as reflect the significant similarities. For although the

---
[2] *Studies*, p. 51.
[3] The introduction to the poem is in nine stanzas, followed by nine speeches of the nine Muses, each speech of ten stanzas, except for that of Euterpe, which has eleven stanzas and who comes fourth among the Muses but fifth in the order of ten-stanza-groups, that is, in the exact middle of the poem. Thus Euterpe's extra stanza brings the whole to an even hundred stanzas.

three poets received a large part of their inspiration from many of the same sources, it is in the reaction to the same stimuli that their individuality and their particular greatness is to be discovered.

This poem of Spenser's is not a great poem. It contains many bad lines characteristic of what C. S. Lewis calls the Drab Age that preceded Spenser. R. E. Neil Dodge comments that the poem "comes near . . . to seeming insufferable," and goes on to say that "in the particular tone or mood . . . one almost suspects an echo of Ronsard."[4] Lest anyone think that such an echo might be felicitous, Dodge says of Ronsard that he "is notably distinguished from his colleagues by an odd faculty of making their common views offensive or ridiculous."[5] Thus the French influence is noted, but is marked down as wholly deleterious.

Certainly the petulance of the Muses' complaint is un-English, but the poem, after all, is called a lament, and its author was more likely following convention rather than inspiration. It is for this reason that the French influence can be more clearly found in *The Teares of the Muses* than in the great poems in which all influences have fused and have been transmuted in the intense heat of creative activity. The differences of tone between the somewhat petulant complaints of Spenser, of Ronsard, and of Du Bellay assume a greater significance because the similarities are so striking at the superficial level, and diverge only beneath the surface, as if French expressions in coming to England had suffered a sea-change by passing through instead of over the Channel pointedly called, by the English, "English."

The French poems cited by W. L. Renwick[6] and J. B. Fletcher[7] are Du Bellay's *La Musagnoemachie* and his *Poëte*

[4] *Spenser's Complete Poems*, p. 70.
[5] *Ibid.*
[6] *Complaints*, notes to *The Teares of the Muses*, *passim*.
[7] "Areopagus and Pléiade," *JEGP* 2 (1889), pp. 429ff. It should be remarked that L. S. Friedland deals also with *The Teares of the Muses* in

Courtisan, as well as his *Deffence*; and Ronsard's *Dialogue entre les Muses Deslogées et Ronsard*, his *Ode x* (*A Michel de L'Hospital*), and his *Ode xii* (*A Bouju*).[8] The analogous passages are quoted extensively in the Variorum Edition of Spenser, and the reader is left to draw his own conclusions. The parallels are so clear in some cases that they constitute convincing evidence that Spenser may have had the French poems in mind at the time of writing. If one assumes this to be true, one may perhaps also assume that he knew the whole poems and not merely the passages cited, and that he knew other poems by the same men which expressed similar ideas, ideas which became a part of the climate of the French Renaissance and which, when Englished by Spenser, were Englished with a difference: a difference that is obviously temporal, partly national, and chiefly individual. Let us consider first Du Bellay's *Musagnoeomachie* and his *Poëte Courtisan*, and the place of their themes in his work; and then the relationship of the poems and the themes to Spenser's *The Teares of the Muses*.

Du Bellay himself says of *La Musagnoeomachie*, in answer to critics of the first edition, "Je n'ay qu'une petite responce à toutes ces objections frivoles: c'est que mon in-

---

his unpublished dissertation, "Spenser's Early Poems," pp. 9/86-11/88; but his discussion contains nothing that is not to be found in Fletcher or in Renwick.

[8] One should note that in the concord of agreement concerning the resemblance of *The Teares of the Muses* to certain poems by Du Bellay and Ronsard, there is at least one jarring discord. Francesco Viglione repudiates the comparisons offered by "il Renwick e il Jones . . . anche Sidney Lee" (*La Poesia Lirica di Edmondo Spenser* [Genoa, 1937], p. 146), and alleges that there is no influence of the Pléiade on this poem of Spenser's. He ignores Du Bellay's poetry completely and points out in a brilliant *non sequitur* that Spenser's thoughts turned more constantly to Sidney than to Du Bellay, and that therefore all influences presumed to be French are in fact Italian. To clinch his argument concerning the impossibility of French influences in England at this time, he points out that England had been making political alliances for three hundred years with the object of humbling the French (pp. 150-151).

tention n'estoit alors d'ecrire une hystoire, mais une poësie."[9] Du Bellay's statement would hold even better for Spenser's poem than for his own, because while the English poet deals with contemporary literature only in the most general way, Du Bellay is very specific in many passages, naming names and making judgments, producing what is at least a catalogue if not a history. It is a youthful work of Du Bellay's,[10] and its immaturity is evident throughout. There has been a tendency to depreciate the poem, which, though it is faulty in construction and though it lacks the grave and gentle music found in much of Du Bellay's verse, nevertheless has a certain *verve* or *élan*, a quality conspicuously lacking in Spenser's poem.

Du Bellay describes the victory of French literature, inspired by the Muses, over Ignorance. Though it ends on a somber and personal note, the poem as a whole is one of faith, hope, and enthusiasm. In its rash forthrightness, in its call to continued battle, and in its preposterous Greek-derived title it is intimate, rousing, and youthful.

Spenser's poem has none of these qualities of juvenile enthusiasm; in tone it differs entirely from *La Musagnoeomachie*. Yet this poem of Du Bellay's is the chief source of analogous passages in Spenser. The English poet must therefore have rejected the spirit of Du Bellay's poem as a whole, while he accepted the propriety of certain passages, to wit, those dealing specifically with the generation of Ignorance. The French poet discourses at length on the horrendous aspect of the monster Ignorance in order to make more illustrious the French victory, whereas Spenser constructs similar passages, almost certainly based on Du Bellay, in order to moralize on English indifference and degeneracy.

Clearly Du Bellay is writing as the self-conscious and con-

[9] *L'Olive, Seconde Préface*, ed. Chamard, I, 24.
[10] The poem was first published in 1550, the year following his first published work, the *Deffense*.

fident initiator of a literary revival, while Spenser, more than a generation later in England, has no sense of the heavy pregnancy of his own national literature.

Du Bellay's poem exemplifies his youthful tendency to cast his poetry of ideas into the form of a myth, a tendency shared by other Pléiade poets, especially Ronsard. But theirs is a dynamic mythology, full of actions and of events, not a static mythological picture, as in Spenser's poem; a myth more closely connected with historical realities, into whose depictions of mythological truth actual persons, either historical or contemporary, freely intrude to alter the course of the myth, symbolically, as in life, they influenced the terrestrial reality.[11]

There is not merely a gap in time and space between Spenser's and Du Bellay's poems; there is a world of difference in outlook. Du Bellay is writing in the flush of a campaign so far successful, waged not alone but first with a "Brigade" and then a "Pléiade"; far from being alone, at this time he has a keen sense of *esprit de corps*. Spenser has on the other hand been more or less isolated in Ireland and has at least for the moment lost faith in the English movement of which he was so important a part and which was to equal and then surpass its French analogue. Du Bellay knows that French literature is renascent and he is celebrating this as a virtually accomplished fact. Spenser is upset and concerned because he fears English literature is not renascent; he may even be looking back on the accomplishment of the Pléiade as a whole and see a disheartening discrepancy between England and France.

In the *Poëte Courtisan*, however, Du Bellay has moved closer to Spenser's position. Almost ten years have passed

[11] Such a method of treatment probably derives from the almost exclusively classical emphasis of Du Bellay's and Ronsard's formal education —a more exclusive emphasis than in the case of Spenser, whose treatment of myth is colored by mediaeval allegorical practice.

since the writing of *La Musagnoeomachie*. The hope and the faith that generated the *élan* of the earlier poem, and of its prose companion the *Deffence*, have become dissipated. Du Bellay is an older and, if not a wiser man, at least a man of far greater experience. The nature of this experience—much of it connected with his public position at Rome and the accompanying disappointment, with illness, and with the lack of personal success, especially at Court—all these tend to produce a mood in its circumstances not unlike that which caused Spenser to write *The Teares of the Muses*.

But the *Poëte Courtisan* is not a lament in form; it is a satire and it makes its points through irony. Thus, close as it is in circumstances to Spenser's poem, its method is radically different, and its aim is more restricted. The courtier poet is merely one of the breed of ignorance, and it is at this poet rather than at ignorance itself that Du Bellay chiefly aims, whereas Spenser at the end of his poem (lines 583 ff.) makes specific though anonymous exception of a certain few court poets, and points his main arguments at ignorance itself.

By ironic inversion, however, the *Poëte Courtisan* is a backhanded *Musagnoeomachie*. It recommends ignorance, lack of artistry, absence of study; it endorses most of the qualities in a poet that both Du Bellay and Spenser in fact deplore. The poem is bitter, but the bitterness is controlled and never spills over into the petulance which mars passages of Spenser's poem. Similar as the mood of disappointment and disgust is in both poets, the total effect reveals Spenser as less mature, less forceful, and less effective than Du Bellay. Perhaps this is partly because Du Bellay is at the end of his hopes for important preferment, whereas Spenser may still entertain hope for material advancement. This draws much of the sting from *The Teares of the Muses*, makes it plaintive rather than bitter, and softens his indictment.

This is not to say, however, that Du Bellay was incapable

of petulance, or that he was always pure and clear of any taint of sycophancy. Several of the sonnets in *Les Regrets* written earlier in his career contain lines whose petulance is comparable to Spenser's in *The Teares of the Muses*.[12] The tendency in Du Bellay, however, was rather toward satire and irony than toward complaint. His literary position was more secure than Spenser's; he was writing as a member of a recognized movement, and his own Muse was more Horatian.

The theme of the reign of ignorance and the threatened degeneration of literature nevertheless haunts Du Bellay's work from the time of his Roman sojourn (1552) to the end of his life. The passages in the *Musagnoeomachie* and in the *Poëte Courtisan* are far from isolated instances of the expression of ideas similar to those in *The Teares of the Muses*. It would be futile to construct a complete catalogue of those instances, but a few might be mentioned in order to demonstrate the continued recurrence of this theme in a poet so admired by Spenser.

In Sonnet CXC of the *Regrets* Du Bellay writes,

Helicon est tary, Parnasse est une plaine,
Les lauriers sont seichez . . .
Phoebus s'en fuit de nous, & l'antique ignorance
Sous la faveur de Mars retourne encore en France . . .[13]

This is the situation of the early 1550's under Henri II; the recently unqualified enthusiasm of the *Deffence* and the *Musagnoeomachie* has begun to become tarnished by a broadened experience of the world, and the mood of com-

---

[12] Chiefly Sonnets XLIII, CLIV, and CXC.
[13] It seems worth noting here the words of Euterpe in Spenser's poem, lines 277-281:

Our pleasant groues . . .
That with our musick wont so oft to ring,
And arbors sweet . . .
They haue cut downe and all their pleasaunce mard . . .

plaint is forming a transition to the later mood of irony. In
A Olivier de Magni, a poem probably written in Rome in
the middle fifties but not published until 1559, he writes
of poetry after the ascent of Henri II to the throne:

> Maïs depuis les premiers Auteurs,
> Un tas de sots imitateurs,
> Enflans leurs vaines poësies
> De monstrueuses fantasies,
> Ont tout gasté: & ceulx qui ont
> Le mieulx escrit, pource qu'ilz sont
> Pressez de la tourbe ignorante,
> Leur gloire n'est point apparente.[14]

There would seem perhaps to be a reminiscence of these lines in some of the words of Terpsichore in Spenser's poem.[15]

The currency of complaints concerning the abuse of the Muses' gifts, as well as Du Bellay's predilection toward this theme, is indicated not only by his original work but by his translations from contemporary Latin poetry.[16] It is in such a trend of his whole work that Du Bellay comes close to the Spenser of *The Teares of the Muses*, as it is in the whole text of *The Teares of the Muses* that Spenser most clearly parallels a theme that was of continuous concern to Du Bellay and, indeed, to the other members of the Pléiade as well as the international group of humanists writing in Latin. The convention in which Spenser's set piece is placed is thus broader than any single national literary tradition. But there can be little doubt here, as elsewhere, that Spenser felt a special temperamental affinity with the second poet of the Pléiade. Both men lived on what might be called terms of intimacy with the Muses; both men complained to

[14] *Oeuvres Poetiques*, ed. Chamard, v, 66 (*Divers Jeux Rustiques*).
[15] See *The Teares of the Muses*, lines 319-324.
[16] See *Oeuvres Poetiques*, ed. Chamard, IV, 190ff. and VI, 113ff.

them, of them, or through them. The Muses for them were more than literary constructions, more than mere personifications of genres; they were living sources either of inspiration or of desperation, and, aside from the poems under consideration, numerous passages in both poets attest to this reality.

A discussion of Ronsard, and of the poems usually associated with *The Teares of the Muses*, as well as of several others which treat the same theme, will further demonstrate the quality of Spenser's connection with the chief Pléiade poets, and the position of his poem in a category that was familiar to his French predecessors.

Three poems of Ronsard's are conventionally linked with *The Teares of the Muses*. The analogies are few, but specific, and all refer to the maleficent influence of Ignorance on poetry.[17] There are, however, between Spenser's poem and these of Ronsard somewhat closer connections than have been observed, similarities of thematic treatment, and other connections probably more interesting and more fruitful for consideration because they are not merely reiterative of the same ideas in other words, but contrasting presentations of the same kind of subject matter. I shall deal successively with the likenesses, but as a preliminary to that note as briefly as possible the general nature of the Ronsard poems in question.

The earliest poem of Ronsard's that has an affinity with *The Teares of the Muses* is his *Ode X, A Michel de L'Hospital, Chancelier de France*, first published in 1552, but evidently composed in the second half of 1550,[18] almost at the very beginning of his career. It is an ambitious poem, in form a careful Pindaric imitation comprising twenty-four strophes, antistrophes, and epodes. While it contains fine

---

[17] *Complaints*, ed. Renwick, notes to *The Teares of the Muses, passim*; and J. B. Fletcher, "Areopagus and Pléiade," cited above.
[18] See Henri Chamard, *Histoire de la Pléiade*, I, 364.

passages, it fails to come off as a whole because it is too ambitious, too overweening in its attempt to comprehend in one lyric poem of 816 lines a complete mythological survey of the birth and early career of the Muses, an historical survey of the Muses' career in the real world from the time of the legendary Greeks to Ronsard's own day, an account of the birth of Michel de L'Hospital cast in mythological terms, and finally a courtly tribute to Michel and to Marguerite de Savoie, the French King's sister and a patroness of the Pléiade poets. The chief purpose of the poem is to justify the new conception of the poet introduced and now put into practice by Ronsard, Du Bellay, and other members of the Pléiade. Chamard writes that the *Ode* is a "vibrante apologie . . . de cette poèsie nouvelle où s'affirme et s'incarne l'Humanisme de la Renaissance."[19] But it is a poem of what was called by the French of Ronsard's time *outrecuidance*, by Spenser, "surquedry," and long before, by the Greeks, *hubris*. Thus in tone it is utterly unlike anything that Spenser wrote.

One part of the subject matter of this ode has been connected by W. L. Renwick with *The Teares of the Muses*, and another by Spenser's Variorum editors, this latter on Renwick's suggestion.[20] Both these passages deal exclusively with Ignorance. A parallel as significant as those above may be drawn between Polyhymnia's lament in Spenser's poem, and antistrophe and epode 17 of Ronsard's:

> Whilom in ages past none might professe
> But Princes and high Priests that secret skill,
> The sacred lawes therein they wont expresse,
> And with deepe Oracles their verses fill:
> Then was shee held in soueraigne dignitie,
> And made the noursling of Nobilitie.

[19] *Ibid.*, p. 368.
[20] *Complaints*, p. 211, and *The Minor Poems*, II, 323.

COMPLAINTS OF THE MUSES

But now nor Prince nor Priest doth her maintayne,
But suffer her prophaned for to bee
Of the base vulgar, that with hands vncleane
Dares to pollute her hidden mysterie.
And treadeth vnder foote hir holie things,
Which was the care of Kesars and of Kings.
(Lines 559-570)

This survey of the degradation of poetry follows in general the laments of the rest of the Muses, but in its concept of sacred and profane poetry it is identical with earlier French concepts derived from the classics, especially from Plato,[21] and in its expression it is closely parallel to the following lines of Ronsard's *Ode*, concerning the early divinity and later degeneracy of poetry:

> ANT. Eux [the divine poets], piquez de la douce rage
>   Dont ces filles [the Muses] les tourmentoyent,
>   D'un demoniacle courage
>   Les secrets des Dieux racontoyent . . .
>   Carolant en rond par les prez,
>   Les promouvoyent Prestres sacrez
>   De leurs plus Orgieux mysteres.
> EP. Apres ces Poëtes saints,
>   Avec une foule grande
>   Arriva la jeune bande
>   D'autres Poëtes humains
>   Degenerant des premiers:
>   Comme venus les derniers,
>   Par un art melancholique
>   Trahirent avec grand soin
>   Les vers, esloignez bien loin
>   De la sainte ardeur antique.[22]

---

[21] The *Ion* and the *Phaedo* appeared in Latin translations in France in 1540. Ronsard, educated as he was by the great Greek scholar Jean Dorat, may have read them in the original.

[22] *Oeuvres*, ed. Cohen, I, 400.

It is perhaps scarcely necessary to point out the relationship between these passages, which like the asymptotes to an hyperbola move in constant rapprochement but never really meet: for example, the "high Priests" and the "Prestres sacrez," the "secret skill/The sacred lawes" and "Les secretes des Dieux," the "deepe Oracles" and the "Orgieux mysteres," and finally the "base vulgar" and the "foulle grande." These are the commonplaces of the Renaissance, similarly expressed and exposed in a multitude of other places, in poetry and in prose, but here divergent in their similarity. There is a dignified restraint in Polyhymnia's words; the verse itself is restrained, as is her description of what E. K. and Spenser refer to as "ἐνθουσιασμός." Not so Ronsard; he is ardent with a reborn "sainte ardeur," and his "douce rage" is really more "rage" than "douce," a "demoniacle courage," and un-Spenserian *forcénement*. If Spenser remembered this poem of Ronsard's, he must have remembered its excessive ardor.

A vague connection between Ronsard's *Discours ou Dialogue entre les Muses deslogées et Ronsard* and *The Teares of the Muses* has been suggested by W. L. Renwick,[23] and a more specific one by J. B. Fletcher.[24] As a whole, Ronsard's poem is a fantasy which expresses a very late disgust[25] with inadequate rewards from a King and a Court which had granted him understanding and appreciation and money that he felt to be totally incommensurate with his merits. The last lines of the poem are paradoxical in that the praise of Henri III is susceptible of a double interpretation, and it is a virtual certainty that in view of Ronsard's well-known

---

[23] *Complaints*, p. 212. Renwick writes, "This [*The Teares of the Muses*, lines 339-354] (and the poem in general) may owe something to Ronsard's *Dialogue entre les Muses Deslogées et Ronsard* . . . but the notion is not very recondite." Again on p. 214 he refers lines 451-460 of Spenser's poem to Ronsard's *Dialogue*.
[24] "Areopagus and Pléiade," *JEGP* 2 (1899), p. 435.
[25] The poem was published in the first part of the *Bocage Royal* in 1584.

hatred of the Court toward the end of his life the pejorative meaning is the correct one.[26]

In this respect Ronsard's poem differs radically from Spenser's; not only is Spenser's praise of Elisa at the end of his poem (lines 571-582) clearly sincere, as are all his references to his Queen wherever they may occur, but one cannot conceive in Spenser the possibility that he might employ *double entendre* or irony in a matter of this kind. There is something brittle and petty in Ronsard's flattery of monarchs (with the exception of Charles IX), which probably does not spring so much from his individual temperament as from his position at Court—one of growing insecurity from the time of the death of Charles IX. His poem has the bitterness of a man who, having made his way to the top, has been displaced and superseded. Spenser's disillusionment is not so personal, nor in fact has he lost his position. Spenser is not disillusioned with the Muses themselves any more than Ronsard was in his *Ode, A Michel de L'Hospital*; he has confidence in them and sympathy for their complaints. But Ronsard in his poem is disillusioned with the Muses themselves; he rejects them, as the final couplet of his poem declares:

> Pource cherchez ailleurs un autre qui vous meine.
> Adieu, docte troupeau, adieu, belle neuvaine.

There is irony in these lines in his calling the Muses "docte" and "belle." In the context of the poem his disgust with them is quite clear, though of course, it is only a reflection of his general disgust with the Court.

Ronsard's whole poem, therefore, is more in the mood of Du Bellay's *Poëte Courtisan* than it is of *The Teares of the Muses*, as the *Hospital* ode is closer to the *Musagnoeomachie*

[26] See letter to A. M. de Sainte Marthe, 1577: ". . . je hay la cour comme la mort."

and the *Deffence* than it is to Spenser. But in certain specific ways Ronsard's *Discours ou Dialogue* is notably close to Spenser. Clio, appropriately, in castigating the English nobility, says:

> But they doo onely striue themselues to raise
> Through pompous pride, and foolish vanitie;
> In th'eyes of people they put all their praise,
> And onely boast of Armes and Auncestrie:
> But vertuous deeds, which did those Armes first giue
> To their Grandsyres, they care not to atchiue.
>
> (Lines 91-96)

Ronsard, speaking to his Muses, perhaps to Clio more than the others, employs a like simile, though turning the criticism back upon the Muses:

> Certes vous ressemblez aux pauvres Gentilshommes,
> Qui, quand tout est vendu, levant la teste aux cieux,
> N'ont plus d'autre recours qu'à vanter leurs ayeux.[27]

Further, the idea expressed in Ronsard's title of the dispossessed, errant, homeless Muses, is the same in both poems. The Muses say to Ronsard:

> Errons, comme tu vois, sans biens et sans maisons,
> Où le pied nous conduit, pour voir si sans excuses
> Les peuples et les Rois auront pitié des Muses.[28]

In Spenser's poem, Terpsichore speaks for herself and her sisters:

> The whiles we silly Maides, whom they dispize,
> And with reprochfull scorne discountenaunce,
> From our owne natiue heritage exilde,
> Walk through the world of euery one reuilde.

---

[27] *Discours ou Dialogue*, second speech of Ronsard.
[28] *Ibid.*, first speech of the Muses.

> Nor anie one doth care to call vs in,
> Or once vouchsafeth vs to entertaine ...
>
> (Lines 339-344)

A final point of analogy—though like most such points in Renaissance writing there is no necessary direct relationship between the expression of similar ideas that were common material and possessed simultaneous ubiquity in the Renaissance atmosphere—concerns the duty of the nobility to be wise and to abhor ignorance:[29]

> It most behoues the honorable race
> Of mightie Peeres, true wisedome to sustaine,
> And with their noble countenaunce to grace
> The learned forheads, without gifts or gaine:
> Or rather learnd themselues behoues to bee;
> That is the girlond of Nobilitie.
>
> (Lines 79-84)

Parallel to this, Ronsard's Muses state the same doctrine by implication:

> Nous avons ouy dire
> Que le Prince qui tient maintenant vostre Empire,
> Et qui d'un double sceptre honore sa grandeur,
> Est dessus tous les Roys des lettres amateur,
> Caresse les sçavans, et des livres fait conte,
> Estimant l'ignorance estre une grande honte ...[30]

The ironic ending of Ronsard's poem consists in the poet's refusal to bother a busy King with what he refers to as the Muses' "vulgaire propos," which is that the King take them in. The irony here is probably more than double; the "propos" for Ronsard both is and is not "vulgaire," and in

---
[29] W. L. Renwick traces the lines that follow to Hoby's translation of Castiglione's *Il Cortegiano*, from which Ronsard himself may well have acquired the idea.
[30] *Discours ou Dialogue*, final speech of the Muses.

this ambiguous sense if it is "vulgaire" for the King who is said to be bringing back the Golden Age, then it must be the King himself who is really "vulgaire." Spenser's feeling for Elizabeth did not hang by such a thin wire, nor was he one to split such hairs. But of course Elizabeth herself was quite a different kind of monarch.

One should note further in the above passages, as well as in both poems as a whole, the strong moral flavor of Spenser's Muses—what one might call the "behoues" motif, contrasted with the light, sarcastic, and ironic tone of Ronsard to and through his Muses. It is this tone of morality in Spenser, not only in this poem but throughout his work, that separates him most clearly from Ronsard and to a lesser extent from Du Bellay. Ronsard's *Discours ou Dialogue* is intended chiefly to be amusing, in spite of the fact that it carries a fairly serious message. It is clever, well-phrased, and witty; it is more *dulce* than *utile*. But for Spenser the message comes first. It was not for nothing that Milton found Spenser a better teacher than Aquinas.[31] It may be assumed that Milton had something more important in mind than the brilliance and variety of metre and of verse form.

In exploring this distinction a little further, one observes at once that none of the French poems so far discussed contains any line remotely resembling the following of Spenser, in moral tone and didactic intent:

> By knowledge wee do learne our selues to knowe,
> And what to man, and what to God wee owe . . .
> (Lines 503-504)
> And banish me [Urania], which do professe the skill
> To make men heauenly wise, through humbled will.
> (Lines 521-522)[32]

[31] Milton was of course referring to the *Faerie Queene*, but the pronouncement may be said to be true of the rest of Spenser's work.

[32] See parenthetically the words of Raphael to Adam in *Paradise Lost*, Book VIII, "Be lowlie wise . . ." etc.

There is a lesson to be learned from Spenser's Muses; the function of Ronsard's Muses is to inspire or incite to a divine madness. Spenser's Muse was usually more Protestant than pagan; Ronsard's often more pagan than Catholic.

A similar divergence which is at once more subtle and more striking, concerns Spenser's attitude as expressed in this poem toward "leawdnes," and toward "dunghill thoughts." This is stated first by Terpsichore, who says of Error, Follie and Spight:

> Faire Ladies loues they spot with thoughts impure,
> And gentle mindes with lewd delights distaine:
> Clerks they to loathly idlenes entice,
> And fill their bookes with discipline of vice.
>   (Lines 333-336)

Erato complains that,

> I ...
> Am put from practice of my kindlie skill,
> Banisht by those that Loue with leawdnes fill ...
>   (Lines 379, 383-384)

and goes on to complain of the "base-borne brood of blindnes" which

> Ne euer dare their dunghill thoughts aspire
> Vnto so loftie pitch of perfectnesse,
> But rime at riot, and doo rage in loue;
> Yet little wote what doth thereto behoue.
>   (Lines 393-396)

Here again is the "behoue" motif, a motif not only largely absent from Ronsard's poetry but one that is actively and flagrantly deprecated over and over again. From the first collection of love sonnets, the *Amours de Cassandre* in 1552, with their unchaste references to Cassandre's breasts (XLIV), to amorous combats (XLVI), to Cassandre's *mons Veneris* (cxv); through the *Amours de Marie* in 1555, with the lyric "Amourette," a carefree poem on immoral delights; to the *Sonnets pour Helene* of 1578, addressed late in life to a frigid lady Platonist twenty years his junior to whom he explains that love is not of the spirit but only of the body—in all these love sonnets the sentiment is often frankly and shamelessly physical and sexual. One might say with some justice that Ronsard spent much of his life trying to spot fair ladies' loves with thoughts impure.

Furthermore, in 1553 Ronsard published anonymously a book of verse called *Livret de Folastries* which contained poems of a thoroughly prurient nature, one being an allegorical sonnet on the penis, and two being short verse celebrations of the male and female *pudenda*: the sort of thing poets may write often enough, but which they rarely publish. It was common knowledge at the time that he was the author of these poems—he is said to have apologized for them, by implication, with several Christian lyrics written the following year—but his attitude toward them was ambiguous if not actually lax, for he included them in successive collected editions of his work until 1584, one year before his death, when for the first time he dropped them from a collection. These indeed were dunghill thoughts; but dunghill thoughts, at least in the case of Ronsard, are far from making a dunghill poet.

One cannot, however, ascribe this aspect of Ronsard's work to juvenility, or to a desire to teach his readers some kind of moral lesson. These poems are more in the ribald spirit of Rabelais; and more directly, in form as well as in spirit, they come from Catullus and from neo-Latin poets of the early Renaissance, imitators of Catullus. Raymond Lebègue has said that they are the "divertissements d'un humaniste en gaité."[33] Spenser was a humanist himself, and his work as a whole can hardly be said to lack joy. There are

[33] Raymond Lebègue, *Ronsard, L'Homme et L'Oeuvre*, p. 39.

few poems in the English language that are more essentially joyous within the context of a chaste morality than the *Epithalamion*; but Spenser's gaiety, except in his marriage hymn, did not apply itself to sexual matters, and even there the sexual references are far from prurient. The sexual passages in the *Faerie Queene*, though they are outwardly physical and sensual, have their own inner decorum, their liberal but rigid moral purpose which precludes salaciousness. Even the incident of Hellenore and the satyrs is part of a moral allegory and has an intent more earnest than the mere provocation of a smirk on the reader's face in response to the titillation of his lower instincts.

This difference between Ronsard and Spenser cannot be bridged; it is absolute. Nor is it a national difference, nor even that between a lax and liberal Catholic and a firm and puritanical Protestant. It is a difference that lies deep within both men, is part of their essence. There is no doubt that both Ronsard and Spenser took their vocation as poets with a high seriousness, but Spenser's seriousness was the more pure in this respect at least.[34]

The Teares of the Muses evokes an additional contrast which is perhaps the most interesting of all from the point of view of comparative literary history: that between Spenser's and Ronsard's attitude toward the drama, as expressed by Melpomene and Thalia in Spenser's poem, and by Ron-

[34] Du Bellay's attitude toward such matters will constitute a pertinent addendum, and will further demonstrate his temperamental affinity to Spenser. His treatment of sexual affairs is exposed in its moral honesty and chaste candor in several sonnets of *Les Regrets*. See, for example, Sonnet LXXXIV (The Romans do not court the Muses, but they do court prelates and whores), Sonnet xc (The impudicity of Roman girls contrasted with the chastity of the Angevines), Sonnet xciv (Happy is he who can spend three years in Rome without becoming infected with the Great Pox), and Sonnet xcvii (Which expresses the poet's disgust with Roman whores and their intimate relations with monks). As a whole, these sonnets might have been written by a negative Spenser; and part of the measure of the two poets may be taken by the fact that Spenser's chastity assumed in its poetic expression a positive or didactic form, whereas Du Bellay's remained negative and critical or one might almost say wholly puritanical.

sard writing in the first person in his liminal *Elegie* to Jacques Grévin. Spenser's tragic Muse, after commenting on life itself as the greatest tragic catastrophe, says:

> So all with rufull spectacles is fild,
> Fit for *Megera* or *Persephone*;
> But I that in true Tragedies am skild,
> The flowre of wit, finde nought to busie me . . .
> (Lines 163-166)

Next in turn, Thalia laments the lack of true comedies, saying:

> In stead thereof scoffing Scurrilitie,
> And scornfull Follie with Contempt is crept,
> Rolling in rymes of shameles ribaudrie
> Without regard, or due Decorum kept,
> Each idle wit at will presumes to make,
> And doth the Learneds taske vpon him take.
> (Lines 211-216)

These two quotations taken together indicate that Spenser had a classical or neoclassical view of the drama, closely akin to that expressed by Sir Philip Sidney in his *Defense of Poesie*. Such a view connects him more intimately with continental concepts than with those held in England, whether one dates the poem early or late between the limits suggested above.

The application of this brief criticism of the drama to the dating of Spenser's poem, that is, the effort to relate Melpomene's complaint of paucity and Thalia's of indecorum and ribaldry to the production of tragedies and comedies in the 1580's has been widely discussed.[35] But what is more interesting and of greater certainty here than the date of Spenser's poem is the concurrence of Spenser's and Ronsard's concepts of the drama, and the divergence between

---

[35] See the notes to these lines of *The Teares of the Muses* in the *Works of Edmund Spenser, The Minor Poems*, II, *passim*.

French and English achievement in the genres, as seen by the poets, and the actual reversal of this divergence, as seen now through the perspective of literary history. If Spenser's view of the drama sometime during the 1580's is uniformly black, then Ronsard's view of French drama in 1561 may be called brilliantly or perhaps dazzlingly white. He writes:

> Jodelle le premier, d'une plainte hardie,
> Françoisement chanta la Grecque Tragedie,
> Puis, en changeant de ton, chanta devant nos Rois
> La jeune Comedie en langue François,
> Et si bien les sonna, que Sophocle et Menandre,
> Tant fussent-ils sçavans, y eussent peu apprandre.
> Et toy, Grevin, apres, toy, mon Grevin encor...[36]

Thus Jodelle is ranked with Sophocles and Menander, while Grévin is proclaimed the continuator of Jodelle and ranked equally high by implication. To call this judgment an exaggeration is greatly to understate the case; it is a blatant absurdity. But as an expression of Pléiade solidarity, of group spirit, the judgment is perfectly sincere. Jodelle's *Cleopatre captive* had been a success in 1553, as had also his comedy *Rencontre*. In his work, the classical drama was recreated in the French language. This had been a major part of Du Bellay's program as stated in the *Deffence*, and its fulfillment, irrespective of the merit of the plays that accomplished it, was of capital importance to Ronsard. He writes to Grévin more as an enthusiast than as a critic.

Earlier in the *Elegie* Ronsard has characterized tragedy as "la plainte des Seigneurs." This had a mediaeval sound, but it changes to a humanist tone a few lines later with:

> L'argument...
> ... du Tragique est de peu de maisons.
> D'Athenes, Troye, Argos, de Thebes et Mycenes...

[36] *Elegie* from Jacques Grévin's *Théâtre*.

He goes on to state that the argument must suit or conform to the scene, and with these vague pronouncements it becomes clear that he is taking an orthodox neoclassical point of view based on Horace's *Ars Poetica* and on Aristotle's *Poetics*. He feels that Jodelle has been a success in the practice of principles derived from classical sources and colored, not to say distorted, by commentators on the classical texts. He excepts Jodelle from the large group of "inventeurs froids," mere "versificateurs" who "riment et composent" without real inspiration from "Phebus Apollon."[37] Jodelle has restored to France a drama of classical exterior, written in French verse. For Ronsard this is richly sufficient; it is a solid cornerstone for the literary movement carefully planned by Du Bellay in 1549, which produced Ronsard's own *Odes* soon after and was ultimately to domesticate the epic in the shape of a *Françiade*, and other genres from Ronsard and from other Pléiade poets. The situation for Ronsard was in every way pleasing, and was a matter for mutual admiration or, better still, intra-coterie adulation.

Spenser's consideration of the drama, through his Muses, is closely similar to Ronsard's. The rigid separation of the two genres tragedy and comedy, with its implied wish for purity within the given genre, is the same, as is the high regard for decorum and classical propriety. The two poets are in accord as theorists; they hold the same orthodox standards for the drama. Ronsard finds them fulfilled in Jodelle, in his amazingly dull *Cleopatre captive*, full of endless talk written out in mediocre verse at best, a play in which the action may be said to have total unity because there is so little of it; a play in which the unity of time, attributed to Aristotle, is pared down to approximately the duration of the talk in the play; a play indeed of stunning monotony, unrelieved by any passages of fine poetry; a play which is now read only by scholars, and even by them per-

[37] Compare *The Teares of the Muses*, lines 213 and 393.

haps not often in full. In such a play Ronsard finds the realization of an ideal which is shared by Spenser.

On the other side of the Channel, Spenser's Melpomene finds nothing at all, and Thalia finds "ribaudrie" and want of "due Decorum." When one considers the earliest date that can be reasonably assigned to *The Teares of the Muses*, it is clear that England had by this date produced more and, from the modern point of view, better work both in tragedy and in comedy than had France. One need only mention *Gorboduc* (first performed in 1561), a better play than *Cleopatre*, for all the neoclassical strictures invoked against it by Sidney; or *The Tragedie of Tancred and Gismund* (written in 1568), which for all its mediaeval vestigial remains, and its failure to observe the neoclassical rules that confined and throttled French tragedy of the time, nevertheless maintains a certain proper dignity in its verse, contains no elements of comic relief, and with its Chorus and its references to the Greek drama seems probably to conform more closely to a true Greek spirit than do French plays that are largely based on a mechanical imitation of principles many of which were unknown to Sophocles. But it is an open question whether Spenser was aware of the existence of these plays.

For comedy there is the lively *Gammer Gurtons Nedle* (presumably written 1553-1554), which, if Spenser knew it, must have offended him with its scatological and sexual humor; and *Roister Doister* (1566), which, classical as it is, contains very little vulgarity of any kind and is influenced though not suffocated by its author's training in Latin literature. If Spenser's Muses had not thought so narrowly, they would have had more cause than Ronsard for self-congratulation. But neither Spenser nor Ronsard knew what the Greeks realized instinctively but never stated explicitly: that it takes more than decorum to make a play. This is why, in terms of literary history, the French sixteenth century is a dramatic failure, while the Elizabethan and Jacobean drama is a brilliant success.

It is a pity that Spenser's own comedies and his book of literary criticism, if indeed he really completed them, have not survived. But, lacking a body of explicit statement of literary theory, one can see through the pronouncements of Melpomene and Thalia the likelihood of a position on Spenser's part as rigid, and if one may say so in respect to the drama, as unfeeling as Sidney's. A lover of Spenser, therefore, failing positive evidence to the contrary, must prefer to date *The Teares of the Muses* 1579-1580, along with W. L. Renwick; but if the poem is as late as 1590, Spenser's position is *a fortiori* that of an intransigent neoclassicist who probably carried a dislike of the English drama to his grave.

The irony of the situation is blatant. The achievement which Ronsard vaunts turned out in the long run to be hollow; his hopes were falsely placed and could not have found a proper fulfillment within his lifetime, in spite even of the work of Garnier. Spenser's despair, in the long view, is equally hollow and false; for it really does not matter in principle whether he excluded Marlowe from the rank of true tragedian, as he may have, or even for that matter, Shakespeare; his neoclassical logic could not be assailed on either score. Unlike Ronsard, he misread the literary temper of his country.

For England was never to find herself in neoclassical drama as France did in the seventeenth century; and England was beginning, before the composition of *The Teares of the Muses,* and continuing during Spenser's lifetime and afterwards, a flowering of a free, perhaps of a romantic but certainly not of a classic, drama such as has never been equalled or even approached since that time. If one can say that Ronsard saw Racine's shadow in Jodelle, one might add that Spenser might have wished to see Dryden, or Addison, in the 1580's. One may be grateful that such a wish never came true, for among these three playwrights even a victim of uncritical national bias cannot deny the high preeminence of Racine.

In conclusion, it is clear that there are both textual analogies and conceptual divergencies between *The Teares of the Muses* and the work of Du Bellay and of Ronsard, the former offering good evidence of Spenser's familiarity with the work of both French poets, the latter clarifying the discrepant nature of this literary relationship. It is equally clear that Spenser's familiarity with the work of these French poets did not in this poem take the form of what is conventionally called an influence. It is rather a combination of attraction and repulsion, certainly a higher form of literary relationship than that represented by pure imitation, and a form more suitable in a great poet, even in the case of a distinctly minor poem.

Spenser is not by any means at his best in *The Teares of the Muses*, moody and complaining poem that it is; but he is true to the best in himself in his constant adherence to the moral value of poetry, in his sympathetic intimacy with the Muses who were his inspiration, and in this case the vehicle of his criticism, and who elsewhere so bounteously repaid his unwavering faith. Spenser was more sober-tempered than Ronsard. Even the gloom of the Muses' literary criticism is alleviated to some extent by what has been referred to as the quasi-palinode at the end of the poem.

In his satiric or ironical work Spenser did not tend toward the personal as did Ronsard and Du Bellay: his concern is chiefly with situations in life and in the world that transcend the personal, and this is clear in the breadth and generality of his criticism even in *The Teares of the Muses*. Ronsard and Du Bellay were narrower in this respect than was Spenser; they were less truly classic, although Ronsard at least specialized in the superficial or external marks of the classic.

COMPLAINTS OF THE MUSES

The discussion of this poem of Spenser's seems to indicate that there was little temperamental affinity between Ronsard and Spenser, and this tentative conclusion will be borne out by further comparisons of their work. On the other hand, *The Teares of the Muses* as a whole does demonstrate the greater closeness of temperament that existed between Spenser and Du Bellay, and this will be further analyzed and substantiated by an examination of *The Ruines of Time* and *Visions of the worldes vanitie*.

V · THE CONQUEST OF TIME

THE initial poem in the 1591 edition of Spenser's *Complaints* is *The Ruines of Time*. There is no poem of his (except for his translations) that has a clearer or more widely recognized connection with the work of the poets of the Pléiade. It follows in the most general way the structure of Du Bellay's *Antiquitez de Rome*: there are ninety-eight stanzas of rhyme royal in all, twenty-six of them composing two separate appended "Visions" at the end, and two final stanzas of "L: Envoy." Du Bellay has thirty-two sonnets in sequence, followed by the *Songe* which is appended at the end, consisting of fifteen sonnets. Thus the proportions of the parts of the poem are approximately equivalent, as the disparity in their total length is also roughly proportional.

Du Bellay's poem, however, has a simpler structure. It is united by a single theme—the inconstancy of all sublunary things—and the final *Songe* is integrated with the main body of the sonnets because it is not, thematically, an addendum or an afterthought but an allegorical or emblematic restatement of an initial theme, thus forming an artistic unit.

Spenser's poem, on the other hand, is unified neither in structure nor in theme. The main body of the poem has three parts,[1] and the appended "Visions" are in two parts. The first section of the poem proper (lines 1-175) deals with mutability, which is lamented by a personification of the ancient city of Verlame; the second part (lines 176-343) deals in a more specific manner with the death of various friends and patrons, Dudleys, Sidneys, and Russells; and the third (lines 344-476) deals broadly with the immortality that poetry can confer upon mortals. The first "Vision" re-

---

[1] The poem is not divided *formally* in the main body, as are the "Visions." The division is thematic.

peats allegorically or emblematically the theme of the first section; the second "Vision" recapitulates part of the theme of the second section, presenting an allegory of the life and death of Sir Philip Sidney.

The transitions from theme to theme are rough and awkward, and the thematic separation as stated above is not absolute or pure; it is merely a working distinction. It does make clear, however, that the structural inspiration, if one may call it that, which is said to come from the *Antiquitez de Rome*, is at best superficial, and has had only the most tenuous influence on Spenser's poem as a whole. Du Bellay's well-knit sonnet sequence has thus inspired a somewhat disjointed series of stanzas on several related subjects; integration has inspired patchwork.

The relationship between *The Ruines of Time* and the *Antiquitez de Rome*, however, goes far beyond a loose structural analogy. For the theme of the first 175 lines of Spenser's poem is not merely the same as the general theme of the *Antiquitez de Rome*, but its expression is in many cases similar, and in some so similar as to amount to a virtual paraphrase. The same holds true of the "Visions" at the end of Spenser's poem, especially the stanzas in the first series. W. L. Renwick has dealt with these resemblances in a vague though suggestive fashion;[2] and Louis S. Friedland, at a much earlier date, culled and collated an imposing series of analogies and paraphrases.[3] Friedland's work especially makes it quite unnecessary to pursue verbal resemblances between the *Antiquitez* and the *Ruines*. He has fully exploited all the important analogies between the two poems, dealing particularly with the first and last sections of the *Ruines*, in which Spenser's matter is drawn copiously from the French poet.

[2] *Complaints*, ed. W. L. Renwick, "Commentary to The Ruines of Time," *passim*.
[3] "Spenser's Early Poems," Chapter 3, *passim*.

As Renwick says of "Vision 2," Spenser's "method here is a kind of continuous *contaminatio*."[4] Spenser was clearly steeped in Du Bellay's poem as he wrote these sections. The two middle parts (lines 176-476), however, are comparatively free of echoes from the *Antiquitez*, except for one analogy by contrast which will be discussed below. It is therefore interesting to note that many of the most melodious lines and stanzas in this uneven poem occur precisely in this central section, in which Spenser's inspiration is somewhat more open, and less shackled by an effort to parallel some particular long poem.

In spite of the lightness of the structural debt owed to the *Antiquitez* by Spenser, and in spite of the relative lack of relationship between Du Bellay's poem and the central 300 lines of Spenser's, there is none the less a profound resemblance between the two poems both in the matter treated and in the temper of the treatment.[5] At his best, Spenser soars beyond Du Bellay in certain passages which deal with similar themes. As a whole, however, the French sequence preserves throughout a more consistent dignity of tone, a musical and a thematic gravity, serious but not ponderous, that is punctuated, especially in the middle section, by a dispersed group of sonnets that are unusual in their quiet melodiousness and remarkable for the striking beauty and freshness of their imagery.[6]

It is curious, as I have pointed out, and perhaps not very meaningful, to note that the best stanzas in Spenser's poem occur not in the first or last section in which Du Bellay's *Antiquitez de Rome* or *Songe* are imitated or paraphrased, but in the central section of his poem in which his theme echoes the European Renaissance at large rather than this

---

[4] *Complaints*, p. 201.
[5] See Appendix II for a recent and possibly spurious interpretation of the relationship between Spenser's and Du Bellay's poems.
[6] Sonnets XII, XIV, XV, XVI, XX, XXVIII, XXIX.

specific poem of Du Bellay's.[7] But, on the other hand, the best sonnets in the Du Bellay sequence are not quite of the standard of the best in the later *Regrets*; nor does any of them quite equal lines 400-406 of *The Ruines of Time*, in which Spenser achieves a marvelous felicity of phrase in the restatement of a Renaissance *cliché*.

Much of the effect of the better passages of Spenser's poem depends on the care, one might almost say the painstaking care, with which the verse is wrought. This is seen in such involuted lines as the following:

> So there thou liuest, singing euermore,
> And here thou liuest, being euer song
> Of vs, which liuing loued thee afore
> And now thee worship . . .
>
> (Lines 337-340)

Veré Rubel has pointed out that the *Ruines* "is outstanding among all the poems in the Complaints for its rhetorical tropes," and that this is especially true of lines 190-259, where one finds that "repeated ploce and traductio on the words 'live' and 'die' are interwoven with epanodos, eclipsis, anadiplosis, apostrophe, hysteron proteron, and epiphonema."[8]

Such calculated, and perhaps to some tastes, overwrought elevation of style is appropriate to the subject, especially in the second part of the poem, in which the elegies are specific, and also in the third part, in which the full meed of praise is accorded to Poetry the immortalizer. It gives the verse a tone of decorum and high seriousness, and it is this tone more than anything else that enables the poem, except in awkward moments of transition, to maintain a high level of melodious and intricate verse, above which stanzas such as

---

[7] Lines 337-358, 400-413, for example.
[8] *Poetic Diction in the English Renaissance, from Skelton through Spenser*, pp. 231-233.

those mentioned above (see note 7) can take flight in clear and simple purity, and can return from greater heights usually with the certainty of alighting on a plateau of consistently superior elevation.

Du Bellay's *Antiquitez*, in contrast, depends on rhetorical tropes only in the more pedestrian sonnets; his best effects come from long, semi-Homeric similes, occasionally several times multiplied in classical fashion within a single sonnet,[9] evoking vivid pictures which live only to be erased in the last half of the sestet. In each case they also represent symbolically the erasure of human constructions in this mutable world. He paints a larger canvas in the fourteen lines of his verse unit, and with less density of language. Spenser, with the smaller unit, writes more densely, and at the same time he achieves a greater continuity (except at the three points of transition) because the flow from stanza to stanza is far more free than that from sonnet to sonnet. All in all, the two poems are quite as different as they are similar, and it is happily unnecessary to make a value choice between them.

Leaving aside now the close verbal links between specific parts of the *Ruines* and of the *Antiquitez*, which have been so fully treated by L. S. Friedland in his unpublished dissertation, but most of which are available to the public in the Variorum Edition of Spenser's *Works*, I shall investigate the relationship between this poem by Spenser and other poems by Du Bellay, which are related in subject and which deal with similar or identical ideas either in the same way or, more importantly, with a divergent nuance. For surely it cannot be too often repeated that the mere fact that Du Bellay and Ronsard, and Spenser, present ideas which are Renaissance *clichés*, and which often seem identical both in conception and in expression, is not sufficient reason for dismissing such parallels as having no significance.

It is clear that many of these ideas did not come to Spen-

[9] See sonnets XIV and XVI, for example.

ser from the Pléiade poets, but that they arrived in France and in England from common sources. Such parallels, however, as are found to give an initial impression of identity do not necessarily have a geometric absoluteness in their equivalence, but for the very reason that they are in language and not in a more precise symbolic form of expression such as mathematics frequently have a subtlety of variation within the general likeness. This variation reveals and emphasizes not only the difference between the poets themselves, but that between the literary milieux of which the poets were a part. Thus the appearance of identity sometimes conceals an illuminating discrepancy beneath the surface.

The erudite W. L. Renwick writes of the central section of *The Ruines of Time* (lines 344-455) that its theme of poetic immortality is "the banner and ensign of Renaissance poets everywhere."[10] He then cites a passage from Ronsard,[11] and one from Du Bellay's *Deffence*,[12] and refers to Du Bellay's *Discours au Roy sur la Poesie*.[13] The reference to the *Deffence* contrasts the immortality of Achilles' fame, through Homer, to the mortality of human monuments. The same general idea is that expressed in the *Antiquitez* as a whole, an idea which pervades Spenser's work and which turns up constantly in other poems by Du Bellay. Spenser's specific statement is:

O fortunate yong-man [Achilles], whose vertue found
So braue a Trompe, thy noble acts to sound.
(Lines 433-434)[14]

[10] *Complaints*, p. 196.
[11] This will be discussed below, p. 104.
[12] *Deffence*, p. 136.
[13] Since this reference is to the poem in general, which indeed does contain pertinent lines *passim*, a few of the more high-flown lines might be quoted as illustration. Speaking of the poet, Du Bellay writes:
Cestuy-la toutefois est trop plus admirable,
Et son oeuvre n'est moins que l'histoire durable,
Pource qu'en imitant l'autheur de l'univers,
Toute essence & idee il comprend en ses vers.
(*Oeuvres*, ed. Chamard, VI, 166).
[14] The exemplary statement of this thought probably reached both Spen-

THE CONQUEST OF TIME

Du Bellay writes in *Contre les Envieux Poetes, A Pierre de Ronsard*, for example:

> Les vers sont enfans du ciel.
> Heureux, qui par un Homere
> A domté la mort amere.[15]

This particular expression of the idea that poetry confers immortality in a world where all else is transitory has thus not only a wide currency during the Renaissance but a pervasive currency within the work of Du Bellay. It is impossible to say with certainty from what source Spenser took it, but it is possible to say that Du Bellay emphasized the idea, and that even if Spenser thought of it himself,[16] this indicates a temperamental affinity.

Now, while the third section of the *Ruines* (lines 344-476) is the one that contains an extended exposition of the theory that poetry immortalizes, there is also one stanza in the second section—which is connected specifically with the elegy upon the death of Ambrose Dudley—that makes the first clear reference to this theory. Unlike the ensuing passage, this stanza makes the reference with a personal note on the poet's part:

> Thy Lord shall neuer die, the whiles this verse
> Shall liue, and surely it shall liue for euer:
> For euer it shall liue, and shall rehearse
> His worthie praise, and vertues dying neuer,
> Though death his soule doo from his bodie seuer.
> And thou thy selfe herein shalt also liue;
> Such grace the heauens doo to my verses giue.
> (Lines 253-259)[17]

---

ser and Du Bellay from Petrarch, Sonnet CLXXXVII, *In Vita di Madonna Laura* (—O fortunato, che si chiara tromba/Trovasti a chi di te si alto scrisse!—).

[15] *Oeuvres*, ed. Chamard, IV, 44.

[16] This is hardly likely in view of E. K.'s citation of the passage in his commentary on *The Shepheardes Calender*, "October," n. 65.

[17] The rhetorical play in this stanza is noteworthy.

This stanza states the power of poetry to immortalize not only an Achilles but any deceased person, not to mention the widow alive at the time of writing. The last two lines are a boast in the classical manner, more often copied by the French than the English. This may be compared with Du Bellay's *A Salmon Macrin, sur la Mort de sa Gélonis*, an elegy on the wife of a friend, a lady certainly less distinguished than Spenser's:

> Et puis la Renommée
> Par le divin effort
> D'une plume animée
> Triomphe de la Mort.[18]

The same boast is made in a specific context, which poets used so much more frequently and conventionally in a more general context. Du Bellay was certainly aware that this was a boast, for in his preface to the second edition of *L'Olive*, his first published book, he writes: "Si en mes poësies je me loüe quelques fois, ce n'est sans l'imitation des anciens. . . ."[19] One may as clearly presume that Spenser too was aware of this, as clearly as one may presume on the other hand that Ronsard did not share the same tendency toward an explicit awareness of the opprobrious vanity of self-praise.

The heart of Spenser's statement on this subject in the *Ruines* lies in lines 400-413; all the rest of the third section is elaboration and particular examples. It will perhaps be best to quote these two stanzas in full before proceeding to make a general distinction between Spenser's and Du Bellay's attitudes toward this theme.

> For deeds doe die, how euer noblie donne,
> And thoughts of men do as themselues decay,
> But wise wordes taught in numbers for to runne,

[18] *Oeuvres*, ed. Chamard, IV, 29.
[19] *Ibid.*, I, 18-19.

Recorded by the Muses, liue for ay;
Ne may with storming showers be washt away,
Ne bitter breathing windes with harmfull blast,
Nor age, nor enuie shall them euer wast.

In vaine doo earthly Princes then, in vaine
Seeke with Pyramides, to heauen aspired;
Or huge Colosses, built with costlie paine;
Or brasen Pillours, neuer to be fired,
Or Shrines, made of the mettall most desired;
To make their memories for euer liue:
For how can mortall immortalitie giue?

Thus poetry, because of its divine origin, is sole possessor of the power to grant immortality in this otherwise all-mutable world. The doctrine is very obviously of pagan origin, but neither here nor elsewhere does Spenser seem to feel that there is any conflict between such a doctrine and the Christian belief that in the terrestrial world only the soul is immortal and that poetry is like all other mortal things in its ultimate evanescence. Indeed, there is no conflict. For Spenser, both statements are true, but on different levels. The immortality of poetry is on a level far below that of the immortality of the soul, but Spenser's belief in it on this level is not merely conventional; within the limitations of its implied separation from Christian doctrine his belief is perfectly sincere, wholly warm and enthusiastic. That Spenser expected his readers to understand this is clear enough from the fact that he never found it necessary to bring the matter to their attention, or to labor an apology for devotion to a pagan idea, lest he be misunderstood. He took it for granted, as did Sir Philip Sidney in his *Apologie*, that Theology was the Queen of the Sciences, and that Poetry held only the highest place in a subcategory. He never felt that his metaphorical excesses called for recantation.

Not so Du Bellay, who was tonsured in his youth and held minor ecclesiastical benefices during his lifetime. As early as 1552 he published *XIII Sonnetz de L'Honneste Amour*,[20] which sound a religious note of apology for the love sonnets of *L'Olive* published two years before. And in the same year he wrote *La Lyre Chrestienne,* in which he abandons his "Muse charnelle" in favor of "la Muse eternelle."[21] In this poem he writes the following lines, which out of context might be found to fit in well with the attitude expressed toward poetry in the *Ruines,* but which in fact refer to Christian hope and faith:

> Bien heureux donques est celuy
> Qui a fondé son asseurance
> Aux choses dont le ferme appuy
> Ne desment point son esperance.
> (Lines 105-108)

And he goes on to make a specifically Christian repudiation of the immortality of poetry:

> Celuy encor' ne cherche pas
> La gloire, que le temps consomme:
> Saichant que rien n'est icy bas
> Immortel, que l'esprit de l'homme.
> Et puis le poëte se nomme
> Ores cigne melodieux,
> Or' immortel & divin, comme
> S'il estoit compaignon des Dieux.
>
> Quand j'oy les Muses, cacqueter,
> Enflant leurs motz d'ung vain langage,
> Il me semble ouyr cracqueter
> Ung perroquet dedans sa cage...
> (Lines 113-124)

[20] *Oeuvres,* ed. Chamard, I, 137-149.
[21] *Ibid.,* IV, 137.

THE CONQUEST OF TIME

Du Bellay loved his Muses far too well, and from the excess of his love, as from the excesses of other pagan statements, there grew up in him a sense of guilt which Spenser never felt; for Spenser loved his Muses well and constantly, but always wisely, and never so well as to have to deny them.

On the other hand, Ronsard is in this respect different both from his French *confrère* and from Spenser. He never sought, for religious reasons, to cancel anything that he had ever written about the immortality of poetry, and he wrote much.[22] If he felt any conflict, or any guilt, we do not know it. What one does know in him, and well, is his total insouciance in such matters except at moments of crisis.[23] All his repudiations of the Muses, or of Fame, or of the immortality of poetry, except one which will be noted below, proceed not from a desire to cancel any impression of pagan sentiment that he may have given or from a feeling of moral guilt for having perhaps denied by implication his true beliefs, but from a materialistic desire to parade his disgust and disappointment with the inadequate rewards received for his immortal productions. It is a curious irony that it is usually the poems written at actual or presumptive Court order about which Ronsard complains, since for them he expected the greatest reward and often got the least, both from the contemporary aristocracy and subsequently from an educated reading public for three hundred years. These poems indeed have an odor of mortality.

It may be said then that with respect to the immortality of poetry Spenser, Du Bellay, and Ronsard occupy divergent positions. Spenser writes of it with a clear Protestant con-

[22] It should be mentioned that the indecorous and wholly ambiguous *Hercule Chrestien*, published in 1556 in the *Second Livre des Hynnes*, was probably written not so much as an apology for pagan expressions—for the poem itself contains numerous thoroughly distasteful Christo-pagan confusions—but as an apology for the *Folastries*, which had caused a scandal quite as much for their lewdness as for their paganism.

[23] The two great crises in Ronsard's life were the Protestant attack on him at the time of the religious wars in the 1560's and his slow death.

science, secure in his Christian beliefs in a country which had not had and was never to have a Protestant-Catholic war; Du Bellay writes with a troubled conscience and with a painful sense of the ambiguity of the position of a Christian poet perhaps too much immersed both in corrupt ecclesiastical intrigues and in classical and pagan theories if not practices; and Ronsard writes, some of the time, with no conscience at all, but with his hand on his purse and his eye on the main chance.

To a certain extent, however, Ronsard's moods and tones are mirrored in *The Ruines of Time*. W. L. Renwick has pointed out the resemblance between parts of Ronsard's *Ode I, Au Roy Henry II*, and Spenser's poem.[24] He does not point out, however, that one stanza of Spenser's poem is virtually a paraphrase of a passage in Ronsard's, as a sequential comparison will show. Ronsard writes to his Prince that his military conquests will all have been in vain,

> Si la Muse te fuit, et d'un vers solonnel
> Ne te fait d'âge en âge aux peuples eternel . . .

He goes on to say three lines later,

> Sans les Muses deux fois les Rois ne vivent pas . . .

and two lines below,

> . . . seulement ceste gloire
> Est de Dieu concedée aux filles que Memoire
> Conceut de Jupiter, pour la donner à ceux
> Qui attirent par dons les Poetës chez eux.[25]

Spenser writes, in turn:

> Prouide therefore (ye Princes) whilst ye liue,
> That of the *Muses* ye may friended bee,

[24] *Complaints*, pp. 196-197.
[25] Renwick quotes the last four of these lines but without specific reference to the following stanza by Spenser.

THE CONQUEST OF TIME

> Which vnto men eternitie do giue;
> For they be daughters of Dame memorie,
> And *Ioue* the father of eternitie,
> And do those men in golden thrones repose
> Whose merits they to glorifie do chose.
> (Lines 365-371)

The similarity of the passages is striking. It is clear also that the usual tonic difference is present, as between Spenser's injunction to Princes, "Prouide," and Ronsard's specific mention of "dons." But the doctrine is the same; it is certainly more similar than these two poets who cite it.

Spenser was not always above the mercenary point of view, however, although he does not reiterate it as Ronsard does, as the following passage will indicate:

> But such as neither of themselues can sing,
> Nor yet are sung of others for reward,
> Die in obscure obliuion, as the thing
> Which neuer was, ne euer with regard
> Their names shall of the later age be heard ...
> (Lines 344-348)[26]

There is a further parallel between a late poem of Ronsard's, and Spenser. Ronsard writes in *Caprice*, a poem that Spen-

---

[26] The following quotations will illustrate Ronsard's reiteration:
> Aussi le Roy, quelque chose qu'il face,
> Meurt sans honneur, s'il n'achete la grace
> Par maints presens d'un Poëte sçavant
> Qui du tombeau le deterre vivant
> Et fait tousjours d'une plume animée
> Voler par tout sa vive renommée.
> (*A Jean de la Peruse, Poëte; Oeuvres*, ed. Cohen, II, 316.)

A further example of this idea occurs in his *Ode XVIII, Au Seigneur de Lanques*, whom he addresses after the nobleman's military victories:
> Tu n'as rien fait si telle gloire
> N'est portraite en mes vers, afin
> Que ta renaissante memoire
> Vive par les bouches sans fin.
> (*Oeuvres*, ed. Cohen, II, 699)

ser probably never read because it was published posthumously in 1604, speaking of the perfect poet who writes eloquent praise of Kings and Princes:

> Par ce chemin, loin des tourbes menues,
> A branle d'aile on vole outre les nues,
> Se couronnant à la posterité
> Des Rameaux saincts de l'Immortalité.[27]

Spenser writes in the *Ruines*, more elaborately and sensuously but in the same spirit:

> But fame with golden wings aloft doth flie,
> Aboue the reach of ruinous decay,
> And with braue plumes doth beate the azure skie,
> Admir'd of base-borne men from farre away:
> Then who so will with vertuous deeds assay
> To mount to heauen, on *Pegasus* must ride,
> And with sweete Poets verse be glorifide.
>
> (Lines 421-427)

And again, a little further in the poem:

> O let the man, of whom the Muse is scorned,
> Nor aliue, nor dead be of the Muse adorned.
>
> (Lines 454-455)

Spenser's man without fame may be contrasted with Ronsard's fortunate man who has "les Muses en partage" and who

> Veinqueuer des ans son nom ne mourra point.[28]

The wings and plumes, the base-born left far behind, the soaring flight, the conquest of death—all these are similar and are similarly diffused throughout the work of both poets. Such instances could be greatly multiplied. The above examples may suffice to substantiate the common generaliza-

[27] *Ibid.*, p. 677.   [28] *Ode II, A Calliope; Oeuvres*, I, 434.

THE CONQUEST OF TIME

tion that the divine dignity of the poet was a subject much reiterated by both Spenser and the Pléiade poets.

It remains only to illustrate more fully the nature of Ronsard's sporadic revolt against the Muses, in order to solidify what has been said above in a general discussion and in order to point out finally that Ronsard was entirely as capable of rising to heights of pure eloquent beauty when writing on this subject as was Spenser.

The primary cause for Ronsard's revolt is financial. Gustave Cohen writes of the following lines, "Explosion d'humeur du poète déçu en ses ambitions matérielles, mais qui restera, à travers tout, fidèle à l'art."[29]

> Hé! Que me sert de composer
> Autant de vers qu'a fait Homere? . . .
> Hé! doy-je esperer que ma vois
> Surmonte des siecles les ailes? . . .
>   Que de suivre l'ocieux train
> De ceste pauvre Calliope,
> Qui tousjours fait mourir de fain
> Les meilleurs chantres de sa trope.[30]

Here the Homer motif mentioned above in regard to Achilles has been reversed, for by implication Time will conquer even Homer; Calliope's followers are an "ocieux train," she herself is poor. The emphasis is on material deprivation, for the penultimate line of my quotation is also the penultimate line of this short, petulant poem.

A somewhat more detached view is taken by Ronsard in the following melancholy lines. Writing of the vanished empires of the Medes, the Greeks, and the Romans, he makes an easy transition to a mood of general melancholy that is not unlike that found in Du Bellay and in Spenser:

> Nostre Empire mourra, imitant l'inconstance
> De toute chose née, et mourront quelque fois

[29] *Ibid.*, p. 1106. [30] *Ibid.*, p. 631.

107

THE CONQUEST OF TIME

Nos vers et nos escrits, soient Latins ou François,
Car rien d'humain ne fait à la Mort resistance.[31]

The poet goes on to say that Fate is ultimately the enemy of the Muses, and it is on this note that he ends. It is interesting to observe that Ronsard cut this poem from collections of his work after 1560. He must initially have taken some pleasure in according mortality not only to things written in French but emphatically also in Latin and by implication in Greek as well. The general melancholy, however, is unlike him; it is an ephemeral mood and is not central to his view of the world as it is in the case of Du Bellay and Spenser. His melancholy is neither gentle nor brooding nor continuous; it is sporadic and is usually provoked only momentarily by some material event in life rather than by reflection on life.

Ronsard is at his best in his positive assertions of the immortality of the poet's work. Some of these statements have the power immediately and forcefully to convince the reader that what the poet says is true and will be true forever. Such an assertion is implicit in the justly famous *Sonnet XLIII* to Hélène, "Quand vous serez bien vieille, au soir, à la chandelle," in which the reader believes at the end with the poet that his immortality, that of the lady, and that of poetry itself has been accomplished absolutely by the very act of writing the poem. Yet the poem is boastful, almost truculent in its assertion, though superbly melodious in its cadence. It is also reflective and nostalgic; the nostalgia and the reflection are Hélène's, not Ronsard's, and yet he has in the act of creating the poem taken possession of them both so that the poem both is and is not reflective. It is overweening in the implication of the final statement by Hélène, "Ronsard me celebroit au temps que j'estois belle," yet the poem itself has justified the statement. One is con-

---
[31] *Sonet, Nouvelle Continuation des Amours* (1556); *Oeuvres*, II, 831.

THE CONQUEST OF TIME

vinced with Hélène in the end that the greatest thing that ever happened to her, or could have happened to a late sixteenth-century woman, was that Ronsard wrote of her in his sonnets, and that this thing was not merely terrestrially great but of permanent and immutable significance.

This is very unlike Spenser, whose best statements about the immortality of poetry are more sober and more cerebral, yet none the less convincing for all that; more convincing perhaps in that they do not demand that the reader commit himself to a personal allegiance to the particular poet, as Ronsard does in the sonnet to Hélène, but are more clearly attached to poetry itself, the abstraction.[32] For Spenser, poetry is words of wisdom; for Ronsard, poetry is words of fire.

Nearer to the mood of Spenser in the third section of the *Ruines*, and about as near as Ronsard ever comes to a mellifluous and intellectual rather than an emotional or a pedantic statement of the transcendent value of poetry, are the following lines from *Ode XXXII*.[33] Ronsard points out that material wealth alters and disappears:

> Mais les beaux vers ne changent pas
> Qui durent contre le trespas
> Et en devançant les années
> Hautains de gloire et de bon-heur,
> Des hommes emportent l'honneur
> Desur leurs courses empanées.

These are fine lines, and not the only ones in this ode, which, early as it is (1550), elaborates at length and with unusual restraint the conception of the immortality of poetry which Ronsard was to state, recant, and restate throughout his lifetime, but more often with protest or with a wild or petulant outcry than with equanimity and with a quiet certainty, as here.

[32] See lines 400-406 of *The Ruines of Time*, quoted above.
[33] *Oeuvres*, I, 644.

109

THE CONQUEST OF TIME

It should be clear now that although the doctrine that poets alone in this world can gain and confer immortality is of classical origin, and found expression in works in Greek and Latin, not to mention neo-Latin, with many of which Du Bellay, Ronsard, and Spenser were unquestionably familiar, there are nevertheless divergencies in the manner in which these three poets gave voice to the doctrine—divergencies which are primarily typical of the differences among the three poets and secondarily typical of the literary atmospheres in which they worked. It would be an exaggeration indeed to say that Spenser was a Puritan or that English literature in the second half of the sixteenth century was in any positive sense the product of a growing Puritan movement which in fact did little else than oppose literature in all forms. But surely Protestantism if not Puritanism in England had wrought some clarification of ecclesiastical issues, and some practical reform of Church abuses which relieved England of the confusion, the uncertainty, and the tension that haunted France during the same period, and which culminated but did not terminate in the Massacre of St. Bartholomew's Eve.

For this reason, perhaps, classical pagan doctrines in England were less radically expressed and were less disturbing both to poets and to readers. A doctrine such as the immortality of poetry and of the poet could be set forth without provoking suspicion on the reader's part that the author was a crypto-pagan, or a Protestant, both of which deviations were in France correlated and confounded with atheism. From the poet's point of view, such ideas could be expressed calmly and without trepidation, and hence they evoked no sense of guilt. Thus on a basis purely national and temporal, there is a difference in atmosphere that accounts for some of the variations between Spenser, and Du Bellay and Ronsard.

Furthermore, the educational background of Du Bellay

THE CONQUEST OF TIME

and Ronsard differed in an important respect from that of Spenser, as has been pointed out. Both French poets were better Hellenists than Spenser, as their master Dorat was a greater Hellenist than Mulcaster. The emphasis on Greek in their education was correspondingly more important, and probably in the case of Ronsard goes a long way toward accounting for his *forcenément* in the attribution of divinity to poetry.

But the temperamental divergence takes precedence over all these generalities; and, besides, it works reciprocally in bringing Du Bellay and Spenser together. For both Spenser and Du Bellay were men of thought, concerned with the senses only insofar as they provide material for the mind to ponder. They are fond of symbols, emblems, abstractions. They are not racked by sexual feelings on the one hand, nor do they tend to confuse themselves with immortal celestial beings on the other. Ronsard is a man of the senses, of strong feelings. Contrary to Du Bellay and Spenser, whose feelings in their poetry take the form of thought, his thoughts in his poetry take the form of feeling. His varying statements about poetry are as unpremeditated, as mercurial, and as assertive as his well-known statement about himself: "Je suis, dis-je, Ronsard, et cela te suffise."[34] He both loves and hates Poetry and the Muses. So also does Du Bellay, but with moral compunctions that Ronsard could not understand, though they were clear to Spenser, and drew him closer to the elder Frenchman, as if he might have been plagued by similar compunctions himself.

Spenser must have read with much sympathy the final sonnet of the *Antiquitez*, which, with its melancholy awareness of the ultimate mortality even of poetry, still expresses a temperate hope, and ends with a boast that is very unlike any of Ronsard's in its quiet and paradoxical modesty:

[34] *Discours I, en forme d'elegie; Oeuvres*, II, 17.

THE CONQUEST OF TIME

> Esperez vous que la posterité
>   Doive (mes vers) pour tout jamais vous lire?
>   Esperez vous que l'oeuvre d'une lyre
>   Puisse acquerir telle immortalité?
> Si sous le ciel fust quelque eternité,
>   Les monuments que je vous ay fait dire,
>   Non en papier, mais en marbre & porphyre,
>   Eussent gardé leur vive antiquité.
> Ne laisse pas toutefois de sonner,
>   Luth, qu'Apollon m'a bien daigné donner,
>   Car si le temps ta gloire ne desrobbe,
> Vanter te peux, quelque bas que tu sois,
>   D'avoir chanté, le premier des François,
>   L'antique honneur du peuple à la longue robbe.

This poem may well be taken as an epitome of Du Bellay's ambivalence and reticence, qualities which not only separate him from Ronsard but which bring him near Spenser. For if this sonnet, which terminates the main series of the *Antiquitez de Rome*, sums up in its hesitant boast the qualification that Du Bellay put on the immortality of poetry, one may also say that lines 400-413 of *The Ruines of Time* (quoted above) considered beside the text of the whole *Antiquitez*—which Spenser undoubtedly had much in mind at the time of writing—and in the context of the *Ruines*, expresses a similarly temperate and similarly qualified attitude toward mortality and the power of poetry to survive.

VI · THE MORAL VISION OF THE WORLD

THE *Visions of the worldes vanitie* is a sequence of twelve dull and colorless sonnets, written in the manner of the emblematic translations of 1569 but printed without accompanying emblematic illustrations. W. L. Renwick has pointed out quite properly that these sonnets are really not visions of the world's vanity "but parables of the limitations of power."[1] This they are indeed and, further, they are heavily moralistic parables or *exempla*; each sonnet is the twin of its neighbor in that it ends with a couplet both ponderous and trite, expressing some quasi-philosophical platitude. Renwick goes on to say that the poems "have little but historical value for us." True as this is, it is nevertheless interesting to note that the historical value is closely associated with the influence of the Pléiade, and that it is especially to Du Bellay that Spenser is indebted—a debt more in borrowings of material than in transference of inspiration. The fact that the poems are among the most feeble that Spenser ever wrote makes any close critical examination of the text a fruitless endeavor; but the close connection that they have as a whole with the melancholic aspect of Spenser's temperament, and the equally clear affinity that this melancholy has with that of Du Bellay—not to mention the contrast with Ronsard—makes a study of these pedestrian verses a matter of interest quite apart from their literary value.

The date of the sequence, like the date of most of the poems in the 1591 edition of the *Complaints*, is uncertain.[2] One would like, for Spenser's sake, to set the date early, but that would be to substitute sentiment for fact. One is forced,

[1] *Complaints*, ed. W. L. Renwick (London, 1928), p. 255.
[2] Harold Stein, *Studies*, p. 69.

therefore, to entertain the possibility that Spenser in his maturity could have been so victimized by melancholic depression as to construct a series of sonnets uniformly without distinction, a series which examines with reiterative monotony only one small area of the general theme of mutability—a theme which Spenser treated elsewhere with such fullness and such ringing eloquence and sweetness.

There is general critical agreement that the *Visions of the worldes vanitie* is "unimportant and derivative."[3] L. S. Friedland has made a full and careful comparison of the many analogies that exist between these poems, *The Ruines of Time*, and the translations of the visions of both Petrarch and Du Bellay.[4] He notes that Spenser ends his poems with the summarizing couplet of Petrarch's visions, and that in more than one place Du Bellay's melancholy note is clearly heard.[5] It would seem, however, in spite of the derivative quality of the poems that since they are not translations and since none of the poems parallels Petrarch's or Du Bellay's to such an extent as to be called a paraphrase one may take the melancholy note of the *Visions of the worldes vanitie* to be Spenser's own—and as clearly individual and peculiar as that of Du Bellay or of Petrarch. Assuming this to be true, I shall examine Spenser's poems in relation to similar poems by Du Bellay and in contrast to others by Ronsard, which are also similar and yet fundamentally different.

All of the poems in Spenser's sequence deal symbolically with animals,[6] with the exception of the first, which is introductory, and the last, which is a kind of summary or conclu-

[3] *Ibid.*, p. 72.
[4] "Spenser's Early Poems," Chapter 3, *passim*.
[5] *Ibid.*, p. 14/49.
[6] In most cases there are two animals involved, a greater and a lesser. The greater is always overcome by the lesser. Sonnets 7, 9, and 11 are exceptions, involving only one animal, respectively a worm, a remora, and some geese, pitted respectively against a cedar tree, a ship, and the ancient Gauls. The implication of the terminal moral is identical in all cases.

sion. These moralistic animal stories are given an Aesopian twist of allegory in the final sonnet, which suggests that Spenser might expect the lessons to be applied in a contemporary social context:

> When these sad sights were ouerpast and gone,
> My spright was greatly moued in her rest,
> With inward ruth and deare affection,
> To see so great things by so small distrest:
> Thenceforth I gan in my engrieued brest
> To scorne all difference of great and small,
> Sith that the greatest often are opprest,
> And vnawares doe into daunger fall.
> And ye, that read these ruines tragicall
> Learne by their losse to loue the low degree,
> And if that fortune chaunce you vp to call
> To honours seat, forget not what you be:
> For he that of himselfe is most secure,
> Shall finde his state most fickle and vnsure.

Such a social interpretation has been made by Francesco Viglione, who presents his arguments with occasional obfuscation and hyperbolic exaggeration, yet whose judgments are often keen. He makes three chief points which are loosely connected with each other. First, a "zelo protestante ispirò anzitutto i 12 sonetti delle 'Visions of the Worlds Vanitie.'"[7] He says further of the sequence as a whole that "la superbia dei grandi, punita e distrutta, simboleggiava la superbia di Roma papale, che si doveva umiliare per una cause altamente nazionale."[8] Connected to this theory of pro-Protestant and anti-Roman nationalistic zeal is the in-

---

[7] *La poesia lirica di Edmondo Spenser*, p. 129. ["It was Protestant zeal above all that inspired the twelve sonnets of the 'Visions of the Worlds Vanitie.'"]

[8] *Ibid.*, pp. 129-130. ["The pride of the great, punished and destroyed, symbolized the pride of papal Rome, which ought to be humbled by a highly national cause (i.e. Protestantism)."]

fluence of Du Bellay and of Petrarch. A contrast is drawn between Spenser and the continental poets because, in the case of Spenser's sonnets, "non sono i superbi che cadono per la mano di Dio, bensí gli umili che abbattono o sollevano i potenti, la quale idea era come una glorificazione delle classi meno abbienti, a cui apparteneva lo stesso Spenser."[9] Thus the initial inspiration of Petrarch and Du Bellay had a curious twofold result in Spenser's poem: the Roman Church was substituted for the Roman Empire and the general theme of destruction that runs through Du Bellay's *Antiquitez de Rome* and his *Songe*, destruction through the inevitable mutability of all terrestrial things, was changed to a specific destruction of the Roman Church, based on Protestant zeal and on wishful thinking. The great who fall in "ruines tragicall" may thus be interpreted, paradoxically enough, as standing for some kind of combination of Lord Burghley and the Church of Rome.

Viglione's final point is that in the most general sense Du Bellay's influence in these poems is toward an "emozione lirica" and toward a sentiment "attegiata a malinconia romantica." The Frenchman's poems "schiusero a lui un nuovo orizzonte."[10] These broad statements seem to have a degree of truth. But Viglione fails to note that Du Bellay's *Antiquitez* and his *Songe* are not in the purely Petrarchan tradition of love sonnets to a lady. Du Bellay did not fail to mark this himself; it was a fact of which he was proud.[11] Spenser's poem, also, stands as the first original sonnet sequence in English that is dedicated to another theme than

[9] *Ibid.*, p. 130. ["It is not that the proud fall at the hand of God, but that they are struck down and subdued by the humble; this idea is a sort of glorification of the class of 'have-nots,' to which Spenser himself belonged."]
[10] *Ibid.*, p. 132. ["Opened to him a new horizon."]
[11] The final lines of the last sonnet of the *Antiquitez* make this clear:
Vanter te peux, quelque bas que tu sois,
D'avoir chanté, le premier des François,
L'antique honneur du peuple à longue robbe.

THE MORAL VISION OF THE WORLD

love, and this is some kind of distinction, whatever it may be worth.

The posture of romantic melancholy that Viglione finds in both poets is pertinent too. Du Bellay's *Antiquitez* are clearly evocative of the engravings of Rome done so much later by Piranesi, standing close to the romantic movement and suggestive also of that most superb sonnet on ruins, the *Ozymandias* of Shelley, which came at the full flood of the movement. Du Bellay was the herald of a sentiment that was to become an integral part of all definitions of "romantic" feeling—a nostalgia for the far past, distant, elusive, and unattainable except through the capacity of the poet or the artist to summon up the memory with vivid poignancy.

So also Spenser; but his evocation of the past occurs not so much in these poems of the *Visions of the worldes vanitie*, as Viglione seems to suggest, as in the *Faerie Queene*, that ancestor of Keats as well as of Milton, and in *The Ruines of Time*. In the present sequence Spenser is not concerned with the past as is Du Bellay in the *Antiquitez*, but with the present, or perhaps with timelessness. In some of his work Spenser stands beside Du Bellay as an ancestor of the romantic feeling for ruins and for ancient, misty magnificences, but not in the *Visions of the worldes vanitie*. On the contrary, the mention of "ruines tragicall" in the ninth line of the terminal sonnet is evocative of the mediaeval definition of tragedy represented by Sackville's *A Mirror for Magistrates*, Lydgate's *Fall of Princes*, and the *De Casibus* tradition of the Middle Ages in general, rather than of the ruins in Du Bellay's *Antiquitez* or even those in Spenser's own *The Ruines of Time*.[12] The new horizon that Du Bel-

[12] Viglione has perhaps been influenced by L. S. Friedland's "Spenser's Early Poems," where Friedland says concerning the final sonnet of the *Visions of the worldes vanitie* that Spenser touches upon Du Bellay's near-romantic theme of "ruines tragicall" (p. 14/49). It would seem that Friedland too, correct as he is in respect to Du Bellay's near romantic theme, misread as did Viglione the implications of "ruines tragicall."

lay opened to Spenser fails to appear in the *Visions of the worldes vanitie*.

If the theory that Protestant zeal caused Spenser to write these allegorical sonnets were true, one might expect to find in the sonnets themselves some clear indication, whether explicit or symbolical, of propagandistic intention. One searches in vain, however, for any implied connection between the bull, the crocodile, the ship, or any of the other examples of pride, and the Roman Church. Far from containing any clear symbols either of Rome or of Protestantism, Spenser's sonnets do not even have a broad or general religious implication, as do those of Du Bellay's *Antiquitez* and his *Songe*. The morality of the didactic aspect of the sonnets is timeless and universal (and, as has been said above, commonplace and trite)—neither nationalistic nor religiously zealous. Spenser's melancholy suggests the more general *lacrimae rerum* of Virgil, a sadness for the ineluctability of fate rather than a specific zeal for the destruction of a Church which had been sufficiently powerful to resist the shock of the Reformation and which could be attacked more effectively in other ways. Nor do these poems lend themselves to the kind of ecclesiastical interpretation that Van der Noot attached to the sonnets of Du Bellay's *Songe*. They are emblematic, after the fashion of the *Songe*, but the implication of the word pictures is nonreligious.

They are also reflective, as are the sonnets of Du Bellay's *Antiquitez*, and they reflect a similar eternal note of sadness. It might be thought that, in taking the material or mechanical aspects of inspiration from these works of Du Bellay and generalizing the specific theme of the fall of Roman monuments, Spenser achieved a larger, a more ample subject. This, however, is not the case. Spenser's subject, the fall of the mighty from high places, is indeed at first glance broader and of greater scope than the more narrow and specific fall of the Roman Empire. But in choosing strange and, in most cases, monstrous animals as victims of a prideful reversal Spenser has dehumanized his subject, a process that he carries further by making small and usually unpleasant animals the agents of the reversal. He has made his subject both monstrous and petty. On the other hand, Du Bellay has imbued a lament for architectural monuments with a deep sense of the melancholy of human works, the futility of human aspiration. Du Bellay's subject has both greater scope and greater depth because his reflections are associated with human life; Spenser has buried his subject in a series of studies of disasters in natural history.[13]

Spenser's poems are pedestrian and simple in their moral expression. They contain no Roman richness, no continental ornamentation, but a grey English bleakness. It is unlikely, however, that the plainness of the sonnets of the *Visions of the worldes vanitie* was intended to make the poem stand in some way as sectarian propaganda; more probably this is simply the result of failure of inspiration, combined with failure to revise a barren work.

Let us consider now the social theme of these unimportant sonnets, in the statement of which Viglione seems closer to the truth. The abasement of the powerful by the humble is said to represent a glorification of the "classi meno abbienti" to which Spenser himself belonged. The final sonnet, quoted above, seems to give substance to this theory; it is the only thread in the tissue of Viglione's suggestions that will hold with very little qualification. In the following lines there is apparently a real exhortation to a democratic point of view that is quite modern:

> Learne by their losse to loue the low degree,
> And if that fortune chaunce you vp to call
> To honours seat, forget not what you be . . .

[13] The fact that Spenser's poems derive from the moralized exempla of mediaeval beast-fables, and thus have a respectable genealogy, does not make them any more human. See J. Th. Welter, *L'exemplum dans la littérature religieuse et didactique du moyen âge* (Paris, 1927).

THE MORAL VISION OF THE WORLD

It is an exaggeration, however, to say that such lines, or the poems as a whole, are a glorification of people of low degree, a kind of full meed of self-praise, if not actually a call to democratic action. In the poems themselves, the final cause of all the falls is pride, and the action of the lowly animal is only the efficient cause. There is no question of glorification.

Spenser's emphasis is certainly not on the revolutionary idea of the humble classes pulling down the mighty, as his phrasing might seem to indicate. To infer this would be to view Spenser in Marxist rather than in Elizabethan terms. The emphasis throughout is on the fall of pride, a moral rather than a social idea, and one ever dear to Spenser, as may be observed almost everywhere in his work. The morality is evidently more internal than Viglione implies, and the external fall is merely the outward form of the inner moral sickness. Thus, though there is expression of concern for persons of low degree, there is no glorification of them. On the contrary, the terminal sonnet is a warning to the lowly, and a warning is more appropriately Spenserian than is either self-praise or self-sympathy.

It is precisely the admonitory aspect of the sonnets of the *Visions of the worldes vanitie*, and especially of the terminal one, that distinguishes the tone of the poems from the sonnets of Du Bellay's *Antiquitez*, his *Songe*, and for that matter, from the melancholy sonnets of *Les Regrets*. Spenser's poems are clearly and deliberately hortatory, and the exhortations temper the quality of the melancholy by the injection of positive moral advice. Du Bellay's melancholy is unequivocally black, unillumined by any suggestion that an alteration in human conduct will improve the state of affairs in this unstable world. Du Bellay is enshrouded in the darkness of Gerard de Nerval's "soleil noir de la Melancholie"; Spenser's sun is merely below the horizon, ready to rise and shine if there be some amelioration in human behaviour. A few examples will clarify this distinction between Spenser's purely didactic purpose and Du Bellay's more purely poetic intention.

In Spenser's series, the terminal couplet of the last sonnet is the epitome of all that has gone before:

> For he that of himselfe is most secure,
> Shall finde his state most fickle and vnsure.

The point here is that security in this world is very uncertain and, not merely that, but a state of seeming security by its very nature lulls the secure person into a condition of unwatchfulness. Security itself contains the germ of the future fall; it leads first to pride, an excessive sense of security, an overevaluation of place. It ripens the victim for destruction. This view is originally Greek and it is fundamentally moral, not social.[14] The purpose of its expression is didactic. Similarly, at the end of the second sonnet Spenser writes, "So by the small the great is oft diseased." At the end of the third, "Why then should greatest things the least disdaine,/Sith that so small so mightie can constraine?" These are the usual types of antithetical endings for all the sonnets in this series. One more will perhaps make this clear to the point of surfeit: "So weakest may anoy the most of might." The poet, thus, is always present at the end of the poem, to make quite certain that the reader shall not miss the point. Each moral is hammered home and, lest the accumulation be insufficient, the final sonnet sums up the preceding eleven.

This is very unlike Du Bellay's method in either the *Antiquitez* or the *Songe*, and though it is partly a difference in genre, it seems to be beyond this also a difference in temperament. In the *Antiquitez*, with the exception of the thirty-second (the last) sonnet, which is entirely personal, and the seventh, which is personal in its final sestet—making

---

[14] Herodotus, *Historiae*, ed. Carolus Hude (Oxford, 1947), I, 32.

what is apparently a reference to the pains of Du Bellay's illness[15]—he indulges in no personal statements of opinion at all, no reflections loaded with moral lessons. He is content to pass from description to description, from image to image, and to leave the reader to draw his own conclusions, though it is always clear to the perceptive reader that the poet thinks Rome has sinned in her excesses.[16] The work is one of nostalgic meditation; most of it is lovely, all of it is hopeless. It is radically unlike the *Visions of the worldes vanitie*, for neither there nor elsewhere in his work is Spenser without hope or without advice. This is perhaps the difference between pessimism and melancholy. In Sonnet LXXVII of *Les Regrets*, a group of poems occasioned by the same stay in Rome that produced the *Antiquitez*, Du Bellay himself makes clear his bitterness, "Car je ry, comme on dit, d'un riz sardonien."[17]

Between the sonnets of the *Songe* and those of the *Visions of the worldes vanitie* there is a closer connection, although even here the affinity is more formal than thematic. Du Bellay's series of fifteen sonnets is governed throughout by the statement of the Daemon in the sestet of the first:

> Puis m'escria: Voy (dit-il) & contemple
>   Tout ce qui est compris sous ce grand temple,
>   Voy comme tout n'est rien que vanité.
> Lors cognoissant la mondaine inconstance,
>   Puis que Dieu seul au temps fait resistance,
>   N'espere rien qu'en la divinité.

[15] Du Bellay suffered from pulmonary tuberculosis all his life, as well as from a painful form of deafness—though he is presumed to have died of apoplexy.
[16] V.-L. Saulnier, *Du Bellay*, p. 138.
[17] This sardonic quality is perhaps shown most plainly in a stanza of Du Bellay's *La Complainte du Desesperé* (1552), lines 475-480. The idea of the desirability of prenatal death must indeed have haunted Du Bellay, for he had written of it earlier, in *Vers lyriques*, Ode XII, lines 25-29. This poem, like so many others of Du Bellay's, and of Spenser's, deals in general with the "caduq' " in life—mutability.

The remaining fourteen sonnets are all descriptive, and never again is there any commentary by the poet that is intended to guide or form the reader's opinion, to instruct him on the proper moral attitude. This is not to say that these emblematic poems are meaningless, or that all the meanings are totally ambiguous; it is merely to say that the symbols remain as symbols, without explanation by the poet. That the poems are broadly didactic is clear, as clear as is the fact that exactly what they teach is so clouded as to be susceptible of a variety of interpretations.

It is this open quality in the symbols that permitted Van der Noot to use these poems, by a Catholic poet, as Protestant propaganda. What the sonnets of Du Bellay teach is not presented in the explicit manner that Spenser assumes in the *Visions of the worldes vanitie*, and for this reason the mood of nostalgia, of melancholy, is more pure and more black, unalloyed by the personal obtrusions of the pedagogue and the moralist. To be sure, Du Bellay recommends hope in God, but he does not pursue his reader throughout with specific suggestions. In this he is more tolerant than Spenser, and in this greater toleration one may see reflected in miniature one of the essential differences between the poetry of Spenser and that of the Pléiade. Though in this case the distinction resides to some degree in a difference of genre, it nevertheless goes beyond this, for after all it is the poet who choses the genre in which he can express his meaning most fittingly. Broadly speaking, Spenser teaches hortatory moral lessons, while Du Bellay and Ronsard, on the whole, tend rather to teach literary lessons. This is not to deny that the English poet is a literary theorist, nor is it to say that Ronsard never gave moral instruction in his verse; it is merely to point out the different emphasis. It should also be observed that this tolerant quality on the part of Du Bellay is confined to the texts under discussion and does not pervade all of his work. It is the pedagogue in Du Bellay the poet that elsewhere brings him so close to Spenser and at the same time separates him from his great contemporary rival, Pierre de Ronsard. It places him in a position intermediate between the wholly moral English poet and the often amoral Frenchman.

Ronsard is never melancholy, nostalgic, or bitter in the same sense as Du Bellay. His melancholy is romantic and unreal; his nostalgia is not for the irrecoverable or the unattainable but for lost pleasures that will very likely return once more; and his bitterness is often that of wounded sensibilities or of wounded pride. In these respects he is more representative of the full flood of the French Renaissance than is Du Bellay; he is closer far to Rabelais, though without Rabelais' pervasive vulgarity. Older and longer lived than Du Bellay, he is always more youthful. His best work is gay and carefree, neither reflective nor dark. When in some of his longer and more pedestrian poems he puts upon himself the mantle of philosophical meditation, he is cheerful rather than melancholy. When he contemplates mutability, corruption, and death, he is more likely to see through them to regeneration and rebirth than to dwell upon the "caduq'" with sadness or pessimism. One of his more gloomy elegies will partially clarify this point. Early in this poem of 138 lines he writes, concerning man in general:

> De tous les animaux le plus lourd animal,
> C'est l'homme, le sujet d'infortune et de mal ...

and thirty-two lines later:

> ... et vouloir tout sçavoir,
> Vouloir parler de tout, et toutes choses voir,
> Et vouloir nostre esprit par estude contraindre
> A monter jusqu'au Ciel, où il ne peut attaindre?
> Tout n'est que vanité, et pure vanité:
> Tel desir est bourreau de nostre humanité ...[18]

[18] *Oeuvres*, ed. Cohen, Elegie xv, II, 77.

THE MORAL VISION OF THE WORLD

This would seem to be an echo of Ecclesiastes, the sort of echo that was dear to the hearts of Du Bellay and Spenser. It is also a castigation of *outrecuidance*. But in the text of the poem itself there is throughout a clear denial of this melancholy middle portion. The mood as a whole is light, though isolated lines may proclaim the sadness, tragedy, and vanity of human life. The poem is presumed to be of early composition, though it was first published in the 1584 edition of Ronsard's collected works;[19] it is an imitation of a poem by Johannes Secundus, whose neo-Latin verse so influenced the early Ronsard. His remarks on the *condition humaine* quoted above are more of a concession to convention than an expression of sincere feeling, just as the further lines which condemn *hubris* in man are the occasion for making a paradoxical contrast with the life of La Haye, to whom the poem is written, and who is specifically stated to have succeeded in surpassing the limits usually set on human achievement. Toward the end of the poem Ronsard writes:

> Mais tout ainsi, La Haye, honneur de nostre temps,
> Qu'entre les animaux, par les champs habitans,
> On en voit quelques-uns, qui en prudence valent
> Plus que leurs campagnons, et les hommes egalent
> De sagesse et d'esprit, souventefois aussi,
> Entre cent millions d'hommes qui sont icy,
> On en voit quelques-uns qui dans leurs coeurs
>   assemblent
> Tant de rares vertus, qu'aux grands Dieux ils
>   resemblent
> Comme toy, bien appris, bien sage et bien discret...

Thus the whole thesis of the vanity of human endeavor is undercut by the example of the surpassingly brilliant La Haye, a man who succeeds in the practice of "surquedry."

[19] *Ibid.*, Notes, p. 1059.

The poem ends not merely with a wholly conventional assertion of faith in eternal life through Jesus Christ, but in the very last line a conclusion is drawn from this faith that is not conventional: "... tu ... me fais cognoistre / Que rien plus sainct que l'homme au monde ne peut naistre." These words belong to the exuberant spirit of the French Renaissance in Ronsard's youth, as a similar exuberance and sense of human certainty had characterized the Italian Renaissance in the late fifteenth century. They imply an overweeningness more typical of the ardor and enthusiasm of an earlier time—an enthusiasm so frequently expressed by Ronsard—less typical of the spirit of the English Renaissance and especially not typical of Spenser.[20]

A further and somewhat more weighty example of this tendency toward cheerfulness in the face of vanity and mutability is Ronsard's "Discours, de l'alteration et change des choses humaines,"[21] from the *Premier Livre des Poemes* (1560), a more ambitious poem in length (216 lines) and in subject matter. It is not an imitation, and was written in the poet's maturity. The poem begins with a very brief survey of historical examples of degeneration, which is immediately followed by eight lines castigating Protestantism as a modern instance. Ronsard then expounds his theory of cyclic regeneration, an idea which permeates the whole body of his more serious work:

> Le temps mangeard toute chose consomme.
> Villes, Chasteaux, Empires; voire l'homme,
> L'homme à qui Dieu fait part de sa maison,
> Qui pense, parle et discourt par raison,
> Duquel l'esprit s'en-vole outre la nue,
> Changeant sa forme en une autre se mue.

[20] It should be pointed out that there are conspicuous exceptions to this generalization, such as Marlowe, Nashe, Harvey, Bacon, and possibly Chapman.
[21] *Oeuvres*, ed. Cohen, II, 376-381.

> Il est bien vray, à parler proprement,
> On ne meurt point, on change seulement
> De forme en autre, et ce changer s'appelle
> Mort, quand on prend une forme nouvelle ...

It should be noted how the third line of this quotation retracts the phrase "voire l'homme" in the second, as if salvation were almost a matter of course (except, naturally, for Protestants). There is no melancholy, no pessimism, no regret in this enumeration of cities, castles, and empires that come and go; their passing is presented with a light air, an air of *tant pis*; nor indeed is it a serious misfortune. Further on in the poem, the question is asked: "Qu'est devenu l'Empire d'Assyrie, / Du Mede et Grec? ..." and is answered in a similar tone of lightness if not actually of levity.

The important point, however, to which the poem as a whole is devoted, is contained in the last four lines quoted above; everything is seen to be in a state of development, and death is only a phase of this, an intermediary phase between the old and the new form. For this reason there can be no sense of loss or of regret, only a sense of *carpe diem* while living and the promise of eternal blessedness in the end, based on a conviction that salvation is no more than the due of the aristocratic poet. This last is clearly expressed in the final ten lines of the poem, which are in the conventional form of a prayer that God protect France, the King, his family, Chauveau (to whom the poem is written), the French people, and the author. The prayer is without fervor and without humility; it is the usual prayer of the professional court poet, and it gives the impression that Ronsard feels that God is by nature a Francophile.[22]

---

[22] Further examples which illustrate the pervasiveness of Ronsard's cyclical theory of life-death-life may be found in his *Hynne de la Mort* and in "A luy-mesme" (*Epitaphes de divers sujets*), among many others (*Oeuvres* ed Cohen, II, 281-289, 480).

Curiously enough, Ronsard seemed to find a sense of security and of well-being for himself in his theory of cyclical change. He loved the variety and the flux of nature, the lavish productivity of spring, the excessive ardor of summer, the fruition and the sickness of autumn, somber but not melancholy, and the frigidity of winter, sterile itself but pregnant with the rich promise of a new spring.[23] It is almost as if he felt himself to be a part of nature, joyously caught up in the eternally revolving wheels of time. In *Ode* xix of *Le Troisieme Livre des Odes* he writes gaily, in the opening lines:

> D'ou vient cela, Pisseleu, que les hommes
> De leur nature aiment la changement,
> Et qu'on ne voit en ce monde où nous sommes
> Un seul qui n'ait un divers jugement?[24]

He is not saddened by mutability, by change, by death, or by corruption; he is invigorated and enlivened. Where Du Bellay and Spenser write *ubi sunt?* Ronsard writes *carpe diem!* Where they write laments, Ronsard writes invectives. Where they dwell in reflective melancholy on the forever lost, Ronsard moves swiftly from blossom to blossom in the present, catching each blossom before it is full blown; and, when it is blasted, sees in it the seed of its regeneration and never fixes his gaze in pensive pessimism on the moment of corruption.

It might be asked at this point with some justification whether the general cheerfulness that Ronsard exhibits implies that he was never serious or earnest in his work; and the reply, of course, is that he was often serious with a deadly earnestness, and earnest with a crushingly exaggerated *livresque* pedantry. This is to be seen in the long poems in self-defense against the attacks of Genevan Protestants, espe-

---

[23] See the *Hynnes* to the seasons, *Oeuvres*, ed. Cohen, II, 230-259.
[24] See Horace, *Satires*, I, 1, lines 1-3.

cially Theodore de Bèze, and in his prose tract written in this bitter quarrel.[25]

Raymond Lebègue points out that Ronsard shared with Du Bellay an intense dislike of the "rigorisme" of Protestantism,[26] and that this dislike was enflamed in Du Bellay by his passage through Geneva in 1557 and his observation of the "avidité," the "envie," and the "pharisaïsme" of the inhabitants. In common with most Frenchmen of their time, Ronsard and Du Bellay saw in the austerity of the Calvinists only a mask for all vices.[27] Ronsard's feeling in this matter, however, exploded for different reasons than Du Bellay's; for Ronsard's life extended through the religious wars and massacres of the 1560's and the 1570's and his temper was provoked by personal Protestant attacks and by the presence of actual warfare in the neighborhood of his native Vendômois. His "Response" to the Calvinists is in the tradition of unbridled theological controversy and is filled with what Lebègue calls "grossières injures."[28] These vulgarities are certainly serious, as were those of Thomas More before him and John Milton afterward; but they are the product of a particular situation and do not represent an aspect of a broad and enduringly contemplative moral view of the world such as both Du Bellay and Spenser held. Ronsard's seriousness here is that of anger produced by personal outrage; it is not based on a comprehensive and philosophical view of the innately and inevitably injurious nature of life itself.[29]

[25] See the *Discours des Misères de ce Temps*, the Continuation of the same, and the *Response de Pierre de Ronsard aux injures et calomnies de je ne sçay quels Predicantereaux et Ministreaux de Genéve*, all in verse; and *Response aux injures et calomnies de je ne sçay quels Predicans et Ministres de Genève, sur son Discours et Continuation des Miseres de ce Temps*, and "Epistre au Lecteur" in *Les Trois Livres de Recueil des Nouvelles Poesies* (1564), in prose.
[26] *Ronsard, l'homme et l'oeuvre* (Paris, 1950), p. 87.
[27] *Ibid.*   [28] *Ibid.*, p. 85.
[29] It should be noted here to Ronsard's credit that, although he was carried away by the religious hatreds of the 1560's, he was not among the

Further, in the long and quasi-philosophical or quasi-scientific poems which flowed so profusely from his pen in the troubled 1560's, though one finds a certain decorous seriousness in the *Hynnes,* the *Poëmes,* the *Discours,* and the *Elegies,* this seriousness is largely a matter of convention, as some of the ideas he expresses are themselves the conventional Neoplatonic theories of the educated man of his time, derived partly from Oriental occultism which reached France through Marsilio Ficino and partly from Ficino's own theories.[30] Ronsard is not a thinker any more than he is a moralist. In the expression of philosophical ideas he is vague and indecisive; he avoids clear answers and takes refuge chiefly in the use of myth as an embodiment for ideas, or perhaps as a substitute.

Ronsard's early tendency toward pedantry of language is associated with this avoidance of clear statements of philosophical questions and an equal reluctance to present incisive answers. This pedantry became a habit which he never fully conquered, though he tried throughout his life to control the *livresque* penchant which began with his youthful classical studies. In his maturity it became not a fault merely, but a vice. It was at an advanced age (1574) that he wrote the notorious line, "Ocymore, dyspotme, oligochronien. . . ."[31]

That he was persistently earnest in such pedantries is beyond question, as both Du Bellay and Spenser were earnest in their own linguistic experiments; but his is a grim and often a ridiculous earnestness of a strictly nonmoral variety. The pedagogue may be pedantic, as Spenser is in the *Visions of the worldes vanitie,* but it does not follow that Ronsard was a pedagogue because he was pedantic. He felt himself called upon by higher forces to be a seer, the

---

poets who celebrated the Massacre of St. Bartholomew's Eve in 1572. *Ibid.,* p. 85.
[30] *Ibid.,* pp. 66-67.
[31] "Le Tombeau de Marguerite de France, Duchesse de Savoie," *Oeuvres,* II, 480.

mouthpiece of divine inspiration; but much of the result of this inspiration was bookish theorizing whose meaning is very little more discernible than that of scattered Sybilline leaves. He could not stoop to be a simple teacher, as could Du Bellay occasionally and Spenser often, because his temperament, which has been called both "épicurien" and "arthritique,"[32] did not admit such a downward step into the real world; he taught nothing simple and straightforward except that one should indulge and enjoy one's senses, because he knew nothing else simple and straightforward that he could teach. His mind was oversophisticated, and all morality except the Epicurean was repugnant to him; he did not find morality elevating, he found it depressing.

All of Ronsard's best work is in the purely lyric vein: short poems, almost thoughtless, amoral or immoral, lovely, delicate, and marvelously melodious, but without weight or substance. The justly famous "A Sa Maitresse," of *Le Premier Livre des Odes*, in its eighteen lines says only one thing: "Cueillez, cueillez vostre jeunesse."[33] As a *carpe diem* poem, it is as fine as any in any language; but *carpe diem* poems, in the end, do not say very much, and they certainly teach very little that could be called moral. An additional and completely parallel example is the best-known sonnet of the series to Marie: "Comme on voit sur la branche au mois de may la rose, / En sa belle jeunesse, en sa premiere fleur. . . ."[34] In this poem the exquisite language is not overburdened with any message of serious import; in a context which mentions death and obsequies and tears there is no feeling of mortality, and corruption is something which takes place in another world.

Ronsard's poetic world is almost wholly sunlit; it is the Graeco-Roman Vendômois countryside of fields, streams, fountains, roses; the caves are dark, but they are not gloomy, because they contain nymphs; it is a world of wine and

[32] Lebègue, *Ronsard*, pp. 139, 143.
[33] *Oeuvres*, I, 420.   [34] *Ibid.*, I, 184.

maidens, songs, odes or sonnets, a world of constant flux in a constant present.

> Verson ces roses pres ce vin,
> Pres de ce vin verson ces roses,
> Et boivon l'un à l'autre, à fin
> Qu'au coeur nos tristesses encloses
> Prennent en boivant quelque fin....[35]

The "tristesse" is evanescent, it is always vaporous and formless, ready to be dispelled by food or drink or poetry, by roses, or by a passing shepherdess. What remains after the "tristesse" is joy, joy which is to be had for the asking.

This is far indeed from Spenser's world of uncertainty and mutability, a world of unexpected falls and reversals, in which joy itself is evanescent and will always be so until a final day shall bring eternal joy—a kind of joy which was no concern of Ronsard's until his illness brought it into the forefront of his mind. For Spenser as for Du Bellay, the past broods darkly over the present, and the sun is obscured. But for Spenser, the sun may come out clear, and it often does, though not in the *Visions of the worldes vanitie*.

Not so for Du Bellay; happiness for him is always elsewhere, or in another time. Although like Ulysse he could return ultimately to Paris and to Anjou, he was always most keenly aware of what had been lost, of what was irrevocable. The familiar "Heureux qui" theme in Du Bellay rarely refers to the poet himself, or to the present, but to some vanished golden moment that is either absolutely past or absolutely unattainable in the present.

Du Bellay lives under a dark sun; Spenser can see not only darkness but also rainbows and an occasional full and stunning light; Ronsard lives under a clear and brilliant classical sun, as unconcerned about the darkness as he is about the morrow.

[35] *Ibid.*, I, 575 (Ode xxxviii, *Quatriesme Livre des Odes*).

VII · PLATONISM IN SPENSER

*I*T IS a commonplace of modern criticism that the love poems and the philosophical or religious poems of the three poets under consideration were strongly influenced by Platonic doctrines. This influence came chiefly from two sources: the work of Plato himself, either in the original Greek or in Latin translations; and commentaries on this work, mainly by Italian scholars and theorists as well as quasi-philosophical expositions of Platonic doctrine by Italian poets and prose writers. Before the end of the fifteenth century the Florentine scholar Marsilio Ficino had made available in Latin all of the Platonic dialogues that were known at that time.

Of these two sources the second was the more important, because the neo-Platonic commentators and expositors were more prolific than their master, and their works were not only in more profuse circulation in the sixteenth century but, in addition, commentaries eliminated the linguistic barriers and reinterpretation tended to assimilate Platonic to Christian doctrine, sometimes blurring the precise meaning of Plato's text and producing a syncretic doctrine that came to be known as neo-Platonism. In sixteenth century England as in France it is always difficult and often impossible to distinguish the correct source of a Platonic passage in poetry, because as a rule neither the poets nor the scholars themselves worried about distinctions between the actual Platonic text and the texts of commentators. The ponderously magnificent Variorum Edition of the Works of Spenser lists as putative sources of the *Fowre Hymnes* five dialogues by Plato himself, the *Symposium*, the *Phaedrus*, the *Timaeus*, the *Phaedo*, and the *Laws*; among the commentaries, principally that of Ficino; the work of Bembo, Pico della Mirandola, Bruno, Benivieni, and Castiglione.[1] Since Spenser in remote England, and in more remote Ireland, was familiar with these texts, one might assume that Ronsard and Du Bellay, living in the continental aura of neo-Platonic speculation, were even more intensely exposed to infection, as, in fact, they were.[2] That two of the poets reacted very differently to the infection, however, was a matter of temperamental divergency and not of geographical distance or proximity.

The *locus classicus* of Platonic doctrine in Spenser is the *Fowre Hymnes*.[3] There, in the space of some twelve hundred lines, is gathered together with a certain coherence all that is dispersed elsewhere, in the *Faerie Queene* and in the *Amoretti* in particular. F. M. Padelford has written that "it is a truism that Spenser never thinks with precision when he gets into the realm of metaphysics, being much more of a poet than a philosopher,"[4] and the same may be said, but more forcefully, of Ronsard. For Spenser does think, even though he sometimes thinks without precision; he is indeed a thoughtful poet. But Ronsard rarely thinks at all. He fol-

---

[1] Works, *The Minor Poems*, Vol. 1, "Commentary," and "Appendix v," *passim*. See also W. L. Renwick, *Daphnaïda and Other Poems* (which contains also the *Fowre Hymnes*): "The difficulty of the 'sources' here, indeed, is like that of the *Amoretti*, that much of the matter is common to several authors all of whom Spenser probably knew" (p. 209).

[2] It is quite clear that Ronsard and Du Bellay, as Frenchmen and as former students of Dorat, were familiar with a much wider range both of Platonic writings and of commentaries. Frances A. Yates in *The French Academies of the Sixteenth Century* emphasizes the lines of inheritance that exist between Ficino's Platonic Academy in Florence and what she refers to as the "'Academy'" at the Collège de Coqueret (p. 4). This connection implies a presumptive acquaintance for Ronsard and Du Bellay with some or many of the medieval Platonists of the Catholic tradition, chiefly St. Augustine and Pseudo-Dionysius, a body of mystical writing that might reach a continental Catholic far more naturally than an English Protestant. For a summary account of the neo-Platonic background of the Pléiade, see Yates's *Academies*, Ch. 1; and for a fuller account of the beginnings of neo-Platonism in France, see A. Renaudet, *Préreforme et Humanisme à Paris* (Grenoble, 1916).

[3] Published in 1596.

[4] "Spenser's Fowre Hymnes: A Resurvey," *SP* 29 (1932), p. 212.

lows a school of thought, or reacts against it with very strong feelings and very weak thoughts. In his serious *Poëmes* and *Hynnes* and *Discours* Ronsard seems to have an uncalculated and wholly natural affinity for disorder, for *mélange*, even for contradiction. Furthermore, it is an exaggeration to credit Ronsard with annexing philosophy to poetry, as Raymond Lebègue does, unless the statement is simply an historical one.[5] Important as it was to have been one of the first to introduce philosophic themes into French poetry, it cannot be said that any of his poems is as purely philosophical as is the second pair of the *Fowre Hymnes* of Spenser. All are tarnished by the obtrusion either of illogical arguments or of irreconcilable contradictions or of personal or anecdotal elements.

On the other hand, a clear vein of Platonism may be seen running through much of the work of Joachim Du Bellay. While there is no single major poem by the younger Frenchman that expounds or elaborates either Platonic or neo-Platonic doctrine at any length, nevertheless an essentially Platonic view emerges here and there in his work and is never subjected to contradiction or recantation. In this respect as in others Du Bellay is as far from Ronsard as he is near to Spenser.

Enmeshed with the statements of Platonic or neo-Platonic theory in all three poets are the elements of their religious beliefs. Some of these interlockings are inseparable, as for instance the following from Spenser:

> Then shall thy rauisht soule inspired bee
> With heauenly thoughts, farre aboue humane skil,
> And thy bright radiant eyes shall plainely see
> Th'Idee of his pure glorie, present still . . .[6]

Or perhaps more strikingly:

[5] *Ronsard, L'Homme et L'Oeuvre*, p. 33.
[6] *An Hymne of Heavenly Love*, lines 281-284.

Faire is the heauen, where happy soules haue place,
In full enioyment of felicitie,
Whence they doe still behold the glorious face
Of the diuine eternall Maiestie;
More faire is that, where those *Idees* on hie,
Enraunged be, which Plato so admyred,
And pure *Intelligences* from God inspyred.[7]

Here the language is Platonic, but the matter and the meaning are wholly Christian, ardently religious, and almost ecstatically devotional. In other passages a separation exists in the structure of the poem, or one can be made without undue wrenching of the text. In the present chapter I shall make an effort to confine myself to Platonic or neo-Platonic doctrine in Spenser, and in the following chapter I shall consider the same elements in Du Bellay and Ronsard. Separately and subsequently I shall deal with the strictly religious aspects of the three poets. That such a separation is artificial is unquestionably true, but it is also convenient. It may to some extent be excused because of the limited degree of separation that exists within the poems themselves, and between the more or less conventional neo-Platonism in the first two of Spenser's *Hymnes* and the intertwined but less predominant Platonism of the latter two.

At the outset, and before considering Spenser's own Platonism, it will perhaps be well to review as briefly as possible that aspect of the Platonic doctrine which is most pertinent to Spenser's own views. The core of the theory of Platonic love is to be found in the *Symposium*, the *Phaedrus* and the *Phaedo*, but for our purposes the speech of Socrates in the *Symposium*, which Socrates attributes to one Diotima, a prophetess, will provide a sufficient background for the theories of Spenser and of continental neo-Platonists.

A. E. Taylor writes of this passage, "The purpose of the

[7] *An Hymne of Heavenly Beavtie*, lines 78-84.

speech, in the language of religion . . . is the narrative of the pilgrimage of a soul on the way of salvation, from the initial moment at which it feels the need of salvation to its final 'consummation.' "[8] To state the burden of the speech in this manner is automatically to make clear the reasons for its easy acceptance and easy assimilation by Renaissance Christians; for here in Plato, the end of human life, its final cause, is ἀντὸ τὸ καλόν, just as it is τὸ ἀγαθόν in the *Republic*, both of which are fundamentally the same and can readily be identified with salvation and with God.

The road to this final beauty has been presented earlier in the dialogue as Eros, which has been treated by Phaedrus as carnal desire.[9] Socrates redefines Eros as a daimon (δαίμων) who aspires to wisdom, neither god nor mortal, living between eternity and temporality and always trying to reach the immutable and to cast off the temporal. Here again we approximate the allegory of the ever-restless soul of the Christian wayfarer, his heart always unquiet in its unremitting search for God. According to Socrates, or Diotima, Eros in man expresses itself in a desire for procreation in the beautiful, and this procreation may be either physical or spiritual. In the former there is an adumbration of Spenser's conception of the chastity of married love, and in the latter, the spiritual procreation, which Socrates exemplifies in one of its senses by mentioning the poems of Homer and Hesiod, there is a clear analogy with the *Fowre Hymnes*. The vision of final beauty according to Socrates comes as a sudden revelation and it is apprehended immediately, not by discursive reasoning and knowledge. Man's life is most true only in the rapt contemplation of this good, which is Beauty pure and unalloyed, sole and absolute, the supreme form. Beside it all other beauties and desires are as dross. Intercourse with it results in spiritual progeny, and this alone is

[8] *Plato, the Man and his Work* (London, 1949), p. 225.
[9] *Symposium*, 178a-180b.

the true achievement of "immortality" in the temporal world.

Such a doctrine might be related to Spenser's work itself in that the *Fowre Hymnes* are spiritual progeny and seem, even in this iron age, to have achieved a kind of immortality for their author. The poems, however, are confused and heterogeneous, and never fully or consistently mystical. Spenser had only brief moments of visionary insight, and they were, as one can see in his whole work, consistently based on a substratum of discursive thought. He was not by any means a real mystic.

In his stimulating and perceptive critical study, *Shakespeare and Spenser*, W. B. C. Watkins writes that Spenser's "whole work is an attempt to harmonize body and spirit."[10] This is true in the broadest sense of the entire *Faerie Queene*, and true in every sense of the *Fowre Hymnes*. Almost everything in all four poems is either Platonic or Christian, with the exception of a few stanzas in *An Hymne of Beavtie* which are moralistic, a category which may easily be included under Christian, and a few lines which are conventionally personal in the Petrarchan-neo-Platonic fashion.[11] The diction throughout is exceedingly simple in comparison to the rest of Spenser's work, as is also the sentence structure. Such simplicity, in combination with the elevation of the thought, especially in the later poems, is particularly felicitous in its effect. It tends to carry the reader away emotionally, to rise above the intricacies and perhaps the confusions of thought, and reach an immediacy of clear and simple communication. This quality is apprehended most lucidly in *An Hymne of Heavenly Love*, but it is present

[10] p. 197.
[11] When the Italian sonnet form reached France and later England in the sixteenth century, the bitter-sweet worship of Laura in the poetry of Petrarch was found to cohabit naturally with the neo-Platonic devotion to the lady's eyes as the first stimulus toward a higher and more spiritual aspiration.

in passages in the other poems. It is not Platonic in essence; its spirit is Christian, and the occasional intrusion of the language of neo-Platonism is merely the body. In this sense too there is in these poems an attempt to harmonize the body and the spirit, to establish a concord, which is wholly successful only in *An Hymne of Heavenly Love*, where the corporeal or linguistic elements of neo-Platonism are minimal.[12]

Spenser's attraction to neo-Platonism was emotional, as W. L. Renwick has pointed out.[13] In the earlier two hymns, his neo-Platonism is conventional, perhaps merely a reflection of the current fashion. In this respect it was like Petrarchism and was indeed closely connected with it; it was all the rage. But one does not have to look far into the earlier poems to find that for Spenser it was more than a mere fashion, for in the poems themselves there is a note of sincerity that transcends the conventional, the secondhand Petrarchan. And just so the later poems might be said to transcend even Petrarch himself, who, ending his *Canzonieri* with a lovely palinode to the Virgin, even then cannot restrain himself from envious glances downward into the temporal world of mutability.

Let us examine the first two hymns, and then the last two, in order to lay a groundwork for future comparisons and contrasts with the work of Du Bellay and Ronsard.

An Hymne of Love is split between aspiration to a love beyond the flesh, and the physical presence of the flesh at hand. Love itself is embodied in Venus and Cupid, not etherialized. But the presence of the poet's lady is minimal, and the theme, rather than wavering between carnal love and spiritual love, resolves itself into a discussion of the dis-

[12] Neo-Platonic speculation in the vernacular tended to develop its own vocabulary. This may be seen in English in Hoby's translation of Castiglione's *Courtier*, especially in the climactic speech of Bembo in Book IV.
[13] *Edmund Spenser*, pp. 163-167.

tinction between two kinds of earthly love, the physical, or Eros as interpreted by Phaedrus in the *Symposium*,[14] and the spiritualized love, or Eros in his earthly manifestation as explained by Diotima.

There has been a great deal of controversy concerning whether this poem and the one following it, *An Hymne of Beavtie*, are together a unit quite separate from the two which follow, which in turn are also alike; or, on the other hand, whether all four poems are progressive and connected units which can be said to fit into a mystical system. The "Editor" of the pertinent volume of the Variorum Edition of Spenser's Works has the final word in this longstanding and still unresolved discussion, and writes an instructive caveat: ". . . Spenser was not following a preconceived plan of philosophical presentation. . . . While he undoubtedly understood the implications of the neo-Platonic stages of progression, he touched them but lightly as he passed along to give an appearance of philosophical development to his theme. In attempting to pierce through to a complete understanding of Spenser, it is well to keep in mind that we are working with a piece of Renaissance art and not a philosophical treatise."[15]

The value of this warning will become evident as we pass through our analysis of the poem, observing the consistent core of Christianity and the temporal (Renaissance) or adventitious quality of the Platonic language and the stages of progression.

Early in the first poem Spenser writes that Love created the world, and holds the elements in accord with each other, keeping them all in order; that Love compels them

---

[14] Though of course without the implications of pederasty that appear in the *Symposium*.

[15] *Works, The Minor Poems*, I, "Appendix v," p. 681. (The "Editor" is apparently both Charles G. Osgood and Henry G. Lotespeich.)

PLATONISM IN SPENSER

> To keepe themselues within their sundrie raines . . .
> But man, that breathes a more immortall mynd,
> Not for lusts sake, but for eternitie,
> Seekes to enlarge his lasting progenie.
>
> (Lines 88, 103-105)

Here is the first indication of the forthcoming rigid distinction between love and lust; and within the language of orthodox Renaissance neo-Platonic expression of a doctrine straight from the *Symposium*, one can see also in the background the *Old Testament* exhortation to increase and multiply. Spenser goes on to write of the aspiring quality of man, and outlines the highest kind of earthly aspiration:

> For sure of all, that in this mortall frame
> Contained is, nought more diuine doth seeme,
> Or that resembleth more th'immortal flame
> Of heauenly light, then Beauties glorious beame,
> What wonder then, if with such rage extreme
> Fraile men, whose eyes seek heauenly things to see,
> At sight thereof so much enrauisht bee.
>
> (Lines 113-119)

Quite properly from the Platonic point of view, the rage and enravishment are penultimate, since their cause is only a reflection of the immortal flame, its appearance in the temporal world. It is merely the frailty of man which makes this less-than-final vision so affecting.

Next, a few fashionable Petrarchisms intervene; but very soon thereafter the individual Spenserian note rings forth, the signature that does not merely translate but transmutes. Speaking of the trials Love imposes in his effort to make the lover swerve, he writes:

> And mayest them make it better to deserue;
> And hauing got it, may it more esteeme.

141

For things hard gotten, men more dearely deeme.
(Lines 166-168)

This typical moral maxim introduces a more extended passage on the unworthy earthly lovers, the men of base-born minds who cannot take fire with love of the truly beautiful, but feel only loose desires. A brief and characteristic passage is interjected at this point, on the higher love, perhaps to make the contrast with the base love more striking:

> For loue is Lord of truth and loialtie,
> Lifting himselfe out of the lowly dust,
> On golden plumes vp to the purest skie,
> Aboue the reach of loathly sinful lust . . .
> (Lines 176-180)

That love should be lord of truth is within the Platonic tradition, but the mention of loyalty is Spenser's own, and is radically in opposition to love as conceived by Ronsard.

Spenser then proceeds immediately to a castigation of the lustful lover:

> His dunghill thoughts, which do themselues enure
> To dirty drosse, no higher dare aspyre,
> Ne can his feeble earthly eyes endure
> The flaming light of that celestiall fyre,
> Which kindleth loue in generous desyre,
> And makes him mount aboue the natiue might
> Of heauie earth, vp to the heauens hight.
> (Lines 183-189)

The language in this passage is reminiscent of the bitterness of *The Teares of the Muses*; Spenser has neither mercy nor sympathy for the immoral. This intransigence is not Petrarchan, and the language is stronger than that of Plato. It is a view perhaps more rigid and uncompromising than that of Dante, who could feel some degree of pity for Francesca in Hell. Spenser is keenly aware of the permanent and unalterable conflict between loyalty and generosity, which are in the image of heaven, and of dirty, lustful, dunghill thoughts, full of the heaviness of this world.

He goes on to describe the heavenly image in terms which recall Christian religious usage:

> He thereon feeds his hungrie fantasy,
> Still full, yet neuer satisfyde with it . . .
> (Lines 198-199)

Here, were it not a mirror-image but the thing itself, the language would seem to echo two things: the vision of God, and what is essentially connected to it, participation in the sacrament of the Eucharist. But in this poem we are still in the world or, to put it in Platonic terms, we have only just turned from a contemplation of the shadows on the wall of the Cave—in the viewing of which we have abandoned the lustful lover—and faced the images of second-degree reality behind us. We are not yet out of the Cave. And lest we mistake the image for more than it actually is, Spenser brings us back in the next stanza to the physical lady "whose sole aspect he counts felicitie" (line 217).

Of these lines (197-217) W. L. Renwick writes, "Spenser begins here with the second stage of ascent, the image of the beloved in the mind, but he does not regard it as an advance, but merely as a concomitant of love of the individual, whom he never discards as the Platonists say he ought."[16] This is Spenser's initial failure to mount the conventional neo-Platonic ladder, a failure that begins the defeat of the theorists who consider that the four poems fit into a consistently progressive mystical system. Spenser remains grounded in material reality; he does not share in the long history of Marian veneration that made the transition from physical woman to ideal beauty and love so much

[16] *Daphnaïda*, "Commentary," p. 216.

easier and more natural for continental Catholics. He betrays, perhaps, a kind of hardheadedness in spiritual matters. His treatment of neo-Platonic material is free and independent; as much as he can conveniently use, he takes. Influenced as he undoubtedly was by the conventions of Italian neo-Platonism, he is not enslaved by them either in any individual poem of this series or in the organization and linkage of the four. He will not etherealize his flesh-and-blood lady; she is not a steppingstone on the wayside, not a rung in an ascent. Spenser's method is allegory, not idealism; and in allegory he can have both the abstractions and the individual.

In the last sixty lines of the poem Spenser remains with the terrestrial situation of the lover, and introduces a long passage on "that cancker worme, that Monster Gelosie" (line 267), who has been so fully treated in the incident of Malbecco and Hellenore in the *Faerie Queene*. The position of the happy lover is contrasted with that of the unfortunate one, and the poem ends with two stanzas of prayer to Cupid:

> Ay me, deare Lord, that euer I might hope,
> For all the paines and woes that I endure,
> To come at length vnto the wished scope
> Of my desire; or might my selfe assure,
> That happie port for euer to recure.
> Then would I thinke these paines no paines at all,
> And all my woes to be but penance small.
>
> Then would I sing of thine immortall praise
> An heauenly Hymne, such as the Angels sing,
> And thy triumphant name then would I raise
> Boue all the gods, thee onely honoring,
> My guide, my God, my victor, and my king;

Till then, dread Lord, vouchsafe to take of me
This simple song, thus fram'd in praise of thee.
(Lines 294-307)

An interpretation of these stanzas is crucial to a general understanding of all four of the *Hymnes*. As I have pointed out, the first hymn is about both heavenly and earthly love, with the emphasis on the latter, and only adumbrations of the former. Especially at the end Spenser turns to the terrestrial situation. The "wished scope" for which he is praying is success in love in a broad and wholly earthly sense, not merely physical possession but a decorous and proper union. This "wished scope/Of my desire," within the context of the first hymn, is clearly a temporal matter, but the desire is not merely sexual, in terms of the castigation of such love in preceding stanzas. Spenser is seeking a chaste union such as is celebrated much later in the incomparable *Epithalamion*, the full and comprehensive union that inspires the principal characters in the *Faerie Queene* as an ideal capable of realization in this sublunary world.

Within the first hymn it is Cupid who can grant the poet's desire, if he will but take pity. Thus Spenser promises to honor him with a heavenly hymn, to honor him above all gods, as guide and God and victor and king. That Cupid receives a capital "G" here as God is no more significant than is the real God without capital letter in the third hymn. The poet's reference is not confusing; the confusion lies in the erratic printing practices of the Elizabethans. Cupid as guide, victor, and king in the third line from the last is entirely appropriate to a poem which begins with a request that Cupid ease the bitter smart of the poet's poor captive heart.

The first hymn, therefore, does not seem to point forward to the third, and is not an explicit stage in the journey toward heavenly beauty in the fourth. But the third does point backward to the first. In a certain sense the third fulfills the promise of the last stanza of the first; but it does not do so in the terms in which the promise was made. It is as if, in the interval between the writing of the first pair of hymns and the last pair, with the passage of time, the growth of maturity, and above all the final success in the realm of love that the *Epithalamion* bespeaks, the poet's mind could now be freed to write of a love without taint of time or place, hardly touched by Petrarchan idealism or by neopagan convention, but liberated from the mutability of human affairs because the tribulations and vicissitudes of this world had now fallen into their proper places in the poet's mind.

Just as the poem we have been discussing is anchored in the terrestrial sphere by the continued presence of the lover and the beloved in their earthly form, so too does *An Hymne of Beavtie* remain as it were grounded, in spite of occasional incomplete soarings beyond the realm of the earth's shadow. In this poem the celestial is shown to have a close and intimate connection with the sublunary, having the same relationship that the stamp has to the wax. Earthly beauty partakes of the heavenly; it participates. The difference seems to be one of degree, not kind. Although the influences in this poem are more preponderantly Italian than in the former, although whole passages seem to do little more than broadly paraphrase passages in Bembo, Castiglione, and Ficino especially, the poem as a whole not only fails to get its feet off the ground in proper neo-Platonic fashion; it seems even deliberately to refuse such flights. In the beginning, the middle, and the end, the poem is held firmly to the earthly situation. Whatever emendations or corrections Spenser may have made in the text in order to please the ladies of the dedication, at least he has not cut his ground anchor.[17]

[17] For an opposing view of this question, see Appendix III.

The poem takes flight in an initial invocation to Venus. The poet is swept away with a fury in his feeble breast, and he cannot slake the raging fire that the goddess of love has kindled in him. This opening is superficially like a good many of the wild invocations at the beginning of Ronsard's poems, especially his early odes; out of context it would read like an example of Ronsardian *forcénement*. But Spenser's spirit, though metaphysical, is fundamentally sane, as the second stanza indicates. The passion is not Venereal; what the poet requests is that Venus' bright beauty,

> The rauisht harts of gazefull men might reare,
> To admiration of that heauenly light,
> From whence proceeds such soule enchaunting might.
> (Lines 12-14)

The poet asks further of Venus:

> Doe thou vouchsafe with thy loue-kindling light
> T'illuminate my dim and dulled eyne . . .
>
> That both to thee, to whom I meane it most,
> And eke to her, whose faire immortall beame,
> Hath darted fyre into my feeble ghost . . .
> (Lines 19-20, 22-24)

The beloved appears with the goddess as corecipient of the invocation. She is connected with the goddess as a kindler of fire; furthermore, the "immortall beame" from the beloved's eyes is a reflection of the beam which originates in beauty itself and is distributed by Venus. (What the archetypal beauty is will not be revealed until the fourth hymn.) The scheme is thus neo-Platonic up to this point, when a Petrarchan request for "Some deaw of grace, into my withered hart" intervenes. This personal remark at the end of the invocation emphasizes the fact that beauty in this poem is still of this world, earthly and natural, a world in which a withering takes place, and pity may be evoked. The main body of the poem then begins with two stanzas of orthodox Platonic doctrine which seems to have come directly from the philosopher, although the doctrine is misunderstood at one point. Spenser refers to the realm of the Ideas as follows:

> That wondrous Paterne wheresoere it bee,
> Whether in earth layd vp in secret store,
> Or else in heauen, that no man may it see
> With sinful eyes, for feare it to deflore,
> Is perfect Beautie . . .
>
> (Lines 36-40)

The pattern that is laid up in heaven is Plato's, but the fact that no man may see it is Spenser's. Lilian Winstanley points out quite accurately that this prohibition implies a denial of the Platonic doctrine of reminiscence, and says that Spenser thus prejudices the core of his Platonic argument.[18] This would be important if the hymn were an expository treatise. The meaning of the poem does not, however, depend on the logic or the veracity of its philosophical argument. In any case, the pattern is seen in the fourth hymn; and not seen, as in Plato, and recognized because it has been seen before, but seen through a vision, for the first time. In the present context the point is not so much that the pattern may not be seen; the emphasis is on the sinful eyes of man, who, of course, in a state of sin could not see the pattern even if it were directly before his eyes. This passage is moral in the Spenserian fashion; the orthodoxy of metaphysical argument is colored by emotion.

The poem goes on to say that every earthly thing "partakes" of perfect beauty "Or more or less by influence diuine" (lines 43, 44). This is purely Platonic, the radiation

[18] *Fowre Hymnes*, ed. Lilian Winstanley, pp. 54-55.

downward of the eternal forms. This orthodox view is continued in the succeeding stanzas in which beauty is stated not to reside in secondary characteristics, as idle wits believe. The language itself seems Platonic:

> ... confesse it then,
> That Beautie is not, as fond men misdeeme,
> An outward shew of things, that onely seeme.
> (Lines 89-91)

The world of appearance decays and becomes corrupt; the lovely hue of the cheek and the roses upon the lips fade away. At this point, where Ronsard would hardly be able to resist an exclamation of *carpe diem*, Spenser indicates the immortal soul as the seat of beauty eternal (lines 93-103); here the soul is the eternal reality, and the eyes are the transient and corruptible appearance, just as in another relationship the fair lamp in heaven is the highest reality and the soul which receives and transmits its light is but the earthly manifestation. Spenser says:

> For of the soule the bodie forme doth take:
> For soule is forme, and doth the bodie make.
> (Lines 132-133)

That is, the soul informs the body, which in itself is inert matter. This is the doctrine set forth in other and more confusing terms in the Canto dealing with the Garden of Adonis in the *Faerie Queene* (III, vi, 37-38), a doctrine shared not only by contemporary neo-Platonists but also by Ronsard. The reader will have noted, however, the discrepancy between Spenser's and Ronsard's tone in the presentation of this theory, which is essentially Christian in Spenser, whether it be associated with Venus, as in this context, or with Venus and Adonis, as in the *Faerie Queene*. The classical setting in Ronsard has been seen to have an implication that points less clearly to Christian symbolism or allegory.

The next extended passage in *An Hymne of Beavtie* (lines 148-182) parallels the moral comparison and exhortation that occupies a similar position in the first hymn. But it is less bitter in its denunciation of lust, and it places a more eloquent emphasis on the love that is pure and true. This difference is in accord with the more metaphysical quality of this second hymn, yet the brief mention of shame and corruption serves to remind the reader that the world is still too much with us. Fair dames are warned that though they are by nature good,

> Nothing so good, but that through guilty shame
> May be corrupt, and wrested vnto will . . .
> (Lines 157-158)

They are urged in admonitory tones to be "mindfull still of your first countries sight . . ." (line 166).

Here Spenser seems to imply an affirmation of the Platonic doctrine of reminiscence. The implication is at least as positive as was the previous implied denial indicated by Miss Winstanley. The ladies are asked to preserve their

> . . . first informed grace,
> Whose shadow yet shynes in your beauteous face.
> (Lines 167-168)

The light from the soul reaches the face with the shadow of the flesh upon it, yet the light is so clear and pure that it may be said metaphorically to shine. The implication seems to be that the soul knows what informed it, has had some kind of vision of its first country. Here the exalted quality of the soul is stressed; in the previous case the emphasis was moral, upon the sinfulness of mankind. In this comparative example it may readily be seen that philosophic doctrines for Spenser were raw material to be recast, to be formed for poetic use; not logical arguments in the coils of which a poet might strangle his creative power, constrained like Laocoon in external strictures.

Spenser next directs his fair dames to the loathing of lustful love:

> Loath that foule blot, that hellish fierbrand,
> Disloiall lust, faire beauties foulest blame,
> That base affections, which your eares would bland,
> Commend to you by loues abused name;
> But is indeede the bondslaue of defame . . .
> (Lines 169-173)

The contrast with a right and proper love follows immediately, as it did in the previous hymn. It is stated in much the same terms, but here the passage is more extensive. A series of variations is played upon the ideal of terrestrial love, variations, and modulations which ultimately evoke some of the joyous spirit of the *Epithalamion*:

> But gentle Loue, that loiall is and trew,
> Will more illumine your resplendent ray,
> And adde more brightnesse to your goodly hew,
> From light of his pure fire, which by like way
> Kindled of yours, your likenesse doth display,
> Like as two mirrours by opposed reflexion . . .
> (Lines 176-181)

The true lovers are thus connected with each other and with love itself by a series of mirror images which modify the stunning beauty of love itself, but do not falsify or pervert its truth or beauty. Spenser proceeds:

> For Loue is a celestiall harmonie,
> Of likely harts composed of starres concent,
> Which ioyne together in sweete sympathie,
> To work ech others ioy and true content.
> (Lines 197-200)

The poet goes on to say that true love is foreordained and prearranged in heaven. Such true love has "pure regard and spotlesse true intent" (line 212). Throughout this part of the discourse one hears echoes of Socrates' voice in his second speech in the *Phaedrus*. In the stanza that begins at line 211 Spenser moves from a personal view of love which emphasizes the dual nature of the true emotion which is both physical and spiritual—of the body and of the soul, yet in both equally pure and chaste—to a wholly Platonic or neo-Platonic statement which is clearly derived or received. The beloved is seen in "her first perfection" (line 216), and "free from fleshes frayle infection" (line 217). This is as close as Spenser comes in his earlier hymns to the disembodiment of the beloved; it is a step beyond any in the first hymn to love. Furthermore, there is no act of disembodiment in the later heavenly hymns, for in them the beloved is God, or the archetype of Beauty which is contained in God.

Jefferson B. Fletcher writes that these lines and their surrounding context (211-238) "virtually telescope Benivieni."[19] One should distinguish, however, between the use of the words and phrases of Italian Neo-Platonists, the reflections of the eyes, the rays, the mirrors, the celestial harmonies; and the things that are generally Elizabethan and personally Spenserian, the concern with loyalty and truth and generosity and true content, as well as Spenser's heavy emphasis on the evil of unworthy and blameful love, the base affection of disloyal lust.

Lilian Winstanley assigns other Italians, Ficino and Bruno, as the source of the same lines.[20] Certainly large quantities of the corpus of Italian neo-Platonic writing had been available to Spenser; and though it is hardly likely that

[19] "Benivieni's Ode of Love and Spenser's Fowre Hymnes," *MP* 8 (1911), pp. 555-556.
[20] *Fowre Hymnes*, p. 61.

PLATONISM IN SPENSER

he had a large library with him in Ireland, this reading must nevertheless have haunted his mind in an isolated and comparatively uncultivated atmosphere. It seems therefore probable that both Fletcher and Winstanley are right to some degree; but it is likewise clear that in bringing his reading to his own creative work, Spenser put upon that work a thoroughly individual, unique stamp.

The perception of the inward beauty of the beloved, the capacity of the lover to see through and beyond the flesh, is explained in conventional neo-Platonic terms as follows:

> For louers eyes more sharply sighted bee
> Then other mens, and in deare loues delight
> See more then any other eyes can see,
> Through mutuall receipt of beames bright . . .
> (Lines 232-235)

At this point, neo-Platonic theory seems to be running away with the poem; in four successive stanzas the pure image of the beloved is held in the lover's mind; the body seems as it were cast aside in the proper neo-Platonic fashion. The two following stanzas, however, play on the lovers' fanciful "conceits" concerning each other's physical appearance; the bodies have returned, and the poet has moved to the Petrarchan method, but marked with a personal print as well:

> Sometimes vpon her forhead they behold
> A thousand Graces masking in delight,
> Sometimes within her eye-lids they vnfold
> Ten thousand sweet belgards, which to their sight
> Doe seeme like twinckling starres in frostie night:
> But on her lips, like rosy buds in May,
> So many millions of chaste pleasures play.
> (Lines 253-259)

It is important to notice the words Spenser uses in this description. The parts of the body that are mentioned are the forehead, the eyelids and by implication the eyes and the mouth. All except the mouth are barren of direct sexual associations, and the mouth is included only in respect to "chaste pleasures." The radiance in the eyes is beautifully and significantly described as not only twinkling and starry, but as on a frosty night; that is, clear, and above all pure. The Graces on the forehead are pure, too, for Spenser's Graces are always purity itself. Fully to understand the meaning of the words in this chaste description, one should compare these eyes to those of Acrasia in the famous "Bower of Blisse":

> And her faire eyes sweet smyling in delight,
> Moystened their fierie beames, with which she thrild
> Fraile harts, yet quenched not; like starry light
> Which sparckling on the silent waues, does seeme
>   more bright.[21]

The difference between a chaste love and a thrilling lust is manifest; it needs no further comment.

The closing four stanzas of *An Hymne of Beavtie* complete the return of the poet to this world after his brief and tentative step in the direction of neo-Platonic ascent. The opening lines of the third from last are gay indeed; the poet's experience has been exhilarating:

[21] *Faerie Queene*, II, xii, 78. In this connection I should point out a similar comparison by W. L. Renwick, of Acrasia (*Faerie Queene*, II, xii, 78) and "the more direct and simple beauty of Una" (*Faerie Queene*, I, iii, 4), *Edmund Spenser*, The R. A. Neil Lecture (Cambridge, 1952), p. 11. Renwick writes: "Perhaps something could be done in the intensive study of Spenser's words; but this is not the proper occasion. I point out only the example of that word *grace* as applied to Una."

By a similar token, this is not the proper occasion for a further comparison. But I, for my part, must note here that Spenser's words are heavily fraught with the meanings they acquire through their repeated use in certain contexts in his whole work. They become as "loaded" as any words a poet ever used. "Chaste" for Spenser has a meaning that was usual in his own time, but is quite different from that commonly accepted today; and in addition it is enriched by his use of it. Like the meaning of "amor" in Dante, or that of διανοια or ἐπιστήμη in Plato, it must be derived from a series of contexts, not from a dictionary.

PLATONISM IN SPENSER

> Then Io tryumph, O great beauties Queene,
> Aduance the banner of thy conquest hie . . .
> (Lines 267-268)

The Greek exclamation and the tone in general seems Ronsardian; but this is false. Spenser has not been wine-bibbing, nor has he come from an amorous combat, nor even has he been gazing at his lady's tempting breasts. He has been contemplating something that Ronsard neither saw nor knew, something that seems also to have been unknown to many of the second-hand Petrarchan sonneteers of the sixteenth century: he has seen love and beauty disjoined from the flesh and yet not divorced from it. He has seen the flesh in its proper place as a means, and not as an end in itself.

The final lines of the poem are entirely personal. The poet is once more at his earthly starting place. He asks his beloved to grant him at length "one drop of grace" (line 277), and prays that Venus his sovereign and the great goddess of his life shall,

> Deigne to let fall one drop of dew reliefe,
> That may recure my harts long pyning griefe,
> And shew that wondrous powre your beauty hath,
> That can restore a damned wight from death.
> (Lines 284-287)

Thus these terminal lines are as earthbound as any in the two poems we have so far considered. Both poems are on the whole earthly and natural; these are the fundamental qualities which they share. In terms of Platonic ascent, the second hymn has moved momentarily a little farther than the first, but even there the ascent is not continued; on the contrary, the descent is almost immediate, and is definitive. The poet apparently intends to keep his feet upon the ground.

In all the welter of classical setting, neo-Platonic theory, and Petrarchan phrasing, Spenser sounds in each poem a clear and individual note; earthly love is loyal and true, generous and chaste; it not only should exist, but it does exist, in this world of mutability and flux. There is nothing in this statement that will conflict in any way with either heavenly love or heavenly beauty. They are all akin, and their difference is one of degree. But Spenser will not rise by a series of steps that may be defined analytically, one after another; he will make a leap to the higher level, and he will stay there for the duration of the heavenly poems.

The *Hymne of Heavenly Love* may be treated with somewhat greater brevity than its two predecessors. I have been able to discover very little, except in the final stanzas, that is of clear and indubitable Platonic inspiration. The initial stanza of the invocation, as has been noted above, is an answering echo and a corrective to the final stanza of the first hymn; the poet asks the god of love, who is manifestly the Christian God, to raise him far above the "feeble reach of earthly sight" (line 5). This act is accomplished by the very asking, and for the entire poem, except for two stanzas of palinode in the invocation,[22] the poet remains on a high level of visionary insight. Toward the end of the poem, the recitation of the history of Christ's life and death, followed by contemplation of His sacrifice, produces a mystic and perfervid vision. The fact that much of the diction here is neo-Platonic does not seem very significant in a total context that is overwhelmingly Biblical.

Further, even at this terminal point the juxtaposition of lines of neo-Platonic phraseology with other lines, pure, simple, and often monosyllabically Anglo-Saxon, is very striking. The simple expression, of indigenous origin, stands out in the broader context of polysyllabic enravishment; not only

---

[22] This palinode will be discussed in Chapter ix in relation to Du Bellay's recantations and to Ronsard's mock-palinodes.

stands out, but for the modern reader raised in the tradition of English Protestantism it evokes translations of the Bible more or less contemporary with Spenser, the devotional poetry of Spenser's successors in the seventeenth century, and the whole body of liturgical literature in the English *Book of Common Prayer*.[23] Such a juxtaposition may be seen in the last lines of the fourth stanza from the end, and in the first lines of the following stanza:

> And giue thy selfe vnto him full and free,
> That full and freely gaue himselfe to thee.
>
> Then shalt thou feele thy spirit so possest,
> And rauisht with deuouring great desire ...
> (Lines 265-268)

This, however, is the last such contrast in this hymn; the final vision is entirely clad in neo-Platonic language. The explanation of the presence of the neo-Platonic terms at the end seems to be that this Mediterranean tradition offered a ready-made series of phrases that were fittingly or decorously suited to appropriate use in poetry, and thus were most proper for the exalted vision at the end of the poem. But though the phrasing of the vision is Platonic, its essence is certainly Christian. Even the steps toward the vision, from the contemplation of the Creation, the Fall, and the Nativity; from that of Christ the human being, to the final vision of Christ in the abstract as God, are Christian not only in essence but in language also, until the very end. The abstraction of the idea of Christ's pure glory from the consideration of His life and sacrifice on earth is not necessarily an abstraction based either on Platonic or neo-Platonic systems of progression; it may well have its background in the

---

[23] The placement of Spenser's simple, indigenous lines in the context of sixteenth century Protestantism is not intended to imply that there was no similar native tradition before the Reformation.

mediaeval Christian mysticism that goes far back of the rediscovery of Plato in fifteenth century Italy.

It is therefore difficult to agree with the opinion stated by Mohinimohan Bhattacherje, who writes of this poem, "Though the ideal is Christian, Spenser's Platonism comes out in the means recommended by him for its realization."[24] The way and the means in this poem, the light that shines in this world that draws the poet onward, is the contemplation of Christ's love, which not only is, was, and ever shall be heavenly, but was also manifested in the world. This manifestation was not Platonic, and a significant part of the poem deals directly with this heavenliness on earth (lines 147-245).

The brief sentence in the Prayer Book in the service for Holy Communion carries by implication in its restrained language the whole movement toward the final vision in this *Hymne of Heavenly Love*: "Let your light so shine before mē, that they may see your good workes, & glorifie your father whiche is in heauen"; and this sentence is not of Platonic origin.[25] The overwhelming stress throughout this hymn is on the love of Christ for man and His presence in man, and not on a differentiation of His human and divine qualities and the process of passage from contemplation of one to the other.

The end of the poem is a vision of Christ's Godhead seen through "the sweete enragement of celestiall loue" (line 286). Related as this final enragement is to Plato's μανία, it is hardly the same thing in the context of this poem, or even in the context of the four poems regarded as a whole. Any connection of this final vision with that of the philosopher in the *Republic* or with that described in Diotima's

[24] *Platonic Ideas in Spenser* (Calcutta, 1935), p. 158.
[25] *The Boke of common prayer, and administration of the Sacraments and other rites and Ceremonies in the Churche of Englande* (Londini, in officina Eoda, vard Wihitchurche [sic], 1552), sig. Miii^r. The original source of the quotation is *Matthew* v, 16.

words in the *Symposium*, can be only of the most loose kind. For this is a ringingly Christian hymn; here more than in any of the other three hymns the neo-Platonism seems adventitious. This is the *locus classicus* of Spenser's public expression of religious beliefs, magnificently and movingly stated; and the poem has been aptly cited as an important source of Milton's great Protestant epic.[26]

It seems only just, however, to give some further indication of the nature of the language in the poem that is questionably that of Plato or of the neo-Platonists. Toward the end of the hymn when Spenser recommends that the reader give himself to Christ as Christ has given Himself to mankind, he writes,

> Then shalt thou feele thy spirit so possest,
> And rauisht with deuouring great desire
> Of his deare selfe, then shall thy feeble brest
> Inflame with loue . . .
>
> (Lines 267-270)

A few lines later he adds:

> Thenceforth all worlds desire will in thee dye,
> And all earthes glorie on which men do gaze,
> Seem durt and drosse in thy pure sighted eye,
> Compar'd to that celestiall beauties gaze . . .
>
> (Lines 274-277)

And finally, in the terminal stanza:

> Then shall thy rauisht soule inspired bee
> With heauenly thoughts, farre aboue humane skil,
> And thy bright radiant eyes shall plainely see
> Th'Idee of his pure glorie present still,
> Before thy face, that all thy spirits shall fill

[26] See Edwin Greenlaw, "Spenser's Influence on *Paradise Lost*," *SP* 17 (1920), p. 347.

With sweete enragement of celestiall loue,
Kindled through sight of those faire things aboue.

(Lines 281-287)

A part of this full quotation of the last stanza has been used above to exemplify the intertwining of the Christian and the Platonic in Spenser. It can now be seen more clearly perhaps that the use of the word "Idee" in this context, though incongruous in one sense, is wholly natural for a Renaissance humanist on terms of familiar acquaintance with Plato and the neo-Platonists. It can be seen further in all of the above quotations that the use of "Idee," of "possest," of "rauish," of "inflame"; the use of the theory that the final vision makes earthly glory seem "as durt and dross," the use of "inspired" and of "pure glorie," all these indicate in Spenser's case that the language of neo-Platonism was most easily and naturally available to him for the description of this sort of vision. There was of course no tradition of Protestant mysticism behind him, on whose language he could draw. So he drew on Platonic language to describe a vision whose cause and whose substance was wholly Christian; a vision whose doctrinal basis, if it is affected by Plato at all, was so affected many years before Spenser, in the distant days of St. Augustine, in the even more remote period of the Church Fathers, and perhaps in the century immediately preceding the birth of Christ, which has recently been the object of so much renewed scholarly attention.

In the final poem, *An Hymne of Heavenly Beavtie*, the Platonic or neo-Platonic influence is both strongest and weakest. This paradox arises because the poem does not deal directly or literally with Christianity but treats symbolically the same subject as the previous *Hymne of Heavenly Love*. In the symbolic approach the use of Platonic language is not so much of an obtrusion upon the essentially Christian content. It seems to fit with such ease and naturalness indeed that a cursory reading might fail to reveal the Christian core. It is there, however, and it is of primary importance to observe that Christian doctrine and not Platonic doctrine underlies the meaning of the poem. The hymn is an allegory; it is not a Platonic myth.

Heavenly Beavtie begins on the same high level which its predecessor maintained. There is no invocation, nor is there need for one. These two poems are thus more closely linked than are the first pair; the invocation of *Heavenly Love* serves for its successor, and heavenly beauty follows heavenly love as a reiteration in other terms. The poem starts with a heavily alliterative ravishment that is sustained throughout (except for the two final stanzas of wholly generalized palinode):

> Rapt with the rage of mine own rauisht thought,
> Through contemplation of those goodly sights . . .
> (Lines 1-2)

Almost at once the order of the contemplation is established. Spenser writes in a vein of Platonic orthodoxy:

> Beginning then below, with th'easie vew
> Of this base world, subiect to fleshly eye,
> From thence to mount aloft by order dew,
> To contemplation of th'immortall sky . . .
> (Lines 22-25)

The end to be reached is a vision of pure and perfect beauty. In the lines following, the hierarchical arrangement is stated in ascending terms, from earth to water to air to fire. This common pre-Socratic order is not confined by any means to Plato. The archetype of beauty will be reached by degrees, Spenser writes, and proceeds to list the degrees by name. The heaven of souls is lowest; more fair is that of the "Idees . . . that Plato so admyred," the "pure Intelligences from God inspyred" (lines 82, 83, 84). Lilian Winstanley points out here that the "Platonism has a curious incongruity with the mediaevalism of the rest. The ideas alluded to are those of Beauty, Temperance, Justice, Wisdom. . . ."[27] This is indeed true, for in the succeeding lines Powers, Potentates, Dominations, Cherubim, and Seraphim are listed in ascending order, a Dantesque group that consorts ill with the Platonic Ideas. The Christian hierarchy swallows up the Platonic. Several stanzas later we find the archetypal beauty, which is certainly also the Christian God, who shows himself to base men only in the "image of his grace, / As in a looking glasse" (lines 114-115). Plato seems to have returned, but now with the philosopher in the *Republic* looking at the reflection of the sun in a pool because he cannot yet bear its full light. It seems quite possible, however, that this might also be an echo of the "through a glass darkly," of St. Paul,[28] and that the two memories may have fused in the poet's mind. In any case, the Christian is inextricable from the pagan, and there is no doubt which Spenser intends, in spite of the Platonic echo.

The general movement in this part of the hymn is both Platonic and Christian. In the stanza (lines 127-133) God is said to be invisible, but susceptible of contemplation in his beautiful works. This is the traditional mediaeval view of the world as the second Book of God, a world which is significant only insofar as it points upward and beyond itself. This attitude is a modified reflection of the sentence quoted above in which the light of the virtuous man reflects some part of that of the Godhead: "Let thy light so shine before men that they may see thy good works. . . ."

In the next stanza, however, Platonic speculation gives wings to the poet so that his mind can

[27] *Fowre Hymnes*, p. 71.
[28] *I Corinthians*, 13:12. The mirror image, of course, is common in the literary discourse of the period.

Mount vp aloft through heauenly contemplation,
From this darke world, whose damps the soule do blynd,
....
On that bright Sunne of glorie fixe thine eyes,
Clear'd from grosse mists of fraile infirmities.

(Lines 136-140)

This is of Platonic inspiration, echoing as it does not only the translated words of Diotima in the *Symposium* but the conventional language that Plato always uses throughout his work when he contrasts the world of the flesh with the mystic vision that transcends both.

In the ensuing lines the vision which the poet does not dare to look upon is perceived to be one of God; not explicitly one of Christ, or of the Trinity, or one of the Father, but of a generalized God who is nevertheless implicitly Christian. He is referred to as "that great *Deity*"; his throne "is built vpon Eternitie," his "seate is Truth," and it is a "mercie seate" (lines 145, 152, 148). There can be no doubt concerning who this is. But the poet does not wish to be specific in this hymn; he has named his God in the previous hymn, and in this one he is symbolizing him. The symbol he chooses is Sapience, a manifestation of God, a female figure who sits in the bosom of the deity, who is infinitely beautiful, so incomparably beautiful that she disposes completely of the pagan figure of Venus in the earlier *Hymne of Love*:

Ne she her selfe [Venus], had she remained still,
And were as faire, as fabling wits do fayne,
Could once come neare this beauty soverayne.

(Lines 215-217)

The sight of Sapience is the initial phase of final vision which has thus been reached by what was stated originally to be a series of Platonic steps, but which has turned out to be a ladder of mediaeval hierarchies. The ascent, therefore, is in no real way Platonic. Nor is it neo-Platonic. F. M. Padelford has pointed out with acuity that, "This is that supreme experience which the neo-Platonic mystics felt to be the ultimate reward of the true lover. But though Spenser had acknowledged it to be the fruits of the contemplation of God's handiwork, the poet is careful not to make any mention of beauty in woman as a part of that handiwork. When he enumerates those works they are all the wonders of external nature, on the one hand, and God's truth, love, wisdom, grace, judgment, mercy and might, on the other. Indeed, the beauty of woman is actually a painful and mortifying memory as mundane and as misleading as love of ostentation or riches."[29]

Padelford goes on to contrast this non-neo-Platonic attitude with that of Castiglione, "who, in the moment of ecstasy, could still hark back to beauty in woman as that which inspired the soul to seek for the beauty which is God...."[30] Thus along with Venus, all of womankind is deplored at the final moment; but it should be noted that she is deplored not in general, nor any more than man is likewise deplored by implication, but only in respect to her not being a rung in the ladder for ascent. This is not only anti-neo-Platonic but, what is perhaps more significant, anti-Platonic as well. For Plato initiated his ascent in the *Symposium* through human manifestations of absolute beauty, and the neo-Platonists through similar evidences, preferably female. In both cases a sort of apotheosis of some kind is granted to this means for ascent. Spenser's ascent is not through woman in this hymn; it is through all of God's evidence in the world, and this is a very different matter. It leaves the clear inference that woman herself may also make

[29] "Spenser's Fowre Hymnes," *JEGP* 13 (1914), p. 426. The main thesis of Padelford's essay, that the first two hymns are neo-Platonic and the second two Calvinistic, interesting as it is, need not concern us here.
[30] *Ibid.*, p. 427.

the ascent, and thus asserts a balance and reciprocity that the mature Spenser always held existed between the sexes.

The figure of Sapience, herself the efficient cause of the ecstatic terminal vision, has been the subject of much controversy. The "Editor" of the Spenser Variorum, answering the plethora of differing opinions expressed in the "Commentary," writes: "As an intelligent churchman Spenser must have been utterly inattentive . . . not to know the traditional identification, both Catholic and Protestant, of the attribute Wisdom with Christ. When he meditated the painstaking symmetry of the quartet of hymns, how could he have selected Sapience for the apotheosis in H.H.B. to correspond with Christ in H.H.L. without thinking of this identification, or indeed without being guided by it?"[31]

This is a welcome voice of reason breaking through the speculations of scholars who try to guess just what Spenser may have intended by making the *"Deity"* a male and Sapience a female. Sapience stands in some sense for Christ; Sapience kindles in man the love of God, leads directly to God. In the final stanza Spenser writes:

And looke at last vp to that soueraine light [Sapience],
From whose pure beames al perfect beauty springs,
That kindleth loue in euery godly spright,
Euen the loue of God . . .

(Lines 295-298)

There can be little doubt that the end of this hymn is essentially parallel to the end of that of *Heavenly Love*; in the latter the final vision is contemplation of the idea of Christ's glory, and in *Heavenly Beavtie* it is the kindling of an ecstatic love of God. Thus the ends, though stated in different terms, are very nearly identical. In the last hymn, however, the nature of the language in the final stanzas tends to obscure the fundamentally Christian concept. The presence

[31] Osgood and Lotespeich, Works, The Minor Poems, 1, 564.

of the vague figure of Sapience further evokes memories of Plato's τὸ καλόν, and the indubitably Platonic quality of much of the phrasing in the last five stanzas might possibly bemuse a reader who was not alert to the accidental quality of the diction in relation to the substantial quality of the vision itself.

Throughout these stanzas there are such lines as these:

> Ne from thenceforth doth any fleshly sense,
> Or idle thought of earthly things remaine . . .
> (Lines 267-269)

Here the prison of the body has been burst, as Plato wished it to be. In the following lines there is Platonic shadow-play; the contemplative's gaze,

> Is fixed all on that which now they see,
> All other sights but fayned shadowes bee.
> (Lines 272-273)

Next, the language of neo-Platonism is used, ironically but probably without intention of irony, to banish the initial human stepping-stone of Florentine ascent:

> And that faire lampe, which vseth to enflame
> The harts of men with selfe consuming fyre
> Thenceforth seemes fowle, and full of sinfull blame . . .
> (Lines 274-276)

There are many short phrases with a Platonic tang, such as "all riches drosse," and "vaine deceiptfull shadowes," and "perfect beauty," and "this vile world" (lines 279, 291, 296, 299). The other-worldliness of the Platonic vision is here indeed, but the Greek is handmaiden to the Christian; Socrates is midwife to the generation of an essentially Christian vision, as he had so often been before. In this last heavenly hymn as in the previous one, Platonism and neo-Platonism are without rational consistency; they are used when they serve the desired end, and they are abandoned at the poet's free discretion whenever he finds a more suitable Christian means. The only consistent pattern in the two poems is that of an humble Christian orthodoxy; all other elements subserve this end. And this end, as has been said above, is not in conflict in any way with that of the two earlier hymns; the higher or heavenly vision is a necessary complement to the earthly and natural adumbration. The pairs of hymns are related to each other as the human is related to the divine; the early hymns, though written first, are the image of the later ones.

One further point deserves now to be stressed because of its significance for the ensuing comparison with Ronsard and Du Bellay. What has been referred to as the peculiarly Spenserian moral emphasis in the central portions of the earthly hymns, the hortatory call to a higher standard of decency in this fleshly world, is not without its counterpart in the heavenly parallels, a counterpart as precise as the nature of the more exalted subject matter will permit. In *An Hymne of Heavenly Love*, such a passage occurs about two-thirds through the poem:

> Then rouze thy selfe, O earth, out of thy soyle,
> In which thou wallowest like to filthy swyne,
> And doest thy mynd in durty pleasures moyle,
> Vnmindfull of that dearest Lord of thyne . . .
> (Lines 218-221)

This is a generalized exhortation, no more influenced in its expression by Plato than by the Bible. It is Spenser's own. The palinode at the beginning of the same hymn is another example of the same sort of expression, only more personal even though it is within the convention of Renaissance recantations.

Similarly in *An Hymne of Heavenly Beavtie*, but tempered this time with the more elevated language of neo-

Platonism, analogous feelings are expressed. For example, in the final vision that aspect of the phenomenal world which in the earlier hymns had been characterized as "dunghill" has now been trimmed to the subject:

> But all that earst seemd sweet, seemes now offense,
> And all that pleased earst, now seemes to paine . . .
> (Lines 269-270)

Further, in the next stanza:

> And all that pompe, to which proud minds aspyre
> By name of honor, and so much desyre,
> Seemes to them basenesse, and all riches drosse,
> And all mirth sadnesse, and all lucre losse.
> (Lines 277-280)

And finally, in the penultimate stanza, which echoes the initial palinode in the poem:

> Ah then my hungry soule, which long hast fed
> On idle fancies of thy foolish thought,
> And with false beauties flattring bait misled . . .
> (Lines 288-290)

> Ah cease to gaze on matter of thy grief.
> (Line 294)

The point of view is now from above downward, and the world should be as inconsequential as the distant, earthly threshing-floor seen from Dante's *Paradiso*, but even at this elevation Spenser cannot utterly abandon his emphatic concern with worldly baseness, even though the concern be negative and remote. The language smooths the emotion, but does not entirely quell it; the emotion is still there, parallel to that expressed in the other three hymns.

In conclusion, one returns inevitably to W. L. Renwick's statement mentioned earlier in this chapter: that Spenser accepted Platonism more as an emotion than as a creed. It can be said that in all of the *Fowre Hymnes* the creed is a consistent Protestant Christianity, while the Platonism and neo-Platonism are adventitious. It has long been a manifest fact that Christian and Platonic doctrine have a close affinity, and that the believing Christian may be drawn with minimal compunctions to an interpretation of Plato that is supplementary to Christianity and in accord with it.

If one may hazard a guess, one might say that the attraction that late fifteenth century Italians and sixteenth century Frenchmen found in Plato was chiefly due to two factors: the reappearance of Plato's works themselves in their original language, and the desire to infuse a new vein of idealism into a concept of love—both heavenly and earthly—that was becoming increasingly debased by clerical corruption and by clerical skepticism, factors which were contributing directly to the Reformation. The Italians of the newly flourishing city states, especially of Florence, were the natural midwives to the Platonic word because it was in Italy that Greek scholarship first returned to Western Europe.

It was here too that skepticism had reached a high point amid the intrigues of the wealthy and cultivated Medici, and it is for this reason that Platonic doctrine was so indiscriminately consumed and redeveloped, even to the extent of tolerating its implied sanction of homosexuality. The attraction of Platonism for the Florentines was emotional too, but it was also intellectual, and sometimes immoral; Platonic doctrine, while it never really challenged Christianity, did come to constitute a kind of secondary religion when it was not fully syncretic. Neo-Platonic study and speculation tended to become something of a substitute for consultation of the Scriptures themselves, Scriptures which in any case had never enjoyed a high degree of popularity with well-organized Catholics. The end result of the infusion of Platonism on the continent was thus not purely a stimulus toward a greater idealism, but partly one toward pagan naturalism. In spite of an abortive movement toward reform within the Church, it was finally left to the Protestants to return directly to the idealism of the Scriptures;[32] and much later in England to produce the Cambridge Platonists.

An outstanding example of the result of neopaganism in France was of course Rabelais, the Christian humanist who could write so enthusiastically of classical studies, who could argue so eloquently for the study of Greek, Hebrew, and Chaldean, but who could also blaspheme the immortal soul in scatological terms. Ronsard is another example, though in a different manner, a more aristocratic fashion. Ronsard did not seek out Platonic idealism; he found it wished upon him, and he usually abused it since his temperament would not let him use it.

Du Bellay is quite separate from Ronsard in respect to his inheritance of Platonic influences; he sought the purity that was to be found in Plato's doctrines, but the circumstances of his time and place had sullied this purity, and after a false start Du Bellay retreated to a personal brand of temperate idealism that might be loosely designated a neo-Platonic heresy. Spenser alone among the three took Plato for what he legitimately might constitute for a believing Christian; he took him for the support and use of Christianity.

[32] It is interesting to note Ronsard's animosity toward putting the Scriptures into the hands of the common people, a donation long since accomplished in England:
> Quand des ayeux la loy est mesprisée,
> Quand l'Evangile est commune aux Pasteurs,
> Femmes, enfans, artizans, serviteurs,
> Mesme aux brigans, qui fils de Dieu se vantent,
> Et quelque Psalme entre les meurtres chantent . . .

(Oeuvres, ed. Cohen, "Discours de l'alteration et change des choses humaines," II, 376).

VIII · PLATONISM IN DU BELLAY AND RONSARD

*J*OACHIM DU BELLAY has repeatedly been shown to have an affinity with Spenser. His understanding of ideas which reached him from sources he shared in common with Spenser, be they classical or Italian, has been shown to be similar in most respects to Spenser's because the ultimate poetic expression of these ideas usually has a general consonance in both poets. The divergences on the whole have been as accidental as the affinities have been substantial. This pattern asserts itself once more in a consideration of their attitudes toward Platonic and neo-Platonic doctrines, asserts itself even more emphatically than in the previous comparisons. To complete the pattern, Ronsard's divergence from both poets in respect to Platonism occupies the usual contrasting and isolated position that it has assumed in the other comparisons. This is not remarkable, for all three poets, different as each was from the other, were alike men of consistent integrity.

Both Du Bellay and Ronsard began their careers as Petrarchan love poets, the one with *L'Olive* (1549) and the other with the *Amours de Cassandre* (1552). In these collections of sonnets there are occasional echoes of neo-Platonic language, resonant and clear in Du Bellay, muted in Ronsard, but the important and dominant strain is Petrarchan: the concentration is on the bitter-sweet quality of the relationship as a first step in a journey which will lead to great heights of spiritual vision. Within a very short time, however, both poets repudiated Petrarchism, each in his own fashion.

Du Bellay passed from Petrarchism directly to neo-Platonism and simultaneously with his tempered adoption of neo-Platonic doctrines he repudiated his previous Petrarchism. The adoption of neo-Platonism is seen in his *Recueil de Poesie* of 1552, the reaction against Petrarchism in the second edition of this collection, published in 1553, the year of his first journey to Rome. At this point his Platonism has reached its full development. His future treatment of either the Petrarchan or Platonic conventions superficially resembles that of Ronsard; he reverts to Petrarchism only very occasionally, probably because of its current fashionableness, and he reverts to neo-Platonism hardly at all because the personal nature of his poetry until the end of his life in 1560 did not admit such a reversion. His own reading of the neo-Platonic ideal, however, remained for him an implicit goal, with Beauty renamed *Honneur* or *Vertu*. An examination of the origin and development of Platonic elements in Du Bellay will clarify these general remarks and demonstrate the significant points of affinity between Du Bellay's Platonism and that of Spenser.

It has been written that Du Bellay was "less a Neo-Platonist than a poet caught in the current of Neo-Platonism."[1] This is to say substantially the same thing that has been said of Spenser's neo-Platonism. Both poets took to neo-Platonism because it offered a sympathetic body of doctrine, some of which they could use in their poetry. They were not philosophers or metaphysicians and hence, as poets, they were not constrained to accept or reject neo-Platonism on an analytical basis. They could be, and they were, emotional about it. R. V. Merrill writes at the end of his brief study of Du Bellay's Platonism that the poet "attempts

[1] Robert V. Merrill, *The Platonism of Joachim du Bellay* (Chicago, 1925), p. 18. In the ensuing discussion of Du Bellay I shall be much indebted to this work for historical material, but I shall, unhappily, find occasion to differ with Merrill's critical opinions. This early book has been followed by a more complete study called *Platonism in French Renaissance Poetry* (New York, 1957), a volume compiled in part from Merrill's own uncompleted version and in part from material prepared by Robert J. Clements, coauthor of the present book. It represents an expansion of Merrill's earlier thesis, rather than an alteration.

to find in the reviving doctrine a theory to raise and amplify the current ideal of human love, and he discards from his active thought whatever fails to contribute toward that end."[2] In this again he is like Spenser—affected but eclectic. He was unlike Spenser, however, in that neo-Platonism and Petrarchism both reached him at the same time, and both came to him far more as novelties than they were in England more than a generation later.

The neo-Platonic theory of ascending and transcendent love and the Petrarchan theory of the yearning but never satisfied lover reached France together during Du Bellay's early youth and had become a part of the native literary landscape less than a decade before Du Bellay himself began to make his own published contributions to both schools of thought. They were new when he had met them; they had not been tried over a period of time and in a variety of places as they had when Spenser encountered them, even if one sets the earliest possible date on the first two of the *Fowre Hymnes*. The only Petrarchan sonnets in French on which Du Bellay could look back were those of Maurice Scève, the *Délie* (1544), published in Lyon, which was then metaphorically an Italian border town.

As neo-Platonist predecessors in the vulgar tongue Du Bellay had primarily Antoine Héroët, whose *La Parfaicte Amy*, published also in Lyon in 1542, R. V. Merrill sets as a cornerstone for his interpretation of Du Bellay's Platonism; and Pontus de Tyard's *Erreurs Amoureuses* (1549), and *Continuation des Erreurs Amoureuses* (1551), both of which were used as the basis for Du Bellay's Platonic sonnets in the *Recueil* of 1552. This is not a rich native background but it is significant in the development of the direction of Du Bellay's neo-Platonism.

More generally, Merrill offers Ficino, Bembo, and Castiglione as important sources of Du Bellay's ideas and, less

[2] *Ibid.*, p. 147.

directly, Petrarch, Benivieni, Pico della Mirandola, Leo the Jew, Marguerite de Navarre, and Lorenzo da Medici. These sources are, of course, secondary; there are, however, few clear paraphrases of Platonic texts themselves in the whole body of Du Bellay's work. Furthermore, as Merrill and Clements state, "Platonism of spirit needs to be distinguished from mere Platonism of expression."[3] Finally, since the *locus classicus* of Du Bellay's neo-Platonism is the *XIII Sonnetz de L'Honneste Amour*, much of which may be traced directly to Pontus de Tyard, one must indeed be wary against exaggerating the real influence of Plato and his commentators on Du Bellay.

In any case the poet's knowledge of Greek and Italian must have placed not only the texts of Plato himself within his theoretical reach, but also the whole corpus of neo-Platonic commentary. One notes with interest, for instance, that Du Bellay can refer to Plato's banishing poets from his republic without adding the conventional and thoughtless Renaissance apologia for the philosopher's act, to wit, the wishful statement that Plato did not intend to banish *all* poets:

>Jadis le fameux inventeur
>De la doctrine Academique
>Chassoit le poëte menteur
>Par les loix de sa republique.[4]

In this context a comparison is drawn between the modern Christian poet in the service of the Christian God, and the "poëte menteur" who claims a specious divinity. Thus Du Bellay approves Plato's act of banishment from a point of view that was unusual in the Renaissance; he correctly interprets Plato's allegations as against all poets, because all poets by the very nature of their calling lay claims to a

---
[3] *Platonism in French Renaissance Poetry*, p. 32.
[4] *La Lyre Chrestienne*, lines 25-28, Oeuvres, ed. Henri Chamard, IV, 138.

divine inspiration that they can neither explain nor understand themselves.[5] It is as if Du Bellay realized that Plato's *Ion* should be taken ironically in terms of his whole work, an idea that apparently never occurred to Ronsard or Spenser or Spenser's sometime mentor Sir Philip Sidney, who found it necessary in his *Defense* to try to explain away Plato's distrust of the lying poet. Such acuity of understanding, combined with the known intimacy that existed with the great Hellenist Jean Dorat, makes it likely that Du Bellay was at least as well versed in Plato's original work as was Spenser.

The native influences, however, are more immediately discernible in the growth of Du Bellay's neo-Platonism than are those from the ultimate source. Let us turn to his expressions of neo-Platonic theory in *L'Olive* of 1550 and in his *XIII Sonnetz de l'Honneste Amour* of 1552; and to other poems in the *Recueil* of 1552 which hint at a dissatisfaction with the neo-Platonic theory of love. It will be seen that these poems suggest that Du Bellay, far from standing on the verge of a more developed and perfected neo-Platonism in 1553 just before his journey to Rome, as R. V. Merrill maintains, stood in fact on the verge of quite another poetic career: that of a Christian religious poet.[6] This career was stifled by the stewing corruption of mid-century Rome, which inevitably turned the poet to satire, to bitterness, and to a hopeless nostalgia.

The *Olive* is a collection of a hundred and fifteen sonnets. As a whole, they are Petrarchan, and they represent the apprenticeship of Du Bellay. Curiously enough, however, the collection loses its consistency in the terminal sonnets: CVII-CXI are religious poems. They constitute an implicit

[5] See Plato, *Apology*, 22.
[6] See Appendix IV for a discussion of Merrill's assertion that Du Bellay's "Elegie" in the second edition (1553) of his *Recueil de Poesie* (1552) represents the "peak" of his Platonism.

palinode within the body of the *Olive* sequence. The poems are not an overt retraction of the orthodox Petrarchism that precedes them; but standing almost at the end of the sequence, they amount to a covert recantation. These five are followed by two others, CXII and CXIII, both clearly of neo-Platonic inspiration. Sonnet CXIV is in blank verse, the only unrhymed poem in the group. It deals with the poet's hope for *L'Olive* and for his future work. The final sonnet is to Ronsard. Du Bellay, the elder, expresses fervid admiration for his junior and wishes that someday under the tutelage of Ronsard he may come to equal him. This last sonnet, like all of Du Bellay's to Ronsard, is filled with unstinted praise and affection, little of which was ever reciprocated.

The two neo-Platonic sonnets are pertinent to the present discussion. Sonnet CXII is said by Henri Chamard to be inspired by the *Phaedrus*; he adds, "mais aux idées platoniciennes du Bellay allie les dogmes chrétiens."[7] The poem states that "Le Prevoyant," who is also called "Le Juste," has ranged the "occultes Idées" in heaven, and "a son Filz les faict quasi egaulx." The ideas are Platonic but it is the Christian God who has ranged them on high: the statement is exactly the same as that which Spenser makes in lines 82-84 of his *Hymne of Heavenly Beavtie*. This is not to say that Spenser took his location for the Platonic ideas from Du Bellay; it is merely to point out that both poets naturally place Platonic ideas in a position inferior to that held by God the Son.

Du Bellay says nothing more about the Platonic ideas in *L'Olive* except in the following sonnet, CXIII, which is completely paraphrased from a sonnet by Bernardino Daniello. R. V. Merrill writes of this poem that "Daniello's imagination excites Joachim to a lyric height which in his own work is never surpassed."[8] This seems rather a strong statement

---

[7] *Oeuvres*, ed. Chamard, I, 121, n. 1.
[8] *Platonism*, p. 41.

for a poem which is after all a close paraphrase, even to the extent of following the soaring movement of the sestet. Furthermore, almost any one of the five purely religious sonnets that precede these Platonic ones reaches lyric heights at least comparable to those reached in CXIII. The octave of the poem expresses a wish to burst the bonds of the flesh and to ascend to "un plus cler sejour" ("a l'eterno alto soggiorno"). In the sestet this region is reached. In the final lines Du Bellay addresses his soul:

> Tu y pouras recongnoistre l'Idée
> De la beauté, qu'en ce monde j'adore.[9]

Here Plato's specific word Idea is used in place of the generalizations in the Italian text. The poem is unquestionably Platonic in a pure sense, but it is an isolated instance in the *Olive* and, in addition, this sonnet is not original.

The Platonism of the *XIII Sonnetz de l'Honneste Amour* is a different matter entirely: it is a Platonic sequence. R. V. Merrill writes that these poems are "a mine of Platonistic terminology and of Platonistic thought."[10] He says further that "human and worldly affection has been sublimated to a celestial quality." It is small wonder, therefore, that this short sequence should constitute the chief source of Du Bellay's Platonist expression. There is a significant difference of opinion, however, between Merrill and Henri Chamard concerning the value of the Platonist expressions in these sonnets dedicated to an honest love. Chamard, a sober critic if there ever was one, writes that in the thirteen poems "nous voyons du Bellay, sous l'influence momentanée de Pontus de Tyard, *verser dans le galimatias*, en s'essayant à substituer, dans sa poésie amoureuse, l'inspiration platoni-

---

[9] *Oeuvres*, ed. Chamard, I, 123. These lines are reminiscent of those of the final version of Spenser's *Hymne of Heavenly Love*, 283-285.
[10] *Platonism*, p. 130.

cienne à l'inspiration pétrarquiste [my italics]."[11] In his monumental *Histoire de la Pléiade,* Chamard elaborates the above statement, saying that Du Bellay takes much even of Pontus de Tyard's language from *Erreurs Amoureuses* (1551). "Il le redit, hélas! de la manière le plus entortillée, la plus alambiquée, la plus quintessenciée."[12] In a footnote to this pronouncement, sonnets I, IV, V, IX, and XI are designated almost unintelligible. Let us consider these sonnets as dispassionately as possible.

The sequence as a whole is what Spenser or his editor E. K. or his friend Gabriel Harvey might have called a "gallimaufry." There is an obvious, honest effort on the part of the poet to bring off a short Platonic *tour de force.* But the direct representations of Plato, taken usually from the *Phaedrus,* are often garbled cryptographs, and the neo-Platonic references have in almost every case been traced by Chamard to Pontus de Tyard's *Erreurs Amoureuses.* So Du Bellay's original Platonism is at best not wholly clear, and the neo-Platonism usually at secondhand.

The first sonnet dedicates the whole work to God. Du Bellay assumes that God has consecrated him as a sort of poet-priest with a mission to sing hymns to the honor and glory of the Almighty. If this is not exactly Platonic, at least the second sonnet makes up to some extent for this deficiency. R. V. Merrill writes of this poem: "here is a Platonic profession with a vengeance, emphasizing in florid style both the divine origin and the spiritual character of the qualities which the poet worships."[13] The poem begins:

Ce ne sont pas ces beaux cheveux dorez,
Ny ce beau front, qui l'honneur mesme honnore ...

Continuing in this renunciatory vein, the sestet says:

[11] *Oeuvres,* I, xiii.
[12] I, 249-250. It is amusing to note that Chamard takes the words "alambiqué" and "quintessencié" from Du Bellay's sonnets themselves.
[13] *Platonism,* p. 52.

Ce ne sont pas ny ces lyz, ny ces rozes,
Ny ces deux rancz de perles si bien closes,
C'est cet esprit, rare present des cieux,

Dont la beauté de cent graces pourvëue
Perce mon ame & mon coeur & mes yeux
Par les rayons de sa poignante vëue.

In its rejection of the body and its assertion of the beauty of the spirit the poem is certainly neo-Platonic. In the manner of the enumeration of the physical beauties which are being rejected the poem is also anti-Petrarchan, since the golden hair, the lilies and the roses and the pearls are all specifically associated with Petrarchan poetry. In addition, Chamard points out that the whole sonnet "n'est guère qu'une réduction" of Pontus de Tyard's *Chant à son Leut*, published the previous year in the *Continuation des Erreurs Amoureuses*.[14] Thus the poem is to a large extent secondhand. It is indeed florid, but ironically, in the manner of Petrarch; and the Platonism, unelaborated, derived, is something less than emphatic.

The third sonnet of the series creates the image of the beauty of the beloved in the memory of the poet. This is pure neo-Platonism, and it does not come from Pontus de Tyard. But following this statement in the octave, the poet says in the sestet that if this image creates in him a "fol dezir," the virtue of the beloved rather than her beauty quickly quells such concupiscence and turns his heart to a "plus grand bien." Such neo-Platonism is ambiguous, involving as it does a momentarily lustful truancy from a purely spiritual adoration. The poet is evidently still not a perfected Platonic lover.

Henri Chamard's accusation of unintelligibility seems justified in the fourth sonnet (it is not my intention to take

[14] *Oeuvres*, ed. Chamard, I, 140, n. 1.

up every one of these sonnets individually). It will perhaps be best to quote the entire poem as a full illustration of the confusion that inhabits most of the sonnets of this series, to a greater or lesser extent:

> Une froydeur secretement brulante
> Brule mon corps, mon esprit, ma raizon,
> Comme la poix anime le tyzon
> Par une ardeur lentement violente.
>
> Mon coeur tiré d'une force allechante
> Dessou' le joug d'une franche prizon,
> Boit à longs traicts l'aigre-doulce poyzon,
> Qui tous mes sens heureusement enchante.
>
> Le premier feu de mon moindre plaizir
> Faict halleter mon alteré dezir:
> Puis de noz coeurs la celeste Androgyne
>
> Plus sainctement vous oblige ma foy:
> Car j'ayme tant cela que j'ymagine,
> Que je ne puis aymer ce que je voy.[15]

The "prizon" in the sixth line is evidently Plato's prison of the flesh, but the "poyzon" in the following line which is bitter-sweet is the same old poison that Laura dispensed to Petrarch. The poet is not entirely free of the Petrarchan banks of the Rhône. The panting desire in the sestet is ambiguous until the Androgyne comes in, remotely from Plato and directly from Pontus de Tyard. The last lines are wholly neo-Platonic. But it is interesting to contemplate what meaning, far from Du Bellay's mind, a reader might put upon the last two lines if he had just come from reading Ronsard, who also loved best in woman what he could not

[15] *Oeuvres*, ed. Chamard, I, Sonnet IV, 141-142.

see, and did not mean by this the spiritual qualities that appear only in the eye of the mind. In the fifth and sixth sonnets there are references to the quintessence of Love, to the distillation of perfection in an "allambic," and to a celestial flight that obscurely recalls the chariot in the *Phaedrus*. Both these poems defy classification because of the difficulty of determining exactly what they mean. Sonnet VII, however, contains in both octave and sestet a straightforward assertion of the orthodox neo-Platonic theory of love:

> Le Dieu bandé a desbandé mes yeux;
> Pour contempler celle beauté cachée
> Qui ne se peut, tant soit bien recherchée
> Representer en ung coeur vicieux.

The second quatrain develops this idea; and the sestet begins:

> Le seul dezir des beautez immortelles
> Guynde mon vol sur ses divines ailes
> Au plus parfaict de la perfection.[16]

The only new element in this statement is that the lover must be pure in heart in order to reach perfection. This restriction is similar to that which Spenser places upon his lover in the *Hymne of Heavenly Beautie*, in which he says that the precious dower of Sapience is for the worthy alone (line 252).

In Sonnet VIII Du Bellay slips into the pitfall of exaggerated overstatement. He begins as none other than the "Prestresse folle" who is "grommelant d'une effroyable horreur"; he is having a seizure, like that of Virgil's Sibyl. In the second quatrain he says that his "estomac gros de ce Dieu qui vole" is frightened by a blind terror. He must speak out, however, and at the end of the poem he bids

[16] *Ibid.*, p. 144.

himself sing better than ever before and bids his verses scatter throughout the world like leaves blown by the wind. This is a grotesque poem, more reminiscent of the paintings of Hieronymus Bosch than of Plato or of Virgil, by whom it is in general inspired.

The next sonnet is among those Henri Chamard has called almost unintelligible; the sestet contains a confused reference to the "Moteur souverain" who moves the "sphere de ma vie." This mover is evidently not Aristotle's, though the phrase is his, nor is it the force at the end of Dante's *Paradiso* "che move il sol e l'altre stelle." It is the immortal lamp of his ladies' "vertuz." The statement, confusing as it is, nevertheless seems to have a neo-Platonic coloration. But the plurality of the virtues indicates that Du Bellay had either not read Plato's *Meno*, which demonstrates that virtue is one, not many, or was not remembering it at the moment.

One may disregard the last four of these sonnets, which can add nothing to what has been said, except an obscure reference to Prometheus. The penultimate sonnet is to Pontus de Tyard; the last is to the immortal aspect of his own lady, and the final three lines are taken almost word for word from Pontus.[17]

The group of *XIII Sonnetz* is derivative in two senses; it comes remotely from Platonic sources, and directly from neo-Platonic sources of which Pontus is by far the most important. All of the sonnets are overwrought; some of them are downright obscure. None of them is up to the standard Du Bellay has set for himself in *L'Olive*, and all of them are far, far below the standard achieved such a short time later in *Les Regrets*.

These sonnets are Du Bellay's only sustained venture

[17] For a scholarly account of the contrastingly successful welding of Platonism and Christianity in the work of Pontus de Tyard, see Frances A. Yates's *Academies*, especially chapters iv, v, and vii.

into the neo-Platonic vein, and it is quite obvious to a present-day reader that the sequence fails to achieve its purpose. Du Bellay has taken his nascent and still undeveloped concept of "honneur" and tried to graft it upon the neo-Platonic theory of love. He has tried to intertwine an idea that is ascendent with one that is transcendent. Probably he himself did not realize clearly, in this crucial year 1552-1553, that "vertu" and "honneur" were not Platonic ideas but were terrestrial standards which he was developing in opposition to Petrarchism for the conduct of his life in this world. Not only would they not fit at the top of the neo-Platonic ladder; they would not fit with the humble, suffering attitude of the Petrarchan lover, nor would they fit with the courtly Provençal tradition.

Unselfconsciously perhaps, Du Bellay was developing an egalitarian principle for love, a principle according to which man and woman would be on a new par with each other, each able to recognize and to love the "vertu" and the "honneur" that was equally an individual and particular part of the other. From this standpoint a lover, of either sex, could transcend himself; there could be reciprocal love on earth on a spiritual level which transcended the sensual. But there is no suggestion in either the "Elegie" or in the *XIII Sonnetz* that the lovers, either alone or separately, would mount the neo-Platonic ladder to union with absolute beauty. His few religious poems will show that Du Bellay reserved this genuine transcendence for Christian religious experience. As in the case of Spenser in his *Hymne of Heavenly Love*, for Du Bellay also the experience of the ultimate reality was concerned with Christ.

In 1552, in the preface to a selection of translations from Virgil's *Aeneid*, Du Bellay expresses an intention which is of capital importance to this discussion. Speaking of his original work, which has been "depraved" by the printer, he voices his regret for the botched editions and his hope for a correct future collection of his works. For the time being, he says: "... j'ay bien voulu recuillir une partie des moins malfaictz: attendant l'entiere edition de tous les autres, que j'ai delibere (afin de ne mesler les choses sacrées avecques les prophanes) disposer en meilleur ordre que devant: les comprenant châcun selon son argument, sou' les Tiltres de LYRE CHREST. & LYRE PROPHA."[18]

That this intention was not carried out is for the moment beside the point. This project was another casualty of the journey to Rome. But what is important is that in the *Recueil* of 1552 there appear three religious poems, *La Monomachie de David et de Goliath*, *La Lyre Chrestienne*, and the *Hymn Chrestienne*, all of which must have been destined to be classified under the generic title *Lyre Chrestienne*. These poems are purely Christian. It seems entirely possible that Du Bellay would have classified the "Elegie" of 1552 and the *XIII Sonnetz* as *Prophane*, and that the devotional sonnets at the end of the *Olive* would have presented a problem, occurring as they do in a work that is otherwise profane. These poems will be discussed in the next chapter, but for the time being they may be seen to constitute a growing body of religious verse which is developing along with a simultaneous rejection of Petrarchism and an equally simultaneous though unsuccessful attempt at poetry in the neo-Platonic vein.

The Roman sojourn put an end to all these embryonic developments. But it would seem from all this evidence that Du Bellay was becoming a religious poet just before he accepted the position with his remote relative the Cardinal Du Bellay at the Papal Court, a position he was to regret very much, which was to make him so eloquently miserable and at the same time was to turn him into a truly great melancholy poet.

R. V. Merrill regards the neo-Platonic strain in Du Bellay

[18] *Oeuvres*, v (2), 253.

in 1552-1553 as the dominant one. He writes that "without Rome he might have become a greater Platonist."[19] I must disagree completely with this proposition. Merrill has put too fine an edge on Du Bellay's Platonism, which was for Du Bellay nothing more than a *tentative echouée*, like his Petrarchism. Its place in his work is very like the place of neo-Platonism in Spenser's; he uses as much as he can. Spenser was more skillful in his use, but he was older and more mature and had a clearer sense of the separation of essentials. Hence Spenser could use more of it without so much confusion, whereas Du Bellay, after a few attempts at neo-Platonism, dropped it entirely, and turned on the terrestrial level to a personal conception of honor and virtue and on the celestial level to poems of purely religious content, almost untouched even by neo-Platonic phraseology. V.-L. Saulnier has written of Du Bellay that, had he not gone to Rome in 1553, "il eût tenté d'être notre premier très grand poète religieux."[20] It seems highly likely, in terms of the foregoing review of this question, that Saulnier is correct.

The reader has probably anticipated that Ronsard's attitude toward Plato and toward neo-Platonism is ambiguous. He rejects with almost unblemished consistency the neo-Platonic view that regards woman as something more than a mere creature of flesh and blood. Yet even here he is not without some sense of the abstract quality of female beauty, although he never dwells upon it except ironically. But in the ironies and in the sarcasms one sometimes senses that the strength of the poet's feelings is capable of betraying him into an implicit and unwilling admiration of woman as a superior being. A poet cannot love one woman or another for most of his lifetime without admitting to himself, however covertly, that woman has a certain elevated power. But

[19] *Platonism*, p. 146.   [20] *Du Bellay*, p. 69.

Ronsard never explicitly accepts the neo-Platonic idealization of woman, nor is even the exalted Petrarchan phrasing which crops up sporadically in his early sonnets to Cassandre and to Marie to be taken as wholly sincere.

Paul Laumonier, in his monumental study of Ronsard as a lyric poet, writes that one need not pause over the few accents of Platonic love that are disseminated in the *Amours* of 1552.[21] For these expressions, like those of Petrarchism, are clearly a matter of fashion. The Petrarchism was abandoned almost at once by Ronsard, as it was by Du Bellay; it had served as it were to give both poets a start on their careers and this was all that was necessary. The anti-Platonic remarks to which Ronsard gave such forthright utterance in the next thirty years of his life make it clear that his relationship with Platonic doctrines of love was a youthful flirtation, and not a mature courtship.[22]

On the other hand, in spite of Ronsard's antipathy to Platonic or neo-Platonic doctrines of love, he does show some sympathy for other Platonic tenets. He refers frequently to the body as a prison, to the flesh as a burden; he accepts the conventional interpretation of the message of the *Ion* in regard to poetic inspiration, though in expatiating on it he shows that he misunderstands Plato;[23] and he is not beyond an expression in at least one instance of what

---

[21] *Ronsard, Poète Lyrique* (Paris, 1923), p. 506. Robert V. Merrill and Robert J. Clements, however, have paused at some length over these accents, see *Platonism in French Renaissance Poetry, passim*.

[22] It should be pointed out that Merrill and Clements recognize this attitude of Ronsard's, though their tendency is to understate it; they write that Ronsard is "less fully addicted to Platonism whether philosophic or amoristic . . ." than is Du Bellay (*Platonism*, p. 44).

[23] Ronsard is not alone in his failure to perceive the irony present in the *Ion*, when it is considered in relation to the statements concerning poetry in the *Republic* and the *Apology*. See A. E. Taylor's discussion of this matter in his *Plato*, pp. 38-41. Renaissance poets and critics did not have a modern analytical point of view in reading Plato; they were carried away by their enthusiasm, and they were prone to make Plato say what they wished to hear. See Sir Philip Sidney's misrepresentation of the doctrine of the *Ion* in his *Defence*, a misreading based on Italian sources.

is perhaps a sincere belief in the existence of a higher, abstract quality in Love itself.[24] His emphasis, however, is anti-Platonic. Let us look first at the nature of his rejection of Platonism, and its putative causes, and then at the statements which seem to some extent to temper this almost intransigent point of view.

Ronsard probably read Plato early in his youth. Raymond Lebègue points out that the *Ion* and the *Phaedrus* were translated into Latin in 1540 and had a considerable influence on French poets after that date.[25] Ronsard could thus have read them before he knew Greek well; and after he achieved this skill under the tutelage of Jean Dorat in the late forties, it may be presumed, bookish youth that he notoriously was, that he read other dialogues in the original: read them, and was repelled by them, for Ronsard's revulsion against Plato does not proceed from ignorance. He makes it clear that he has read the *Symposium* and the *Republic*, and probably the *Timaeus*. He damns them because he knows them and does not like them. He also knows the neo-Platonists, the Italians from Ficino to Castiglione to Bembo; he knows the Platonizing poetry that they inspired in his French predecessors such as Maurice Scève, and his contemporaries such as Héroët and Du Bellay; he probably contemplated the confusion of *XIII Sonnetz* with small pity and much delight.

The cause of Ronsard's rejection of Platonism is dual. He maintained throughout his life an increasingly cordial dislike of all Italian influences in France. In his maturity this applied to the deleterious atmosphere that Italians created at Court, an atmosphere in which Ronsard found his own position more and more jeopardized as he grew older. But his dislike originated in the debt that the early Pléiade owed to the Italians: Petrarch was an Italian, the neo-Pla-

[24] Examples of these references will be discussed in this chapter, below.
[25] *Ronsard, L'Homme et L'Oeuvre*, p. 149.

tonists were Italians, literary criticism was Italian, even the sonnet was of Italian origin. The headstrong young poets had to break away from the parental influence that threatened their independence. Because of the strength of his national feeling, Ronsard was unable to subjugate himself for long to contemporary Italian literary influences, or even to the influences of older work in his native language. So the Brigade that became the Pléiade enslaved itself to Rome and to Greece, neither of which carried the same stigma because the time was remote and the language was classical.

Beyond this, there was Ronsard's own personal orientation toward the physical world in which he lived, a world of aristocrats and of charming women in Paris, of shepherdesses and rural nymphs in the Vendôme countryside. Ronsard loved not only the ladies of higher birth; he was not averse to excursions into what was probably the lower-class, or at least the small bourgeoisie.[26] He was seeking only one thing in womankind: the warm flesh and the admiration of himself that surrender would signify. Paul Laumonier points out that Ronsard, like almost all the neo-Latin and Italian poets from 1450-1550, had "goûté infiniment les poètes du paganisme, et les plus voluptueux." He goes on to say: "Comme eux il avait négligé le caractère surnaturel et divin que Pétrarque avait exalté dans la femme [and here the neo-Platonists might be added]; il ne l'a pas consideré comme d'une nature superieure à la sienne; il a été beaucoup plus épris de ses charmes materiels que de sa valeur morale et les a décris beaucoup plus volontiers."[27]

A single example from Ronsard's first book of love son-

[26] See Gustave Cohen's discussion of the identity of the Marie of the sonnets, and also Pierre de Nolhac, *La Vie Amoureuse de Pierre de Ronsard*, Chapter 2, *passim*. It is fascinating for the English reader to observe the avidity and enthusiasm with which French critics address themselves to these questions and others, such as the exact degree of success Ronsard may have achieved in his seductions.

[27] *Ronsard, Poète Lyrique*, p. 499.

nets, the *Amours de Cassandre* (1552), will serve to illustrate his early anti-Platonic irony. He writes:

> Pardonne moy, Platon, si je ne cuide . . .
> Que . . . il n'y ait quelque vuide.[28]

Here the poet is playing with the ancient doctrine of the void. The above lines are the first and fourth of the octave of the sonnet, an octave which is devoted to an elaborate and somewhat pedantic exposition of the conceit that there must be a void which is empty enough to receive the flood of unstinted tears and sighs which the poet in his love-smitten grief casts heavenward. Platonic physics and geography are used as a butt for ridicule in this sonnet, which is a fluffy *jeu d'esprit*. It may have succeeded in its time, but today it seems rather flat. Its carefree treatment of Plato, however, is significantly typical.

A further early example will demonstrate Ronsard's anti-Petrarchism, which is evidently connected with his anti-Platonism, since it was the same element of both fashionable modes that most offended him: the ethereal, the abstract. He writes, in a short, light poem called "Odelette à sa Maistresse" (1555):

> Les amans si frois en esté,
> Admirateurs de chasteté,
> Et qui morfondus petrarquisent,
> Sont toujours sots, car ils meprisent
> Amour qui de sa nature est
> Ardent et pront . . .[29]

Here is Spenser's word "chastity," but in a context that presents a polar contrast to Spenser's use of it. Though Petrarch is the explicit victim at this point, it is quite clear from Ronsard's work as a whole that there could not be any

---

[28] *Sonnet* LXXXI, *Oeuvres*, ed. Cohen, I, 35.
[29] *Les Meslanges*, *Oeuvres*, ed. Cohen, II, 797-798.

objection to including the neo-Platonic lover as a "sot" also, and for the same reason.

Another example of similar sentiment, written much later, shows the persistence of Ronsard's denial of the Platonic nature of love. It contains as well a certain element of the growing bitterness that has come with age. Written to Hélène Surgères, the lady-in-waiting to Catherine de Medici, who is said almost always to have had a volume of Plato in her hand, the poem expresses not only the poet's specific irritation at being ordered to woo a frigid and much younger woman, but also his more general disgust at the new wave of Petrarchism and neo-Platonism that had arrived with the growing Italianization of the Court.[30] Perhaps even more generally within this context it expresses his dislike for the rising young Desportes, who was being showered with laurels because he was reflecting the mood of the time far better than the older Ronsard. The poem was later significantly withdrawn from reprints of the 1578 edition of *Le Premier Livre des Sonets pour Helene*: Ronsard seems perhaps to have been unwilling to defend such an explicit denial of fashionable Court doctrine:

> En choisissant l'esprit vous estes mal-apprise,
> Qui refusez le corps, à mon gré le meilleur:
> De l'un en l'esprouvant on cognoist la valeur,
> L'autre n'est rien que vent, que songe et que feintise.
> Vous aimez l'intellect, et moins je vous en prise . . .[31]

Paradoxically, however, another sonnet which states the same beliefs in terms more radical than the above was left in future editions of the sonnets for Hélène. This is perhaps because the statement here is not explicitly directed against Hélène herself, but is expressed in general terms. A more

---
[30] See Frances A. Yates's *Academies, passim*, for a full discussion of these influences.
[31] *Oeuvres*, ed. Cohen, II, 919.

sweeping denial of the doctrines both of Platonic and neo-Platonic love would be difficult to find:

> Bien que l'esprit humain s'enfle par la doctrine
> De Platon, qui le vante influxion des Cieux,
> Si est-ce sans le corps qu'il seroit ocieux,
> Et auroit beau louer sa celeste origine.
>
> Par les sens l'ame voit, ell'oyt, ell'imagine,
> Ell'a ses actions du corps officieux;
> L'esprit incorporé divient ingenieux
> La matiere le rend plus parfait et plus digne.[32]

The sestet continues in the same vein, likening the Platonic lover to Ixion in the myth. A conscientious translator would have to say that here Ronsard states the human mind to be bloated with a Platonism that pretends to be of divine origin. The poet's emphasis on the materialism of the spirit is overwhelming. It is matter that gives value to the spiritual; it is, as it were, the body that animates the soul. Such an exaggerated reversal of the usual relationship of soul and body, according to Christian as well as to Platonic doctrine, probably must be regarded not so much as a statement that results from a thoughtful consideration of the human situation as an expression of bitter animosity against life itself, proceeding from the frustrations of encroaching old age and diminishing influence in the world. The eight lines are probably even more anti-Platonic than Ronsard really was.

Ronsard's sarcastic view of the Platonism of the *Republic* is related to the above examples. It is the lack of a material or practical attitude that Ronsard deplores in Platonic writings. In a formal court poem to the Governor of Paris at the time of writing (1567), Ronsard says:

> Je m'esbahis des paroles subtiles
> Du grand Platon, qui veut regir les villes

[32] *Ibid.*, "Sonnet L" of *Le Premier Livre des Sonnets pour Helene*, I, 236.

Par un papier et non par action;
C'est une belle et docte invention,
Qui toutesfois ne sçauroit satisfaire;
Elle est oisive, il faut venir au faire . . .[33]

While the poem is an exercise in the art of flattery, as are all of Ronsard's Court poems, it is nevertheless significant that in choosing an example of bad government to contrast with Montmorency's good, Ronsard naturally fastens on Plato. A parallel sarcasm appears in the first sonnet of the second series to Hélène, in which Ronsard writes:

Lecteur, je ne veux estre escolier de Platon,
Qui la vertu nous presche, et ne fait pas de mesme . . .[34]

In this case it is not clear exactly what in Plato is being criticized, but the cause of the criticism, the discrepancy between preaching and practice, is the same. The *Republic* is a "docte invention," a "papier"; it does not satisfy because it does not go beyond the theoretical to the practical, from thought to action. For this reason it is "oisive," just as love without the body is "ocieux," which is the same thing. Ronsard wants deeds, not words; action, not thoughts; practice, not theory; matter, not spirit. This is why he excels at the poetry of the senses, the tactile, the here-and-now. In this he is very unlike Du Bellay, who always seems at least one remove from physical reality. And it is interesting to note that in respect to this quality Spenser comprehends both Ronsard and Du Bellay, being able in the greater breadth of his understanding of this world and the next to embrace both what is immediately apprehensible to the senses and what is perceptible only to the eye of the mind. For it has been shown how Spenser converted Platonic idealism into an instrument for the expression of his own

---

[33] *Ibid.*, "Discours à tresvertueux Seigneur François de Montmorenci, Mareschal de France," *Le Bocage Royal, Premiere Partie*, I, 859.
[34] *Ibid.*, I, 243.

metaphysical beliefs; and it is a well-known and incontrovertible *cliché* of criticism of the *Faerie Queene* that Spenser, especially in the sixth Book, shows an instinctive and realistic appreciation of the beauties of the here-and-now in nature.

Two further quotations will complete the survey of Ronsard's anti-Platonic attitudes. The first will fill out in contrasting colors the kind of love which above all others moved the French poet; the second will definitely characterize his opinion of womankind.

The "Discours I, en forme d'elegie" of *Les Elegies* is a long narrative semi-autobiographical poem (470 lines), written to a certain married lady called Genèvre, with whom the poet is purported to have had an affair from 1561-1562. The poem, one of Ronsard's most famous, is a romantic short story in verse. It asserts in forthright fashion the orthodox mediaeval doctrine of courtly love with the concomitant requirement of adultery,[35] the same doctrine that brought so much eternal trouble to Dante's Francesca.[36] Near the beginning of the poem Ronsard says to the lady (to whom, it might be added, he has never been introduced):

> Aussi Dieu ne fait point une femme si belle,
> Pour estre contre Amour de nature rebelle,
> Cela me fait hardi de m'addresser à toy,
> Puis que tant de douceur en ta face je voy.[37]

Ronsard is speaking to Genèvre in the street. He had seen her only once before, the previous evening, dancing on the banks of the river Seine, in which the poet was bathing. On that occasion, all naked as he was, he had impulsively rushed to kiss her hand and, having accomplished this, had dived into the river again. One sees now what Ronsard

[35] See C. S. Lewis, *The Allegory of Love*, Chapter I, *passim*.
[36] *Inferno*, Canto v.
[37] *Oeuvres*, ed. Cohen, II, 15.

means by action, by saying that love is ardent and ready. In the twenty-four hours intervening between the first meeting and the second stage of the seduction quoted above, Ronsard had fallen madly in love with the lady. He is moving with alacrity toward the practical end of love conceived in his own terms: there is nothing "ocieux" or Platonic about his approach. His mind is stripped for action; as symbolically, perhaps, his stripped body at the initial meeting foreshadows his forthcoming success, which, however, is not achieved in this elegy but is mentioned in retrospect in a later poem to the same lady.[38]

In the elegy Genèvre is represented as a recent widow whose husband has bid her take a "gaillard" lover after his death, so that it may never be said of him that his successor was a "sot." Ronsard shows himself a "gaillard" by the mere mention of his name and by giving a summary of his previous affairs with Cassandre and Marie. He proclaims with pride that he is a man who flits from love to love, and in the next breath he swears that he will be forever faithful to Genèvre if she will but love him. This she ultimately does, and his last elegy to her, though a retrospective evocation of their happiness together, is, as one might expect, neither nostalgic nor regretful.

The "morality" on which this poem is based is evidently neither Platonic, neo-Platonic, nor even Petrarchan. It grew up as an escape from the confining Christian conception of Chastity. In Ronsard it is a rebellion not only from the rigidity of Christian morals but from what he probably conceived to be the vaporousness of neo-Platonic morality. It is the morality of Roman poets and of the neo-Latin poets, who as predecessors or contemporaries so influenced the

[38] "Elegie xx, troisiesme pour Genèvre," published in 1571; *Oeuvres*, ed. Cohen, II, 88-95. It is interesting to observe that the last line of the poem, which recapitulates the consummation of their relationship, reads as follows:
Rien n'est si sot qu'une vieille amitié.

youthful Ronsard.[39] It would not be difficult to form a correct estimate of what destiny Dante would have accorded to a man who persisted in Ronsard's amatory activities. Perhaps also it would be no less easy to divine Spenser's hypothetical opinion.

A final commentary on Ronsard's general attitude toward woman may be seen in his fairly lengthy and ambitious treatment of the Venus-Adonis myth in an elegy called "Adonis," published in the same collected edition as the above elegy to Genèvre in 1567. This poem ends with a moral of a sort. When Adonis is dead, Venus goes off lightheartedly with a Phrygian shepherd called Anchises. The poet concludes:

Telles sont et seront les amiticz des femmes,
Qui au commencement sont plus chaudes que flames:
Ce ne sont que souspirs, mais en fin telle amour
Resemble aux fleurs d'avril qui ne vivent qu'un jour.[40]

If the message of the *Fowre Hymnes* were not sufficient to present the contrast between Spenser's view of woman and Ronsard's, one might mention the different treatment of the Venus-Adonis myth in the *Faerie Queene*, or parade a galaxy of female characters such as Britomart, Amoret, Belphoebe, and Una; or, finally, hold up the *Epithalamion* as the most perfect contrast between the ephemeral quality of the earthly love which endures one April day and the earthly love which transcends all time.

It might be inferred that there are few solidly orthodox statements of Platonic or neo-Platonic doctrine in the entire work of Ronsard. As a poet he was generally honest in his convictions, however amoral they were. Except in his adolescence he never made any real effort to pretend that he was

---

[39] In all justice it must be pointed out that the first elegy to Genèvre is a fine and moving poem if read without moralistic bias. Its fresh enthusiasm and its honesty sets it apart from the rest of the amorous poetry of the sixteenth century in France.

[40] *Oeuvres*, ed. Cohen, II, 33.

either a Platonist or a Petrarchist and, as has been observed before, these early hints of the one strain or the other are of negligible importance in the total body of his work. Even in his comparatively youthful *Hynne de la Mort* (1555) in which one might expect some infusion of Platonism, if any remained in the young man, one finds that the poet takes consolation from his theory of cyclic regeneration at least as much as from his Christian beliefs. Further, one of his few mentions of philosophic theory that may have had its origin in his reading of Plato is undercut some hundred lines later by a specific jibe at Plato. Near the beginning of the poem he writes:

Où est l'homme çà-bas, s'il n'est bien miserable
Et lourd d'entendement, qui ne vueille estre hors
De l'humaine prison de ce terrestre corps?[41]

The reference is as clearly Platonic as anything in Ronsard. The sentiment might have been expressed in the same terms by Du Bellay or by Spenser. But Ronsard goes on to point out that the "Platoniques," the philosophers who are so full "de propos magnifiques," will be found to cry and groan as much as the next man when they come to the moment of death, in spite of the fact that they "voudroyent, s'ils pouvoyent, leur trespas differer."[42]

There is in Ronsard, however, one fairly consistent exposition of neo-Platonic doctrine that must by its nature occupy a unique place in the Ronsard canon. Gustave Cohen refers to it as "ce beau discours platonicien sur l'amour."[43] The poem is entitled "Discours, d'un amoureux desesperé, et de son compagnon qui le console, et d'Amour qui le reprend"; it is dedicated to Scévole de Saincte-Marthe, a fellow poet. The Platonism is contained in the

[41] *Ibid.*, II, 282. See also a similar reference to the body as a prison, "Hynne des Astres," *Les Hynnes* (1555), II, 846.
[42] *Ibid.*, II, 285.   [43] *Ibid.*, "Notes," II, 1082.

final speech of "Amour" who is scolding "l'amoureux desesperé." Since this is the most unambiguous presentation of Platonic doctrine that I have been able to find in Ronsard's work, I shall quote the crucial and somewhat lengthy passage in full:

> Quand du haut Ciel les ames abaissées
> Dedans les corps languissent oppressées
> De la matiere et du pesant fardeau,
> Je leur esclaire aux rais de mon flambeau;
> Je les resveille et leur preste mes ailes
> Pour revoler és maisons eternelles
> Par le bien-fait de contemplation.
> Car de l'Amour la plus belle action
> Est de rejoindre en charité profonde
> L'ame à son Dieu tandis qu'elle est au monde.
> Plus ta Maistresse est belle, et d'autant plus,
> Laissant ton corps impotent et perclus,
> Devois hausser tes yeux outre la nue
> Pour voir le Beau dont ta belle est venue;
> Mais t'amusant à la beauté du corps,
> Et aux couleurs qui plaisent par dehors,
> Qui comme fleurs en naissant se fanissent,
> As abaissé tes esprits, qui languissent
> Lourds, engourdis d'un sommeil ocieux,
> Sans envoyer ton ame jusqu'aux cieux,
> Estant plongée en l'amour furieuse,
> Brutale amour, charnelle, vicieuse.
> Donc, de ton gré te liant en prison
> As desrobé toy-mesme et ta raison.[44]

If any proof were needed to demonstrate that Ronsard was familiar with the doctrine of Platonic love, it could be found here. These lines contain all the elements that are found in the first two of Spenser's *Fowre Hymnes*: the

[44] *Ibid.*, II, 361.

Platonic, the neo-Platonic, and, strangely enough, the moral castigation of "brutale amour, charnelle, vicieuse."

These elements, however, appear nowhere else in this long (470 lines) poem, and the above quotation represents their full development. The theory is not expatiated upon; the castigation of the lustful love is confined to two lines, emphatic but brief. To point out the proportional shortness of this presentation of perfectly orthodox Platonic doctrine is not, however, to explain it away. Nor is this indeed necessary, for the final lines of the poem which follow almost at once explain away the presence of Platonic doctrine, probably better than any critic might hope to do:

> Scevole, amy des Muses que je sers,
> Icy je t'offre en lieu de tes beaux vers
> Un froid discours, larron de ta loüange.
> Tu n'es premier qui te trompes au change,
> Glauque jadis s'y deceut devant toy;
> Et toutefois pren ce present de moy,
> Pour tesmoigner d'une encre perdurable,
> Que mon vers fut à ton vers redevable.[45]

It seems clear that these terminal lines may be said effectively to undercut the Platonic passage that immediately precedes them. The poet has made a garland of verse for his friend. He apologizes for it; in mentioning the discrepant value of the exchange, he refers in Ronsardian fashion to the blindness of Glaukos in his armor exchange with Diomedes in the *Iliad*, one of his favorite books;[46] and in the last couplet he makes it quite clear that the beautiful Platonic discourse, which consorts so ill with the rest of his work, has been put in the poem as a concession to Scévole

---

[45] *Ibid.*

[46] It should be noted that Gustave Cohen seems to mistake the reference to Glaukos as referring to "Glaucus, le pêcheur, métamorphosé en Triton" (*Oeuvres*, II, 1082). The proper reference is, of course, to *Iliad*, VI, 234-236.

de Saincte-Marthe, a Platonizing poet, in order to substantiate the final statement that Ronsard's verse is in debt to Saincte-Marthe. It is significant that when Ronsard is in such debt, it is only because he has deliberately contracted the debt in honor of the particular occasion.

In conclusion, the similarity of Du Bellay to Spenser in respect to their Platonism must be stressed. Spenser sought and achieved in his *Fowre Hymnes* a reconciliation between devout Protestantism and neo-Platonic language. His principal deviations from orthodox neo-Platonism consisted in his substitution of Christ and of the Christian symbol Sapience for absolute beauty, or the τὸ καλόν of Diotima; in his refusal to mount the conventional ladder alone, or indeed at all, conventionally; and in his refusal to use womankind as a way or as a means only. The harmony that exists in the *Fowre Hymnes* between the Christian and the pagan elements is the result of the careful, serious, and above all mature skill of a much-practiced poet at the peak of his powers.

Du Bellay in his *XIII Sonnetz* was apparently seeking a similar reconciliation. He was, however, a poet of small experience at the time, barely in his late twenties, with only a single Petrarchan sonnet sequence behind him. In addition, his thinking was immature; he was fresh from plunges into the pagan classics, from the burning outbursts of the *Deffence*, and from the quasi-serious neo-pagan cerebrations and celebrations of the *Brigade*. His neo-Platonism is confused; his ideas are chaotic, and the discords in his verse reflect the confusion in his mind. Not skillful enough to present neo-Platonism in harmonious terms, Du Bellay turns to the purely religious verse which had succeeded two years earlier with the five devout sonnets at the end of *L'Olive*. The idealism that Spenser could express partly in neo-Platonic language in the *Fowre Hymnes*, Du Bellay expresses in Christian terms unaided by the neo-Platonic vocabulary.

Each has used Platonism and neo-Platonism according to his ability; each has arrived at a conception of woman as the spiritual equal of man, a doctrine that is probably an offshoot of the Bembist exposition in Castiglione's *Courtier*, and is in radical contra-distinction to Ronsard's attitude. And each will be seen to have reserved for his most serious religious statements a simple, native diction, starkly bare and clean of foreign accretions, non-neo-Platonic and non-Platonic. For both Spenser and Du Bellay are in the last analysis neo-Platonists *manqués*.

Ronsard, on the contrary, cannot even be called a failure at neo-Platonism because he never really tried it out, except once for the sake of a friend, and perhaps also to see how it looked in the mirror he constantly held up to himself. It did not please him because, besides being a Christian in minor orders, he was after all a pre-Socratic pagan who could involve himself with more enthusiasm in Homer and in Pindar and in early Greek mythology than he could in the soft, late, and degenerate mythology of Plato the moral philosopher.

In the following chapter a comparison of the basic religious orientations of the three poets, as reflected in their verse, will be seen to yield an analogous conclusion; and any value judgment that may be passed on the poets, except in respect to their verse, must be the reader's, if anyone's, and not the critic's.

IX · DEVOTIONAL VERSE IN THE THREE POETS

*T*o discuss the religious orientation of any poet is at best a perilous venture. More perilous still is a comparison of religious attitudes in several poets, especially when two are Catholics and one is a Protestant. In addition, there is the fact that the religious wars in France in the 1560's produced in Ronsard a very strong anti-Protestant feeling.[1] Similarly a journey through Switzerland produced a kindred animosity in Du Bellay, and political circumstances during the reign of Elizabeth from time to time stimulated Spenser's natural English anti-Catholic animus.[2] It would seem, therefore, that the two Frenchmen must be pitted unalterably against the Englishman, and that the situation of all three must be divisive and productive only of contrasts.

It is hard to believe, nevertheless, that the task of comparing poetic expressions of religious feeling is entirely foolhardy. It should be stressed, however, that the comparisons which follow will not constitute attempts to judge the position of a man before his God. They will compare the poets' expressions of religious feeling as found in their poetry, in their creative work. A literary critic can hardly hope to look into the very soul of a poet; such an activity may be left to

---

[1] One should note Ronsard's expression of regret in his *Remonstrance au Peuple de France* (1563), for having at some time early in his career flirted momentarily with poisonous doctrines:

> J'ay autrefois gousté, quand j'estois jeune d'âge,
> Du miel empoisonné de vostre doux breuvage;
> Mais quelque bon Démon, m'ayant ouy crier,
> Avant que l'avaller me l'osta du gosier.

(*Oeuvres*, ed. Cohen, ii, 578). The violence of his anti-Protestant feelings was probably fortified by a lingering sense of guilt for a youthful indiscretion.

[2] One should perhaps mention also that Spenser's official position in Ireland during most of his mature life kept him at or near the center of armed conflict between the Protestant English and the Catholic Irish.

the scientific psychoanalytic scholar. What I seek to define is the representation each poet makes of his religious attitude, in his work not in his self. Furthermore, as I have pointed out above, Ronsard and Du Bellay were both tonsured in their youth, in the middle of the 1540's, in order to make themselves eligible for ecclesiastical benefices; they became minor Church officials and hence might be expected to express their religious thoughts more frequently and more explicitly in their verse than the average lay poet.

On the other hand, as an Elizabethan Protestant, Spenser was in a sense his own priest and theologian. All three poets take a position in their poetry that is clear in the most general way. This is not to say that Spenser's position is at all obvious in relation to a precise degree of Puritanism or of Calvinism; nor that the exact nature of Ronsard's youthful excursion into Protestantism is fully understood; nor that all the facts are known about the quarrel that Du Bellay had with the Cardinal of the same name. The broad lines, however, are fairly definite, and to try to draw them with some accuracy should contribute to a full comprehension of the relationships among the three. The dividing lines will be seen to be not so much Protestant and Catholic or English and French as temperamental and personal, lines which both divide and connect in defiance of national and religious boundaries. Such distinctions can be seen in their verse itself because the poets themselves regarded these matters as of primordial importance.

Spenser's religious views are expressed with grave and straightforward honesty in *An Hymne of Heavenly Love*. In comparing Spenser to his French predecessors, Elizabeth Jelliffe Macintire has written that: "The Pléiade writers, though mostly Catholic, mix their religion curiously with paganism, and this same mixture of Christianity and paganism is visible in Spenser's *Four Hymns*."[3] Applied to the

[3] "French Influence on the Beginnings of English Classicism," *PMLA* 26 (1911), p. 518.

Hymne of Heavenly Love this statement has a ring of specious plausibility, for the hymn is overwhelmingly Christian. Not only is it an implicit exaggeration to call the Platonism and the neo-Platonism in the *Fowre Hymnes* "pagan," but in this hymn far more than in any of the others the Platonic elements are minimal and the neo-Platonic theories are almost totally abandoned in a fervent paean of Christian praise. The pagan mixture may apply to Ronsard, less to Du Bellay, and substantially less to Spenser, as an examination of this hymn will indicate.

After the opening lines of invocation, the poem begins with two stanzas of palinode which express shame for "passed follies" and for "old fault" (lines 20, 21). On the positive side, the recantation asserts that this poem, unlike the poet's past work, will be truly religious:

> Many lewd layes (ah woe is me the more)
> In praise of that mad fit, which fooles call loue,
> I haue in th' heat of youth made heretofore,
> That in light wits did loose affection moue.
> But all these follies now I do reproue,
> And turned haue the tenor of my string,
> The heauenly prayses of true loue to sing.
>
> (Lines 8-14)

W. L. Renwick writes of these lines that they are "in the vein of the repentant sonnets of Petrarch such as ccclxiv (*Tennemi Amor*)."[4] The absence in Spenser's work of anything that might be designated a "lewd laye" would seem, however, to indicate that this palinode is probably conventional, or a concession to the ladies of the dedication, rather than a sincere expression of guilt for past poetic sins. These lines are much more in the vein of Du Bellay's *La Lyre Chrestienne* (1552), in which the poet states his intention to sing the "Muse eternelle" instead of the "Muse charnelle"; Spenser's lines may perhaps also be related to Du

---
[4] *Daphnaïda and Other Poems*, "Commentary," p. 220.

DEVOTIONAL VERSE

Bellay's intention expressed in 1552 to divide his published work into categories of Christian and Profane.

At the end of the first stanza of the main body of the poem, Spenser launches at once into celestial topography as it is conceived to have been before creation, before Time. Here the spheres are moved by a force that contrasts with Du Bellay's "Moteur souverain" in Sonnet IX of the *XIII Sonnetz de l'Honneste Amour*, and compares with the mover in Dante's *Paradiso*:[5]

> That high eternall powre, which now doth moue
> In all these things, mou'd in it selfe by loue.
>
> (Lines 27-28)

Spenser's mover is "loue," and Dante's is "Amor"; for both poets, God is Love. The concept in the quotation may contain a grain of Aristotelianism, but it is by now wholly Christian. In this context Spenser's "loue" is hardly touched by Platonism, whether classical or Renaissance; love is God, not τὸ καλόν.[6]

In the following stanza the Created Son is mentioned, and the fact that He is crowned equally with God the Father is attributed to two causes, one of which is that no "pride was to be found (line 34) in Him. Thus here at the core of Spenser's religious beliefs one finds what is certainly the root and probably the final expression of his continuous bitter hatred of pride, which he stated so baldly in the *Faerie Queene*. The emphasis here is moralistic and perhaps Puritanical; it seems to have been freshly strengthened by the

---

[5] This is the first of many allusions in this and the next poem that seem to point to a familiarity with the *Divina Comedia* on Spenser's part. But since this study is concerned only with French analogies, Dante is mentioned merely for the sake of emphasizing the Christian as against the Greek origin of some of Spenser's phrases.

[6] See Edwin Greenlaw's remarks on this subject: "To him love is the source of the universe, of every living thing, and of every spiritual value in this world and the world to come." ("Some Old Religious Cults in Spenser," *SP* 20 [1923], 243.)

Reformation. It is very unlike the poetic expressions of aristocratic bias that Ronsard carried into his relationship even with God. These lines of Spenser's should be correlated with those that follow a little later, which echo the same idea in regard to Lucifer's rebellion:

> But pride impatient of long resting peace,
> Did puffe them vp with greedy bold ambition . . .
> (Lines 78-79)

And a few lines later:
> . . . fell from aboue
> Through pride; (for pride and loue may ill agree)
> And now of sinne to all ensample bee . . .
> (Lines 93-95)

Here the connection with the moral message of the *Visions of the worldes vanitie*, which is expressed in non-religious terms, is seen in its original Christian context.

After the Fall of Satan, the creation and fall of man is briefly reviewed. Next, in the middle of the hymn, is the coming of Christ. A stanza opens with the following line, which has been characterized by B. E. C. Davis as "the worst line in *An Hymne of Heavenly Love*":[7]

> O huge and most vnspeakeable impression
> Of loues deepe wound . . . (Lines 155-156)

These polysyllables are indeed awkwardly placed in this line, and the poet, introducing that part of his argument in which he has the deepest and most emotional involvement, is carried away for the moment with the immensity of his subject. It is not a line of poetry that he speaks; it is a "grone in grieued thought" as he says later (line 252), as if he were present at the Crucifixion.

For the main emphasis falls on the Crucifixion; this is

[7] Edmund Spenser, A Critical Study (Cambridge, 1933), p. 140.

the subject from the middle of the poem until the third from the last stanza. The life of Christ is reviewed in terms of the final sacrifice; the sacrifice is reviewed in detail. It is from the contemplation of the physical events and their meaning that the final ravishment at the end of the poem proceeds. But the transition from Christ in the world to Christ as pure glory in the sky is a leap, not an orderly neo-Platonic progression. The sheer disproportion between eighteen stanzas on the life and the Crucifixion, and three on the blinding vision at the end, makes it patently evident that the poet's stress is on the former.[8]

The hortatory lines and stanzas that follow concern themselves principally with the infinite value of the redemption, and the infinite obligation that Christ's sacrifice has placed on all mankind. The language is filled with echoes of English Protestantism, the *Book of Common Prayer* and the various liturgies, as well as with English translations of the *Bible*. The language is resonant, grave, earnest, and above all simple, personal and moving in its English tendency toward monosyllabic expression, far from the polysyllabic complexities of Latinate diction. The following quotation will demonstrate the simplicity and immediacy of the language that comes to Spenser from the native tradition:

> How can we thee requite for all this good?
> Or what can prize that thy most precious blood?
> (Lines 174-175)

And two stanzas later:

[8] It should be mentioned that Mohinimohan Bhattacherje, in *Platonic Ideas in Spenser* (pp. 158-161), and John Smith Harrison, in *Platonism in Spenser* (pp. 75-76, 95-97), disagree with this interpretation, and see in this poem a perfect example of the grafting of orthodox Platonic theory upon Christian theology. Denis Saurat, however, agrees with my emphasis on the preponderantly Christian aspect of the two Heavenly hymns ("Les Idées Philosophiques de Spenser," *Arsbok* 1924, Yearbook of the New Society of Letters at Lund [Lund, 1924], pp. 41-43).

> Ne ought demaunds, but that we louing bee,
> As he himselfe hath lou'd vs afore hand,
> And bound thereto with an eternall band,
> Him first to loue, that vs so dearely bought,
> And next, our breathren to his image wrought.
>
> (Lines 185-189)

This directness is not only linguistically antithetical to the rich neo-Platonic expressions in the final vision ("sweete enragement of celestiall loue"); it is pre-Renaissance and wholly English, though no more English Protestant than English Catholic, as the work of Chaucer and Thomas More attest.

> Learne him to loue, that loued thee so deare,
> And in thy brest his blessed image beare.
>
> With all thy hart, with all thy soule and mind,
> Thou must him loue, and his beheasts embrace.
>
> (Lines 258-261)

And, at the end of this stanza, the last before the three terminal ones which deal with ravishment and possession:

> And giue thy selfe vnto him full and free,
> That full and freely gaue himselfe to thee.
>
> (Lines 265-266)

All these lines are moralistic in the highest sense that Spenser could achieve. They are not mystical. They are sententious and hortatory in a tradition that before Spenser was established in the English language by his master Chaucer and by Langland, that was continued after Spenser by Donne, Herbert, Vaughan, and many others in the centuries following.

It is a tradition more natural and more native to the English than that of neo-Platonic mysticism, or the baroque lushness that Crashaw imported from Italy, or any other foreign manner of approaching religious experience. It is the tradition of the prayer book of Edward VI, of the King James Bible, a tradition that was debased but not lost by such nineteenth century writers of devotional verse as John Keble and J. M. Neale. It continues up to the present day in the private religious verse of English men and women in all walks of life, who occasionally publish, such as the late Maud Cherrill, whose small book of nature poetry in the Wordsworthian manner is combined with devotional verse in the tradition of Spenser and Herbert.[9] Spenser did as much to set up this tradition as any other poet, both in his work and in his influence.

Spenser's exhortation to an awareness of man's humility and his immense indebtedness to Christ is in close thematic relationship to moral castigations of dunghill thoughts and lustful love in the two early hymns, and to the similar references to "durty pleasures," "soyle," and "filthy swywn" in this hymn (lines 218, 219, 220). They are indicative of a strong sense of sin, both personal, and inherited, or original. It is man's almost total lack of desert that makes the gift of salvation doubly rich and valuable. For Spenser the thought that he might be saved is infinitely affecting not because it will be such a fine thing to be saved or because he has in some measure deserved it but precisely because he knows that he does not deserve it and because he does not expect it. The sum of his hope is that he may go to eternal rest, not to glory, but to the peace that Piccarda found in the third Canto of Dante's *Paradiso*. He writes, at the end of the unfinished *Faerie Queene*, probably among the last lines that he ever composed:

> Than gin I thinke on that which Nature sayd,
> Of that same time when no more Change shall be,

[9] *Padstow Lights* (Oxford, 1949). Miss Cherrill was the headmistress of St. Petroc's School, in North Cornwall.

DEVOTIONAL VERSE

But stedfast rest of all things firmely stayd
Vpon the pillours of Eternity,
That is contrayr to Mutabilitie:
For, all that moueth, doth in Change delight:
But thence-forth all shall rest eternally
With Him that is the God of Sabbaoth hight:
O that great Sabbaoth God, graunt me that
    Sabaoths sight.

(VII, viii, 2)

These lines are, as it were, a prayer. They follow not long after the achievement of marital happiness celebrated in the *Epithalamion*. Douglas Bush writes of this poem that he will venture to call it: ". . . the finest love poem in the language. It is a wedding hymn in the tradition of Catullus and other Roman poets and their French imitators, in the form of a stately Italian canzone, a series of processional pictures with a mingling of Irish and mythological allusions, of Irish and Roman festivities, *all wrought into a ritualistic offering worthy of a Christian marriage altar* [my italics]."[10]

Thus perhaps Spenser may be called a religious poet in something more than the most general sense of this term. There is a vein of high religious seriousness that runs through all his work. In his final poems he is concerned with mutability and change and flux on the one hand, and with eternity, with constancy, and with rest on the other, just as he was in his earliest translations from Du Bellay's *Songe*. His religion has been an integral part of his work throughout his life; as God is imminent in the world, so is Protestant Christianity imminent in Spenser's work. It is the basis for all of his morality, and it is the inspiration for much of his finest poetry. Yet though it is English and Protestant and Spenserian, it will be seen to have evident analogies with Du Bellay's religious expressions. Finally, the con-

[10] *Classical Influences in Renaissance Literature* (Cambridge, Mass., 1952), p. 46.

trast with Ronsard will be manifest: Ronsard, who lived by far the longest life of the three and seems to have been able to support a surprisingly carefree attitude up to the very end.

Du Bellay may be called a religious poet in the same general sense as Spenser, but with this difference; that in his youth he took more extended and more serious excursions into realms of purely pagan mythology than did Spenser, and that in his years of greatest maturity and productivity he wrote a great deal of verse that was light and playful, having no real moral basis (*Divers Jeux Rustiques* [1558]), and some of *Poésies Diverses*, an arrangement by Chamard of miscellaneous verse (1547-1559).

His most famous work, the *Regrets*, is melancholy and satirical and, at the end, verse of empty flattery. In the satire and the melancholy, however, there is always a moral note, not strictly religious, but often with religious implications. Moreover, he tends toward gnomic expression throughout his work, a penchant which probably originated with the *Songe* to which Van der Noot found it so easy to add emblems. He had a fundamentally moralistic temperament as did Spenser, but with it he had also the tendency to satirize rather than inveigh, to impale vice by ridicule rather than by allegory or by exemplars; and above all, he had a light, joking side that Spenser lacked almost entirely.

V.-L. Saulnier writes that Du Bellay's "humeur . . . est toujours capricieuse. Malade, il sait rire; poète de Dieu, il sait badiner."[11] He was less consistently earnest than Spenser. In Rome, he could take a Roman mistress, Faustine, and write verse in Latin in her honor in the style of Catullus. This is indeed to do in Rome as the Romans do: and this Spenser could never have done. It is perhaps the difference between a lay Protestant Englishman with Puritanical leanings, and a Gallican Catholic in minor clerical orders.

[11] *Du Bellay*, p. 66.

DEVOTIONAL VERSE

This does not mean, however, that Du Bellay was not fundamentally an orthodox believing Christian. It has been said that there is very little of the orthodox Christian in Du Bellay's work, and that much of it is clear of the Christian tradition.[12] It should be stressed, however, that in some of his poetry he is not clear of this tradition at all, and that the presence of this verse, which is manifestly and earnestly within the tradition, occurring as early as *L'Olive* and as late as the last years of his life, implies that the Christian tradition should be assumed to stand behind the more vague and generalized poems that seem to be clear of it. I shall now examine the five devotional poems that occur near the end of the *Olive* (cvii-cxi) sequence and together constitute a series within a series, standing apart from the main body of sonnets which are elaborately Petrarchan.

The note of personal devotion in these sonnets is remarkably like that in the lines quoted above from Spenser's *Hymne of Heavenly Love*. The moral tone of contrition and the simplicity of the language is entirely in accord with Spenser's; the added implication of conflict, of violent feeling, recalls the *Holy Sonnets* of Donne. If the following lines were inserted in translation, into Spenser's hymn, they might deceive even a careful reader:

> S'il a servi pour rendre l'homme franc
> S'il a purgé mes pechez de son sang,
> Et s'il est mort pour ma vie asseurer,
>
> S'il a goûté l'amer de mes douleurs,
> Prodigues yeulx, ne devez-vous pleurer
> D'avoir sans fruit dependu tant de pleurs?[10]

The following sonnet, cviii, is almost a summary of the second half of Spenser's *Hymne to Heavenly Love*:

[12] Robert V. Merrill, *Platonism*, p. 40.
[13] *Oeuvres*, ed. Chamard, Sonnet cvii, 1, 117-118.

O seigneur Dieu, qui pour l'humaine race
As esté seul de ton pere envoyé!
Guide les pas de ce coeur devoyé,
L'acheminant au sentier de ta grace.

Tu as premier du ciel ouvert la trace,
Par toy la mort a son dard etuyé:
Console donq' cet esprit ennuyé,
Que la douleur de mes pechez embrasse.

Vien, & le braz de ton secours apporte
A ma raison, qui n'est pas assez forte,
Vien eveiller ce mien esprit dormant.

D'un nouveau feu brusle moy jusqu'a l'ame,
Tant que l'ardeur de ta celeste flamme
Face oublier de l'autre le torment.[14]

Except for the last line, which hints either at the torments of illness (Du Bellay was painfully deaf, and a lifelong victim of pulmonary tuberculosis—though he died of apoplexy); or at mental torments; or even perhaps at the possibility of Hell-fire; this sonnet resembles Spenser's religious statements in its directness and in its expression of humility and of guilt. It would be difficult to construct a more orthodox Christian sonnet.

Petrarch seems to preside over the opening lines of Sonnet CIX:

Pere du ciel, si mil' & mile fois
Au gré du corps, qui mon desir convie,
Or que je suis au printemps de ma vie,
J'ay asservi & la plume & la voix . . .[15]

[14] *Ibid.*, p. 118.
[15] *Ibid.* The lines from Petrarch are:
Padre del ciel; dopo i perduti giorni
Dopo le notte vaneggiando spese

DEVOTIONAL VERSE

And John Donne seems to enter in the final lines:

> Qui me pourra deffendre de ton ire?
> Mon grand peché me veult condamner, Sire,
> Mais ta bonté me peult bien excuser.[16]

These lines recall the last two of *Holy Sonnets*, IX, "If poysonous mineralls . . .":

> That thou remember them [the poet's sins],
>   some claime as debt,
> I think it mercy, if thou wilt forget.

The next sonnet is a tour de force constructed on only two rhymed words, "la vie" and "la mort." It is a fairly close translation of a similarly artificial sonnet in Italian by an unknown author.[17] As a translation it does not have the significance of the others, except to show that Du Bellay was not above being clever about his religion (as George Herbert could be, almost a hundred years later).

The last of the series is a sonnet written upon Easter. It is fervently devotional, simple and direct; immaculate in the orthodoxy of its Christian sentiments and the sincerity of their expression:

> Voicy le jour que l'eternel amant
> Fist par sa mort vivre sa bien aimée:
> Qui telle mort au coeur n'a imprimée,
> O Seigneur Dieu! est plus que dyamant
>
> Mais qui poura sentir ce doulx torment,
> Si l'ame n'est par l'amour enflammée?

        Con quel fero desio ch'al cor s'accese
        Mirando gli atti per mio mal sí adorni . . .
(*Le Rime di Francesco Petrarca*, LXII in Vita di Madonna Laura.) Du Bellay's poem is not a paraphrase of Petrarch's, or even a recasting. But the tone of both, the sense of time lost and the sense of repentance, is similar.
  [16] *Ibid*, 119.   [17] See *Oeuvres*, p. I, 119, n. 3.

DEVOTIONAL VERSE

Soufle luy donc, pour la rendre allumée,
L'esprit divin de ton feu vehement.

Pleurez, mes yeulx, de sa mort la memoire,
Chantez, mes vers, l'honneur de sa victoire,
Et toy, mon coeur, fay luy son deu hommage.

O que mon Roy est invincible & fort!
O qu'il a faict grand gaing de son dommage!
Qui en mourant triomphe de la mort.

In this poem the sweet torment of the soul enflamed by love, and the flame itself kindled by the breath of the divine spirit, a part of the divine fire itself—all these have initial Petrarchan connotations and, secondarily, neo-Platonic suggestions. But the sestet clarifies the meaning of the octave and places the poem squarely in a Christian context. The non-Christian implications of the second quatrain are thus seen as specious in the light of the sestet. This, in miniature, is like the relationship of neo-Platonic language to Christian thought in Spenser's hymns. The shadows are dispelled in the light of the full meaning.

The *Recueil* of 1552 contains three poems dealing with religious subjects. This does not make the collection as a whole by any means religious, but it does amount to a continuation of the religious note that has been sounded at the end of *L'Olive*. R. V. Merrill writes that the *Complainte dv Desesperé*, the *Lyre Chrestienne*, and the *Hymne Chrestien* in this collection "give a vivid picture of Joachim's period of despair followed by a *temporary* religious consolation [my italics]."[18] Since one must always reckon with dissenting opinion if it seems to be based on scholarly competence, this statement deserves an answer.

The religious sonnets in *L'Olive* provide partial evidence that religion was a consolation to Du Bellay before 1552,

[18] *Platonism*, p. 130.

and the second *Hymne Chrestien*, which was written late in his lifetime (and will be discussed below), should constitute a rounded reply to Merrill's implication that Du Bellay turned to religion only briefly in 1552 as consolation for a temporary period of despair. Henri Chamard is on firmer ground, when he says that "Dans ces chants nouveaux, deux notes résonnaient, qui dominaient toutes les autres: une note élegiaque, une note religieuse."[19]

The *Hymne Chrestien*,[20] as Merrill indicates, is associated with the *Complainte dv Desesperé*. The latter is a long (510 lines) and deeply pessimistic poem in which the poet wishes that he had never been born and bewails both his physical pains and his mental "souciz cuyzans."[21] The sad winter of old age is upon him before he has seen the summer of middle-life. He is in despair. The *Hymne* is his answer to this despair, and the answer is strongly and assertively Christian. The poem opens:

> O Seigneur Dieu, mon rampart, ma fience,
> Rampare moy du fort de pacience
> Contre l'effort du corps injurieux,
> Qui veult forcer l'esprit victorieux.[22]

Du Bellay is retracting his despair. Henri Chamard writes that this poem is in itself "un acte de contrition."[23] The poet continues:

> Ailleurs en vain je cherche mon recours.
> Car ta main seule invinciblement forte
> Peult des enfers briser l'avare porte,
> Et me tirer aux rayons du beau jour
> Qui luyt au ciel, ton eternel sejour.[24]

---

[19] *Histoire de la Pléiade*, I, 303.
[20] It should be pointed out that with this poem Du Bellay founded the genre of the religious hymn in France. (V.-L. Saulnier, *Du Bellay*, p. 148.)
[21] *Oeuvres*, IV, 93. [22] *Ibid.*, p. 111.
[23] *Ibid.*, n. 1. [24] *Ibid.*, p. 111.

DEVOTIONAL VERSE

This passage is followed by a brief description of the creation (16 lines) and an account of Original Sin of the same length. Next comes a lengthy commendation of the faith of the ancient Hebrews and a review of Old Testament history. In the stanza that begins at line 119, a little more than halfway through the poem, Du Bellay renounces the "vains soupirs" and the "vaines chansons" of love, and the "songes antiques" which poets are wont to elaborate. He declares his future dedication to a different kind of poetry:

> Car le Seigneur m'a commandé sonner
> Non l'Odissée, ou la grand' Iliade,
> Mais le discours de l'Israëliade.[25]

This intention was, of course, never carried out; it fell by the board after the journey to Rome in 1553, along with the poet's intention to separate his work into sacred and profane categories. The two intentions are certainly related, and together are significant; these resolutions are the outward signs of an inner conflict that remained unresolved throughout the poet's short lifetime. He was a creature of enthusiastic and mercurial moods when he was young, and since he died at the age of thirty-eight one cannot tell what effect the settling quality of middle-age might have had upon the summer of his life.

Very near the end of the poem, following a brief sample of what might have been the germ of an "Israëliade," Du Bellay begs that God free him from the bonds of the flesh as he freed the Hebrews from the Babylonian captivity. He returns momentarily to his earlier despair. But in the final lines he promises sacred verse in return for the forgiveness of his sins.

As a whole, the *Hymne Chrestien* is the ambiguous expression of a troubled man, racked by physical illness and a sense of regret, not to say of guilt, for the truancy of his

[25] *Ibid.*, p. 116.

secular verse, and probably of his way of life. It is an uncertain poem; hope and despair jostle each other, as do history and autobiography. The poem is not cohesive. It is a tormented poem in which the poet is perhaps too much present, too sincere in his apparent hope that he can justify himself through the good works of sacred poetry. His faith here is hardly spotless, and he seems to know it. But it is faith, and the fundamental convictions are intact.

The next religious poem in this collection is the *Monomachie de David et de Goliath*: the pedantic title announces a partial carrying out of his resolution to write a sacred epic on the Old Testament. He invokes the God of War, Jehovah, not on behalf of Greek or Trojan but on behalf of David the shepherd-boy. He cannot, however, remove himself entirely from the ancient epic manner: though he refers to the poems of Homer and Virgil as "les vieux sons d'une fable moizie,"[26] he still has the Seigneur, the Christian God, "Heureusement tonnant à la senestre,"[27] as Zeus was wont to do. The protestation against the ancient epic and the subservience to ancient symbolism remind one of Milton's God weighing Satan in the divine scales, as Zeus in the *Iliad*. But unlike Milton's theft from Homer, Du Bellay's disturbs the reader; his protestations raise the suspicion that his poem is forced, that it is the fulfillment of a promise to write sacred verse, rather than the spontaneous outpourings of sincere conviction. If this were Du Bellay's only religious poem in 1552, R. V. Merrill's remarks mentioned above would seem to have some justification. But it is not, not by any means.

There is also the *Lyre Chrestienne*, which in verse corresponds to the statement in prose in the preface to the *Aeneid* translations, quoted above: that the poet will sing the sacred muse, not the profane; the eternal, not the carnal. The poem is expository. The future satirist of *Les Regrets*

[26] *Ibid.*, p. 129.   [27] *Ibid.*, p. 125.

emerges in the vilification that is heaped upon the Muses of profane verse. All Greek and Roman culture is deplored in contrast to Holy Writ. Here again, in brief, the thought resembles that in *Paradise Regained*, where Milton rejects Greek culture on the same grounds. Du Bellay's protestations are in some sense Protestant. One feels that in 1552 at least he was fully disgusted with the affectations of both classical and Petrarchan verse in France.

The final lines of this poem, in which the poet speaks of his native river, bring contrasting memories of Ronsard on his Loir, playing gaily or dreaming sensuously; or Ronsard again on the banks of the Seine with Genèvre. Du Bellay writes:

> Desormais sur les bordz du Loyre
> Imitant le sainct pouce Hebrieu [David],
> Mes doigtz fredonneront la gloire
> De celuy qui est trois fois Dieu.[28]

The image of Spenser and his Thames arises also—not to mention his Irish rivers—on which he saw visions at the opposite pole from Ronsard's; but not unlike those that Du Bellay wished to see on his river, and wishing, never saw, because it was the Tiber that lay in his future—not the Loyre, and not the Jordan. The surcease of religious verse remained almost complete. That spirit within Du Bellay which had provided the initial impulse, however, remained latent; it spent itself in satire of Roman prelates and the Papal Curia; but it burst out once more near the end of Du Bellay's life after his return from Rome, in a second *Hymne Chrestien* which seems to bring the Frenchman back into close proximity to Spenser, a proximity from which his doubts, his uncertainties, and his truancies had never really removed him.

The *Hymne Chrestien* is a resounding expression of Chris-

[28] *Ibid.*, p. 144.

tian faith, couched partially in language both simple and direct, some of which, as in the devotional sonnets of *L'Olive*, is draw from Latin versions of the Psalms. Henri Chamard points out that this poem has a rapprochement with "les sonnets de *l'Olive* cvii-cxi."[29] This indeed they do have, and apparently at a distance of ten years; for though the date of this poem is unknown, it seems only reasonable to accept the opinion of Chamard, who is without question the leading authority on Du Bellay, and who writes: "J'incline à croire qu'il [the hymn] se rapporte aux derniers temps de la vie du poète."[30]

Granting then that this poem dates from the late fifties, a time when Du Bellay had returned from his sojourn in Rome and was settled in Paris in physical circumstances more comfortable than he had ever known before, it is significant that such a Christian poem should emerge from a more normal background, rather than from one of distress, as in 1552.

The poem opens with a completely orthodox Christian statement, in majestic alexandrines:

O grand Dieu souverain, dont la divinité,
Chrestiens, nous adorons dessous triple unité,
Qui as pour ton palais ceste voute etheree
Ou des Anges te sert la troppe bienheuree,
Qui formas, tout-puissant, le grand tour spacieux
De ce divin chef d'oeuvre admirable à nos yeux,
Qui tournes d'un clin d'ocil ceste grand' masse ronde,
Qui lances de ta main la fouldre par le monde,
Pardonne nous, Seigneur, & nos pechez lavant,
En ta juste fureur ne nous vas poursuyvant.
  Que si tu mets nos faicts en egale balence,
Et veux à la rigueur condamner nostre offense,

[29] *Oeuvres*, ed. Chamard, v, 409, n. 2.
[30] *Ibid.*, p. 407, n. 1.

DEVOTIONAL VERSE

> Qui pourra supporter le terrible courroux
> De ce grand Dieu vivant animé contre nous?[31]

The reference to the guilt of man in line 12 is the first of several that run throughout this poem of 62 lines, and together establish the theme of the Hymn. He goes on to say:

> Car ou est cestuy-là qui ne soit criminel
> Par son propre peché, ou par l'originel?[32]

Here the generalized sin is made personal. A little later man's culpability is reiterated:

> Coupables sommes nous, si ta severité
> Regarde seulement à nostre iniquité.[33]

The idea of redemption is suggested; thirteen lines later it is emphasized and salvation quite properly becomes a possibility but not a certainty. Writing of God the Father, the poet says:

> Qui a peu le Seigneur du ciel faire descendre,
> Et les membres de Dieu dessus la croix estendre,
> Pour laver nos pechez par l'onde & par le sang
> Que le fer inhumain fit sortir de ton flanc.[34]

The emphasis has now shifted to the love and the mercy of God, the substance of the poet's hope. He concludes:

> Affranchis nous, Seigneur, de l'odieux service,
> Qui nous a si long temps fait esclaves du vice:
> Esteins en nous l'ardeur de nostre vain plaisir,
> Et fais de ton amour croistre en nous le desir,
> A fin qu'ayant parfait le cours de nostre vie,
> Lors que devant son Roy l'ame sera ravie,
> De son partage heureux jouissant avec toy,
> Tu luy sois comme Pere, & non pas comme Roy.[35]

---

[31] *Ibid.*, p. 407.   [32] *Ibid.*, pp. 407-408.
[33] *Ibid.*   [34] *Ibid.*, p. 409.   [35] *Ibid.*

DEVOTIONAL VERSE

The whole poem represents not so much a return to the spirit of the devotional sonnets in *L'Olive* and the sacred poems of 1552 as evidence of the latency of such Christian verse in the poet during his years of preoccupation in Rome. Chamard prints this poem in the final volume of Du Bellay's original verse. Surely it would not be wholly unreasonable to suggest that had Du Bellay lived, more poetry of this kind might well have come from his maturity.

The sense of the guilt of man, of his slavery to vice and to vain pleasures, resembles the moral passages in Spenser's *Fowre Hymnes*. The hope that the poet may share happiness and joy with a God who in his mercy will be more Father than King is not unlike Spenser's expression of final hope in the last stanza of the *Faerie Queene* quoted above. As the poets have been united in their pervasive concern for the mutable and the *caduq'*, so, near the end of their lives, they are still united in a hope to rise above the sublunary flux and change to a heaven of beneficent joy.

Let us now proceed to the contrast which Ronsard offers to this view, both during his long life and at the significant time of slowly approaching death.

Ronsard stands almost as far apart from his French fellow poet as he does from the English. Paul Laumonier says of him that "Il a mis dans l'amour terrestre le bonheur suprême et ne s'est point soucié de celui d'au-delà."[36] This generalization is true in the broadest sense, but within its breadth there are modulations that are essential to a full understanding of Ronsard's religious orientation.

In "Les Daimons, A Lancelot Carle," from *Le Premier Livre des Hymnes* (1555), a poem which is interesting chiefly in terms of its references to occult mediaeval superstitions, and its evocation of the paintings of Hieronymus Bosch and

[36] *Ronsard, Poète Lyrique*, p. 499.

DEVOTIONAL VERSE

Pieter Breughel the Elder,[37] there is a perfunctory eight-line prayer at the end, a prayer that initially takes the reader by surprise in a poem of this kind, but that turns out, in the reading, to be self-explanatory:

> O Seigneur Eternel, en qui seul gist ma foy,
> Pour l'honneur de ton nom, de grace donne moy,
> Donne moy que jamais je ne trouve en ma voye
> Ces paniques terreurs, mais, ô Seigneur, envoye
> Loin de la Chrestienté, dans le pays des Turcs,
> Ces Larves, ces Daimons, ces Lares et Lemurs,
> Ou sur le chef de ceux qui oseront mesdire
> Des chansons que j'accorde à ma nouvelle lyre.[38]

The prayer is playful and practical rather than devotional; in the last four lines the tone changes to one of *badinage* between the poet and his good friend God, with whom he is apparently on terms of easy familiarity. This lightness of tone and this sense of ease recall the attitude of Homer toward the gods in the *Iliad* and the *Odyssey*: he could laugh with them, or even at them, because he had no sense of original sin, no Christian sense of the abyss that separates the human and the divine. Though Ronsard cannot laugh at God, he can as it were laugh with Him, something that neither Spenser nor Du Bellay could do; in this he is more classical than they are; his attitude toward God in this poem is colored by neo-paganism.

A similar lighthearted mingling of the pagan and Christian traditions occurs in a short poem entitled "Les Hynnes," which was published in 1587 in a posthumous edition of Ronsard's collected works, the first that he could not edit personally. In this hymn Ronsard urges that since the genre "hymn" itself was first devised for gay celebrations at Greek

---

[37] See Gustave Cohen's note on this poem. *Oeuvres*, II, 1065, and *L'Hymnes des daimons*, ed. Albert Marie Schmidt (Paris, 1939).
[38] *Oeuvres*, II, 174.

religious festivals, the same should be done for Christian holidays. There should be hymns and flower-decked heads and food and wine and song, all in a Christian context. If this were instituted, Ronsard says that "L'age d'or reviendroit."[39] The poem has a pleasing gaiety; the pagan association does not seem really to conflict with Christian belief in any offensive way. A Puritan might find the suggestion in bad taste, but a modern Calabrian or Sicilian would recognize it as a long-established Mediterranean custom.

In the "Hercule Chrestien,"[40] however, the mixture of pagan and Christian is more radical. The poem, as the title indicates, represents an attempt to wed two traditions. Hercules is taken as an analogue of Christ. The poem is fairly long (296 lines). It is interesting to observe that this is approximately the average length of each of Spenser's four hymns. But in his linking of two traditions Ronsard, unlike Spenser, succeeds only in producing a series of parallels that are at best distasteful, and at worst, positively outrageous. It should be pointed out that a comparison such as this between Hercules and Christ was exactly the sort of allegorical interpretation that Dorat had instilled into Ronsard in his years at the collège de Coqueret and that, furthermore, such interpretations of pagan myth in the Renaissance were sanctioned by mediaeval tradition. These facts, however, seem only very slightly to mitigate the outrageousness of the comparison as presented by Ronsard. Certainly Du Bellay was familiar with the traditional allegorical reading of pagan myth, and it is probable that the tradition was not entirely strange to Spenser; yet neither indulged himself in such interpretations in the manner and spirit that characterizes Ronsard's treatment, as I shall attempt to demonstrate.

[39] *Ibid.*, p. 652.
[40] *Ibid.*, pp. 206-212. From *Le Second Livre des Hymnes*, 1556.

The poem begins with a statement that Du Bellay had made four years earlier:

> Est-il pas temps desormais de chanter
> Un vers Chrestien, qui puisse contenter,
> Mieux que devant, les Chrestiennes oreilles?
> Est-il pas temps de chanter les merveilles
> De nostre Dieu? . . .[41]

The echo is clear. It is probably not unreasonable to suspect that Ronsard is consciously following in Du Bellay's footsteps, as he had done with the sonnet form, and with the hymn itself. But he very soon asserts his own individuality.

The hymn continues in this devout vein for eighteen more lines in the last of which Ronsard, speaking of his lyre and his God, writes:

> Je la consacre à tes pieds pour jamais.[42]

This promise, like Du Bellay's, was never fulfilled. But in Du Bellay's case the poem that followed the protestation was in itself a partial fulfillment. Ronsard's "Hercule Chrestien" is a very ambiguous effort to make a poem match a promise. In the twenty-six lines that follow the promise, Ronsard explains at length the various benefits God has conferred upon man. Such a series of acknowledgments would seem to parallel the expressions of obligation that both Du Bellay and Spenser state with simple humility.

Ronsard, however, in the very manner of his acknowledgment, mitigates the expression of his gratitude. The phrases "nous" (to us), "à nous," "pour nous," "pour nous encore," "pour nous encor, pour nous" and "certes nous," occur fifteen times altogether within this short space of twenty-six lines. The third time such a phrase is used, it is "nous, tes elus." As the "pour nous" series builds up, the reader carries

[41] *Ibid.*, p. 206.
[42] *Ibid.*

the idea of election with him, and the repetition impresses him more and more as a restrictive phrase. The absence of humility and the absence of explicit expressions of gratitude make the reader feel that the repetitions are fraught with a sense of election, as if God had made the natural world and had created all of subsequent history simply for the sake of the poet and his coterie. The "nous" seems to carry no implication that it is all of mankind for whom the creation was made. Nor does there seem to be any sense of personal obligation, either explicit or implicit, on the part of Ronsard. All these gifts of God seem in the end to be only a series of factors that bolster an improper sense of self-esteem. From the proximity to Spenser and Du Bellay of the initial lines, the hymn has now moved rather far away from their spirit of humble gratitude to God.

The poem then proceeds to a comparison between events in Greek mythology, and events in *Old Testament* and *New Testament* history. A striking example of such an analogy is the following:

> On les pensoit tous deux estre fils d'hommes,
> Et purs humains ainsi comme nous sommes,
> Et par le peuple enfans les nommoit-on,
> L'un de Joseph, l'autre d'Amphitryon,
> Bien que Jesus eust pris de Dieu son estre,
> Et Jupiter eust fait Hercule naistre.[43]

These lines are a juxtaposition of pagan mythology and Christian belief that seem in the baldness of their statement, in spite of the mediaeval tradition, to place both upon the same level. This was certainly not Ronsard's intention, but one wonders how it may have impressed Odet de Coligny, Cardinal de Chastillon, to whom the hymn was dedicated. The entire poem constitutes a gross lumping together of

[43] *Ibid.*, 209-210.

DEVOTIONAL VERSE

Christian and pagan elements, without discrimination and without taste, as a further quotation will indicate:

> Qu'est-ce d'Hercule ayant repudié
> Sa vieille espouse, à fin d'estre allié
> D'une nouvelle estrangiere conquise,
> Sinon Jesus, qui l'ancienne Eglise
> Des premiers Juifs pour femme refusa,
> Et des Gentils l'Eglise il espousa?
> Hercule print l'habit de son espouse,
> Et Jesus-Christ fist la semblable chouse,
> Car il vestit l'humain habillement
> De son Eglise, et l'aima tellement
> Qu'en sa faveur receut la mort cruelle
> Estant vestu des habillemens d'elle.[44]

It would seem difficult indeed to move any closer to absurdity in an allegorical comparison. Near the end of this long poem, however, there is a final *coup de grace*:

> Hé! qu'est-ce apres d'Hercule qui alla
> Sur le mont d'Oete, et par feu s'immola
> A Jupiter, sinon Christ à son Pere,
> Qui s'immola sur le mont de Calvere?[45]

This is a comparison to please a modern free-thinker, and there can be no explanation for it other than that Ronsard was calloused to its implications. Had he seen the Crucifixion as Du Bellay and Spenser saw it ("O huge and most vnspeakable impression . . ."), he could not have written these lines. But dedicating them as he did, from a minor ecclesiastic to a Cardinal, he must have been madly inspired by his Muses to an unawareness of the appalling disparity in a one-to-one comparison of Hercules' "sacrifice" and that of Christ.[46]

---

[44] *Oeuvres*, II, 211.   [45] *Ibid.*, pp. 211-212.
[46] Frances A. Yates in *The French Academies of the Sixteenth Century* takes a radically different view of this poem. She places her emphasis on

226

DEVOTIONAL VERSE

These are by no means the only examples of indecorous comparison in this hymn, but they are sufficient to indicate the direction that Ronsard's religious verse could take in the fifties.

Further evidence of the ambiguity of Ronsard's religious attitude is to be found in a poem that is called, curiously enough, "Le Chat."[47] As a whole, the poem is a miscellaneous assortment of elements that seem incompatible but which are linked with an air of plausibility for the apparent purpose of reaching a conclusion which is false and self-contradictory within the total context of the poem. It is worth a careful examination not only because it is interesting, like all of Ronsard's poetry (except for what he wrote at court order), but because it is representative of the way in which Ronsard's mind so often teemed with a superabundance of partly digested ideas, in this case Christian, pantheistic, Platonic, materialistic, naturalistic, and superstitious.

The poem opens with thirty-four lines on the immortality of the soul, lines as eloquently and as sincerely devotional as any that Ronsard ever wrote. Speaking of God as "ce grand Tout," the life-giving soul, he writes:

Car de tout estre elle est commencement.[48]

He goes on to say:

---

the mediaeval tradition, insists on the validity of the comparison of Hercules and Christ, and chides both modern critics and Protestant critics contemporary with Ronsard for their misunderstanding of the poem. She concludes, "Ronsard's use of mythology gains vigor from its organic connection with his living Catholic faith" (pp. 192-193). A view contrary to the above, which emphasizes not the synthesis of pagan and Catholic but its division, is taken by Morris Bishop in *Ronsard, Prince of Poets* (pp. 168-171, 251). While Bishop's book is not studded with scholarly footnotes, it nevertheless seems to contain as sensitive a judgment of Ronsard as that propounded by Miss Yates; as sensitive, certainly, and in my own opinion, more perceptive and more free of prejudice.

[47] *Ibid., Le Premier Livre des Poemes* (1567), pp. 331-336.
[48] *Ibid*, p 332.

DEVOTIONAL VERSE

> Des Elemens et de ceste ame infuse
> Nous sommes nez; le corps mortel qui s'use
> Par trait de temps des Elemens est fait;
> De Dieu vient l'ame, et comme il est parfait,
> L'ame est parfaite, intouchable, immortelle,
> Comme venant d'une essence eternelle;
> L'ame n'a donc commencement ny bout,
> Car la partie ensuit tousjours le tout.
> Par la vertu de ceste ame meslée
> Tourne le Ciel à la voûte estoilée,
> La mer ondoye, et la terre produit . . .[49]

These descriptive lines indicate a view of the nature of man of the world with which no Christian, Catholic or Protestant, could quarrel, and this in spite of certain Platonic overtones. There is nothing in the poem up to this point (line 21), except the title, to lead the reader to believe that it might not be a hymn as sincerely and as fundamentally Christian as any of Spenser's hymns. But almost immediately, describing the earth, Ronsard shows a preoccupation that would perhaps not be significant in this context if it did not also permeate the rest of his work. He refers to the earth as:

> Mere benigne, à gros tetins, feconde,
> Au large sein . . .[50]

While there is nothing unusual in the metaphor of the Earth as Mother, with the proper motherly equipment, it is the use of "tetins" and its repetition in "sein" that marks the stress: it reminds one of the myriad references in the sonnets to this part of the female anatomy, and of other references, like this one, obtrusive in their emphasis. For Ronsard, the earth is sexual, and in something more than a merely symbolic fashion; life itself is a symphonic orchestration of sexual motifs.

[49] *Ibid.*   [50] *Ibid.*

It is precisely at this point too that the poet descends from the metaphysical and places his feet firmly upon more familiar ground. He next mentions diamonds, pearls, rubies, and sapphires as created things in which some occult power may reside. He has a double interest in precious stones: superstitious and materialistic. He does not regard them as terrestrial baubles, as would Spenser in a philosophical poem, or as decorations more fitting for a heavenly hierarchy. He fingers them sensuously, and at the same time wonders what power the "grand Tout" has infused into them.

Next he mentions the gift of prophecy that was conferred upon the ancient Hebrews, and explains this by an odd interpretation of a Roman maxim. The physical circumstances of this world make it possible that:

> Les Regions, l'air et le corps y servent,
> Qui l'ame saine en un corps sain conservent;
> Car d'autant plus que bien sain est le corps,
> L'ame se monstre et reluist par dehors.[51]

Thus there may be augurs, prophets, Sibyls; and the poet turns at once from the Hebrew prophets to augury from animals and plants. He then recounts the story of a laurel plant that he himself had fostered but that he saw uprooted by a "Démon." The result of this occult mischance was slow to follow, but, he writes:

> Deux mois apres, un cheval qui rua,
> De coups de pied l'un de mes gens tua,
> Luy escrageant d'une playe cruelle
> Bien loin du teste la gluante cervelle . . .[52]

The description of this accident is strikingly vivid; the last line produces an immediate physical sensation in the

[51] *Ibid*. The Latin reference is to Juvenal, *Satires*, x, l. 356.
[52] *Ibid*., p. 334.

reader, as from a physical stimulus. At the short distance of some sixty lines from the theological or metaphysical beginning of the poem, the sticky brain that is splashed far from the skull is especially striking. A few lines later, he states that eleven months after the riding accident he was racked with fever. He regards this still as a result of the withering of the uprooted laurel plant, in spite of the lengthy time-lag between the two events. He does not dwell on his illness, however, but passes abruptly to the question of the position of cats among the ancient Egyptians. Here we have the justification for the title of the poem, the title which seemed strange in terms of the opening lines, but began to appear more rational with the mention of augury from animals.

Having pointed out that cats were highly honored in Egypt, Ronsard says:

> Homme ne vit qui tant haysse au monde
> Les chats que moy d'une haine profonde...[53]

and a little later:

> Le chat devin miaulant signifie
> Une fascheuse et longue maladie.

The poet has now reached the crux of his real subject, that cats *par excellence* possess occult and maleficent powers. He is now about to state his pantheistic conclusion. He will set, or perhaps better, he will root his feet deeply in his native, animal earth, the land to which he belongs, almost as do the trees, the vegetable gardens, and the roses of Vendômois:

> Enfans de terre: ainsin il plaist à Dieu,
> Qui ses bontez eslargist en tout lieu,
> Et pour aimer sa pauvre creature,
> A sous nos pieds prosterné la nature

[53] See Appendix v for a note on the relationship of Ronsard to Du Bellay in respect to cats.

Des animaux, autant que l'homme est fait
Des animaux l'animal plus parfait.[54]

Passing from Christian theology slightly colored by Platonic metaphysics, through pagan philosophy and divination, through mediaeval superstition, and a kind of pantheistic view of the created world, Ronsard has reached the conclusion that man is an animal of a type higher than other animals. Man's position is thus undermined as it is in Montaigne's *Apologie de Raimond Sebond*;[55] to be sure, Ronsard finds nature "Prosterné" at man's feet, whereas Montaigne finds man himself prostrated in the animal world, but nevertheless the breakdown in the dignity of man is similar. The connection with God has become tenuous in its dilution.

Ronsard's poem is a compendium of uncoordinated and dissonant beliefs, linked by what we would today call free association. The doctrinal confusion and the Christian heterodoxy that has been alleged against Spenser's *Fowre Hymnes* appears mild and wholly inoffensive beside this "gallimaufry" of received and unreconciled ideas. The moral difference, as usual, is obvious; but further, even though it is generally agreed that neither poet was a thinker, it is easy to see which was the poorer metaphysician. There is a certain consistency in Du Bellay's aspiring idealism, though it seldom transcends the world; and there is a consistency in Spenser's idealism, more often transcendent. But there is no consistency in this poem of Ronsard's; it comprises too many elements without comprehending them.

There is, however, in all of Ronsard a consistency of another kind, not of aspiration, but of exuberant vitality. His more serious and longer poems surge with a glowing energy, a teeming plethora of ideas that the poet cannot tame or

[54] *Ibid.*, p. 336.
[55] *Essais*, ed. Albert Thibaudet (Paris, 1946), II, 12.

DEVOTIONAL VERSE

reconcile intellectually but that he can confine in flowing periods of verse that give an impression of containment, an impression that the poet has overpowered and mastered them. Under analysis they fall apart once more, having been held in an equilibrium that is magically specious. But the vitality and sheer energy of Ronsard's verse is even more powerful than that of Spenser, much more so than much of Du Bellay's.

We now come to Ronsard's *Les Derniers Vers* published posthumously in 1586 by his friend Claude Binet, which contains the poems written at the end of the poet's life, including those written *in extremis*; and others that had remained unpublished during his lifetime, but appeared in the *Oeuvres* of 1587. Let us first examine two of the latter, which are pertinent to the subject of this chapter.

In a poem called "Elegie II, A Philippes Des-Portes, Chartrain," Ronsard discourses for eighty-eight lines on the finality of death and on the certainty of the death of fame. Since the poem is dedicated to Ronsard's arch-rival, it is obvious that the poet has an ax to grind, but his expression of personal feeling about the future, the present, and about death, is in accord with the rest of his work and is such a succinct and forthright representation of an important aspect of Ronsard that it is worth quoting here:

> Quant à moy, j'aime mieux trente ans de renommee,
> Jouyssant du Soleil, que mille ans de renom
> Lors que la fosse creuse enfouyra mon nom,
> Et lors que nostre forme en une autre se change,
> L'homme qui ne sent plus n'a besoin de loüange.[56]

On one level, Ronsard is privately letting off steam at Desportes, who is stealing his reputation. But on another level he is saying *Carpe diem!* with his usual sincerity. What is most interesting is that between the "fosse creuse" and

[56] *Ibid.*, p. 649.

the "ne sent plus," which are so vivid, there is a reference to the theory concerning cyclical regeneration of form. In this context it seems almost meaningless because of its juxtaposition with the end of all sensation and the open grave. This theory of generation from corruption which as a vague philosophical idea had seemed to offer a certain consolation to Ronsard, which had seemed to be an element of happy permanence in a dazzling world of flux, now appears as the yawning "fosse." Whereas the theory itself bears a resemblance to that expressed by Spenser in the Garden of Adonis Canto of the *Faerie Queene* (III, vi), in the present context the mythical value is emptied of all meaning in face of the absolutcness of death. Ronsard ends this elegy with the line:

    Le futur est douteux, le present est certain.

Regeneration and the consideration of death as merely another aspect of life, a transitory phase between one life and another, here seem to fall into the "douteux" category. Spenser on the other hand takes up his early statement of the same theory at the very end of the *Faerie Queene*, in the second of the two final *Cantos of Mutabilitie*. Jove speaks to Mutabilitie:

> I well consider all that ye haue sayd,
> And find that all things stedfastnes doe hate
> And changed be: yet being rightly wayd
> They are not changed from their first estate;
> But by their change their being doe dilate:
> And turning to themselues at length againe,
> Doe worke their owne perfection so by fate . . .
>   (VII, vii, 58)

Here Spenser infuses the theory with Christian implications. Ronsard in his context remains as classical as a Greek or Roman untainted by either Plato or Plotinus.

The second example from the posthumous edition of

DEVOTIONAL VERSE

1587 is in sharp contrast to almost everything else that Ronsard wrote, and yet at the same time it is typically Ronsardian. "Hynne XII, Des Peres de Famille, A Monsieur S. Blaise, Sur le Chant 'Te rogamus, audi nos,' " is a simple, appealing, melodious song, based on the repetition of "Garde nous" at the beginning of the stanza and the refrain, "Je te pris, escoute nous" at the end. It is a poem of some length (134 lines) and of much charm. The subject is religious, and the diction is that of simple rustic sincerity. Almost any stanza is as worthy of quotation as its neighbor:

> Garde nos petits vergers,
> Et nos jardins potagers,
> Nos maisons et nos familles,
> Enfans, et femmes, et filles,
> Et leur donne bons espous;
> Je te prie, escoute nous.[57]

Ronsard has turned his talent for light verse to the cause of prayer, diversion for the author of so many famous light secular poems ("La Salade," the early "Odes," the "Blasons," the "Chansons"). The poem does not seem contrived: it appears to emanate from a limpidly clear religious conviction. It may be hardly fair to ask, rhetorically, why the publication of the poem had to await the death of the author.

Finally, we come to the *Derniers Vers*, written *in extremis*, intimate, and profoundly revealing. This group of nine short poems sums up the whole enormous body of work that occupied a long and prolific lifetime. I shall pay particular attention to two of the sonnets, and to these must be added the final three couplets that Ronsard dictated a few hours before his death.

"Sonnet v" is immediately touching because of the poet's

[57] *Oeuvres*, II, 659.

situation: he is dying, and he knows he is dying. He says in the first quatrain:

> Quoy! mon ame, dors-tu engourdie en ta masse?
> La trompette a sonné, serre bagage, et va
> Le chemin deserté que Jesus-Christ trouva,
> Quand tout mouillé de sang racheta nostre race.[58]

One has the impression that the poet enjoys a sense of being saved, that in travelling Christ's road he is going to the same destination. The next lines say that the road is "facheux," thorny, narrow, "tracé de peu de gens." These lines exhibit a somewhat unseemly concern for the difficulties of the journey, as if the poet deserved something better; though in the circumstances Ronsard had more than sufficient excuse for emphasizing his suffering. The sestet twice repeats the statement that one must finish what one begins, that one should not look back when the hand is on the plow. There is no prayer, only an exhortation to courage. There is no expression of personal guilt or sin, explicit or implicit, or even of unworthiness. Ronsard seems to feel that God, unlike the French Kings and the nobles, is absolutely just, and will naturally recognize his merits, and give him the due that has so often been denied him in the terrestrial world.

This is the only one of the six final sonnets that is without at least one classical allusion. The remainder refer to Ixion, to Lethe, to Cocytus, and to Apollo, among others. The

[58] *Ibid.*, p. 636. This and the sixth sonnet were both dictated to "un de ses religieux" on the day before Ronsard's death, according to Claude Binet (*Critical Edition of the Discours de la vie de Pierre de Ronsard par Claude Binet*, ed. Helene M. Evers [Philadelphia, 1905], p. 88) Binet is at some pains to point out that Ronsard died "chrestiennement." (See pp. 82 and 115 especially.) He protests so much that one's suspicions would be aroused even if Miss Evers had not devoted the introduction of her critical edition of the *Vie* to a thorough destruction of the veracity of Binet's account not only of the death scenes but of much that is contained in the rest of the book.

chief complaint is that there is no relief from pain; sleep cannot be induced even by opium. Of the remaining poems, one is an epitaph which summarizes the poet's career: he has brought the Muses back to France, but he has been unable to resist Death; his soul is for God, his body for the earth.

The first of the *Derniers Vers*, called "Stances," is a combination of a complaint of pain, and a *carpe diem* poem in the classical manner. The last, "A Son Ame," is a coy poem in six couplets constructed in Ronsard's early style:

>Amelette Ronsardelette,
>Mignonnelette, doucelette...[59]

It ends in the classical manner, urging the passer-by not to trouble the rest of the sleeping corpse. But coy and artificial though it is, one feels a certain sadness that it should be a death-bed poem.

Of the nine poems, only the epitaph quoted above, and the two sonnets which will be quoted below, mention God or Jesus Christ. The emphasis in all the poems is upon the pain, and upon the classical allusions which are pertinent to suffering and to death. "Sonnet III" contains the only outcry:

>Miscericorde, ô Dieu! ô Dieu, ne me consume
>A faulte de dormir...[60]

These are the only lines that constitute an appeal to God, that resemble a prayer; and they are isolated between references to the "ruisseau d'Oubly" and complaints about the inefficacy of opium in any form.

"Sonnet VI," the last of the sonnets, is a weighted combination of classical allusions in the octave and Christian allusions in the sestet, not wholly pure, because even at the end the classics adhere to Ronsard from long habit:

[59] *Ibid.*, p. 637.   [60] *Ibid.*, p. 635.

DEVOTIONAL VERSE

Il faut laisser maisons et vergers et jardins,
Vaisselles et vaisseaux que l'artisan burine,
Et chanter son obseque en la facon du Cygne,
Qui chante son trespas sur les bors Maeandrins.
  C'est fait, j'ay devidé le cours de mes destins,
J'ay vescu, j'ay rendu mon nom assez insigne,
Ma plume vole au Ciel pour estre quelque signe,
Loin des appas mondains qui trompent les plus fins.
  Heureux qui ne fut onc, plus heureux qui retourne
En rien comme il estoit, plus heureux qui sejourne,
D'homme fait nouvel ange, aupres de Jesus-Christ,
  Laissant pourrir çà-bas sa despouille de boüe,
Dont le Sort, la Fortune, et le Destin se joüe,
Franc des liens du corps pour n'estre qu'un esprit.[61]

Here the poet sees himself already an "esprit," free of the vicissitudes of a life he dearly loved; yet even as a "nouvel ange, aupres de Jesus-Christ" he seems not to be entirely without regret, though he will continue to exhort himself not to look back at "le Sort, la Fortune, et le Destin," those strange and fascinating forces which he both loved and hated.

Ronsard's last poem was written at the poet's dictation within a few hours of his death. It is the best commentary that one could possibly find on the *Derniers Vers*:

> Toute la viande qui entre
> Dans le goufre ingrat de ce ventre,
> Incontinent sans fruict resort,
> Mais la belle science exquise
> Que par l'ouye j'ay apprise
> M'accompagne jusqu'à la mort.[62]

Here again at what is apparently the very last moment, is the dual concern with the physical aspect of death and

[61] *Ibid.*, p. 637.   [62] *Ibid.*, p. 667.

the persistent awareness of personal value. We have no such final poems from either Spenser or Du Bellay; but if we did, it would not be difficult to guess what tone they would take.

For Spenser possessed a measured sense of his own value, and his poetry expresses a temperate hope of salvation. Du Bellay was a proud man in respect to his work as a member of the Brigade and the Pléiade, but while his sense of self-esteem was not always as proper as was Spenser's, it was never as exaggerated as Ronsard's. Unlike Ronsard's, it was always coupled with a strong sense of humility and contrition.

A final quotation from Ronsard will demonstrate the consistent placidity of his heart, the sense of self-satisfaction and of complacency. This is the characteristic that distinguishes him most sharply from both Spenser and Du Bellay, and from the tradition of restless seeking that has always marked the truly ardent Christian:

> Je suis ce que je suis, ma conscience est bonne,
> Et Dieu, à qui le coeur des hommes apparoist,
> Sonde seul ma pensée et seul la cognoist.[63]

The poem dates from 1562, when the poet was at the height of his fame and in the prime of his life. He died hating the frigid court, overshadowed by the rising Desportes, challenged by Du Bartas. But even so he saw no reason for a humble appeal in his poetry to God, with whom he had always been on such good terms, and who he suspected would not let him down in the last analysis.

There is little doubt that such a final attitude would have disturbed Du Bellay. There is no doubt at all that it would have shocked Spenser. One thinks of the statement of Paul Laumonier quoted above, that Ronsard placed his hope for supreme happiness in this terrestrial world and not in a

[63] *Ibid.*, "Discours, A Loys des Masures," p. 571.

world above. Except for the momentary outcry at the end he was content in the world of mutability: he could settle down in the corruscating flux of earthly affairs and feel no wish to rise above it. In this, and in the cultivation of the Self, the "Moi," Ronsard achieved a classically quiet heart; with a minimal aspiration toward the changeless and the immutable, he was able to take root in mutability and to extract a vivid joy from flux.

In this respect Ronsard is far more typical than Du Bellay of an extraordinarily important part of the Renaissance in sixteenth century France. For it was in this century that one aspect of French humanism began to separate itself from the Christian tradition of life as a perpetual quest. Ronsard and Montaigne in the second half of the century represent this nascent split. The capacity of man to remain rooted in the physical world was a prerequisite to a scientific reexamination of matter, and it was not by accident that the withdrawal of France's greatest poet and greatest master of prose from the life of questing Christian aspiration preceded the development of science in the seventeenth century, a development that was radically to alter the religious orientation of most Europeans from that time forward.

Thus in the most general sense Spenser and Du Bellay may be said to represent the Renaissance that looked backward through humanism to the Christian tradition and upward in aspiration toward God; while Ronsard represents that new element in the Renaissance that, while it looked backward to the classics, looked forward to a scientific world and downward to matter itself and was content to enjoy the flux and to set a natural, not a supernatural order upon mutability.

CONCLUSION

As the Renaissance period itself throughout Europe (including England), may be divided into phases, so also may its expression, or effect, within individual persons: artists, poets, essayists, scholars, and writers of fiction. Renaissance humanist studies at the time of their inception in Italy, France, and England were all Christian in the sense that the purpose of such study was the purification and rejuvenation of existing doctrines of the Catholic and universal Church. Humanism was supplementary to Christianity.

Boccaccio in the fourteenth century recanted his truancy from the straight and narrow Christian path and contemplated burning his *Decamerone*. Petrarch's break from what is called the Mediaeval synthesis was not entirely clean or wholehearted. It took another century of humanist studies before Machiavelli and Ariosto could immerse themselves in this-worldliness without serious *arrières pensées*.

Similarly in France at the beginning of the sixteenth century the humanism of Budé, though pedantic, was nevertheless Christian. Marguerite de Navarre apologized for her *Héptameron* with her final work, the *Mirroir de l'âme pécheresse* (which, incidentally, the young Princess who was later to be Queen Elizabeth translated into a beautifully handwritten copy for her last stepmother). Bishop Briçonnet and Lefèvre d'Etaples were Christians first and humanists afterwards.

Finally, the humanism of the first Englishmen of the Renaissance—Grocyn, Linacre, Colet, and More, was likewise Catholic and universal, wholly and indubitably Christian. Their knowledge of the classics is in no sense a substitute for Christianity. The twentieth century canonization of Thomas More is a late recognition of this fact.

CONCLUSION

It is in the second phase of the Renaissance in each country that the split begins. This is not to say that the humanism of the early phase was in every case consistently Christian but that a general movement toward carelessness, toward a *nonchalance du salut*, becomes increasingly evident with the passage of time and with the trend from scholarly to creative humanist literature.

Ronsard and Du Bellay were second-generation humanists in France. The Reformation began before either was born. The Italian Renaissance was very nearly over during their childhood; Copernicus published his discoveries during their youth. Montaigne's doubts were published throughout Ronsard's maturity, and Galileo's activities began shortly after Ronsard's death. The Renaissance had begun to change from a mainly single and undivided movement. The Reformation widened a split which had been implicit in Italy and was to become explicit in France and in England. On the continent the emphasis shifted toward a growing naturalism, but in England, at least during Spenser's lifetime, Protestantism placed a renewed emphasis on the Christian interpretation of classical studies. Christian humanism was to survive in Spenser and beyond him to Milton; but in the time-gap between these two poets, and more especially after the Restoration, it was to become diluted and was never again to win a creative exponent of the stature of either of these two towering Renaissance figures.

Perhaps the dual aspect of Renaissance culture may now be distinguished with greater exactitude, although the division in neither France nor England is sharp and salient in the sixteenth century but, on the contrary, is subtle and underground rather than overt and plain.

Ronsard, for instance, must not be seen as a conscious skeptic who erected a tight bulwark between his real beliefs and a formalized, automatic, and almost empty Christianity which he set aside as insurance against his dying day. Nor

CONCLUSION

must Spenser be seen as a militant Christian poet whose full integration of humanist study and Christian belief is a defensive act, performed as it were to hold back a flood of skeptical thought that seemed to be moving toward him. Ronsard did not know that in a later historical perspective his enthusiastic concern with the outside world might be considered to contain a significant germ of the future; nor could Spenser be aware that he was the next to last great English poet fully in possession of the Christian humanist balance between his religion and his classical learning, and that even Milton would be forced by the progress of science to cope more explicitly with the question of man's *libido sciendi*.[1]

The Christians of the Renaissance who accorded such a warm welcome to the revival of classical studies could not be expected to have any awareness of the ultimate meaning of the separate investigation of man as man, and of the world as matter, terrestrial, and comprehensible by the terrestrial mind of man himself. The poets and essayists and other writers of the sixteenth century who are often represented today as crypto-skeptics would probably be as astounded at the culture of the twentieth century as the Christian humanists of the same period would be appalled. If Ronsard was a man who showed no great burning desire to rule and control his own emotions and passions, he, however, was not one of those who longed to subdue nature and establish human sovereignty over it. He did not wish to dominate; he wished to enjoy. It was for Bacon, Descartes, and Galileo in the next century to seek this hegemony over the material world. Yet there is nevertheless a connection between the view of nature taken by Ronsard the poet and by Descartes the scientist.

There is no such connection between Spenser and Bacon.

[1] See, for example, *Paradise Lost*, Books v, vii, and especially Raphael's speeches in Book viii.

CONCLUSION

Spenser established a sovereignty over himself, a control that was conspicuously lacking in Bacon, "the Moses of scientific progress,"[2] who sought to establish a method for man's conquest not so much of himself as of outside nature. The world of the future, of course, belonged to Bacon, and as Spenser leads to Milton, so Bacon leads to Newton. Similarly, the work of Descartes points toward Bayle and Fontenelle; the Cartesian spirit separated from its metaphysics dominates the French eighteenth century.[3] The capacity, not so much to separate out metaphysics, as the negative capacity to fail to integrate metaphysics, is first seen in the sixteenth century in Montaigne and in Ronsard.

Thus Spenser seems to come near the end of the old aspect of the dual Renaissance, while Ronsard stands at the beginning of the new. A similar beginning may be distinguished in England also, at the end of Spenser's lifetime, in the overweening characters of Marlowe's plays and in the negative, occasionally dispassionate view of Christian morals in Shakespeare, in whose *Antony and Cleopatra* "a guilty love is, in part at least, pardoned because of its force and splendor."[4] As Lilian Winstanley says in her sharp contrast between Shakespeare's treatment of Antony and Cleopatra and the Christian ethics of Spenser: we may see "the difference between the unadulterated spirit of the Renaissance and the spirit of the Renaissance touched with Puritanism."[5] Such a contrast, however, needs to be qualified by the reminder that Spenser's Christian humanism, although Protestant, is in the main line of Catholic Christian humanism, and though after the Reformation it flourishes chiefly in

---

[2] Douglas Bush, *The Renaissance and English Humanism*, p. 94. In regard to Bacon, I refer to his personal misconduct.

[3] Léon Brunschvicg, *Descartes et Pascal, Lecteurs de Montaigne* (New York, Paris, 1944), p. 222.

[4] Lilian Winstanley, "Spenser and Puritanism II," *MLQ* 3 (1900), p. 106.

[5] *Ibid.*, p. 105.

CONCLUSION

England, its provenance is not wholly English or Puritan, but international or, in an older sense, universal.

Sixteenth century skepticism in France and later in England, therefore, is not positive, active, or militant. It is negative and inactive, preparing the way for the scientific point of view not by the rejection of Christian metaphysics but by a casual and negligent acceptance of Christian convention.

It finds its origin, perhaps, in a similar negligence of Christianity coupled with an intense involvement in the business of this world which had been visible in Italy early in the sixteenth century, in such a play as Machiavelli's *Mandragola* (1512) and in Ariosto's *Orlando Furioso* (1516).

The humanist Renaissance which is still with us today was originally an unselfconscious liberation of mankind from authority. It was not in itself a revolutionary act of excessive pride, but it led to such acts over the course of centuries, acts which have been a continuous cause of concern to men whose loyalties have never deviated from the original Christian humanism of the early Renaissance. For, as I have said, all humanism, whether in Italy, France, or England, was originally Christian and its goal, as Douglas Bush has written, was "a universal church . . . as the channel of a purified universal faith."[6] It was only later that nationalism and skepticism obtruded themselves upon the early idealism.

The difference between the humanism that one finds in Ronsard, and the Christian humanism of Spenser, may be seen in their attitudes toward the Horatian idea of the *dulce* and the *utile* in poetry. Ronsard read the classics for pleasure; he read them seriously, of course, but it was nevertheless the *dulce* that attracted him: the creative, the joyous, as against the didactic or moral, the *utile*. His own work on

[6] *The Thought and Culture of the English Renaissance*, ed. Elizabeth M. Nugent (Cambridge, 1956), introduction to Part 1 by Douglas Bush, p. 5.

CONCLUSION

the whole is a fervent acknowledgment of the sweetness in literature and in life. His famous sonnet on reading Homer, from the *Continuation des Amours* of 1555, is an appropriate example of this double interest in the *douceur* of the past and of the present:

> Je veux lire en trois jours l'Iliade d'Homere,
> Et pource, Corydon, ferme bien l'huis sur moy . . .[7]

He wishes to be alone with the Greek poet. Yet at the end of the sonnet he bids his servant admit at once any messenger from Cassandre. The pleasure of reading must give way to the greater pleasure of loving.

In similar fashion in the later phase of the Italian Renaissance, Machiavelli, in exile and engaged in the composition of that most modern of sixteenth century political treatises, *Il Principe*, would sit alone many an evening, dressed in his finest clothes, reading the wisdom of the Roman classics with love, respect, and humility[8]—a more antique figure than the average Christian humanist and at the same time almost as modern as the twentieth century skeptic.

In contrast, Spenser's work shows a predominant concern with the moral and educational value of literature. His interest in the classics is mainly in their teaching. He is a didactic poet himself, and didactic in a Christian context; he is as concerned as were Plato and Cicero with the moral usefulness of literature. This is not to deny that he worked long and hard over the element of the *dulce* in his work, or to deny that he valued this element. He did indeed, as hundreds of beautifully wrought lines will testify. But for him the heart of his work was earnestly *utile*, whereas for Ronsard, though many long poems are unquestionably didactic and *utile*, the heart of his work is the *dulce*, uncontrolled

---

[7] *Oeuvres*, ed. Cohen, II, 820.
[8] See Niccolò Machiavelli, *Il Principe*, ed. Luigi Russo (Florence, 1951), pp. 29-30.

CONCLUSION

and unaffected by any discernible vestige of Christian morality.

It has been said at the very beginning of this study that the difference between these English and French poets may to a large extent be measured in their attitudes toward love, death, and mutability. But these criteria have shown not so much a purely national difference, as the anonymous author in the *Edinburgh Review* maintained,[9] as a temperamental divergency, and in the widest sense a divergency within the European Renaissance itself.

The Edinburgh author (whose anonymity requires such unfortunate periphrases) makes some further distinctions that are interesting for their acuity, though their patriotic bias sometimes diminishes their validity, if not their wit: "The Pléiade wrote lines—and very dull they often are—in praise of virtue, but the English made poems about goodness."[10] Such a statement, sweeping though it is, draws a nice contrast between Ronsard and Spenser, as also does the following: "The English, more slipshod in thought and more imaginative, heavier-hearted and more strenuous, have the sense of mystery strong within them; dwell rather on what may be than what is. They are idealists—gloomy idealists—where the French are cheerful pessimists."[11] He goes on to say that for the English, God represented "mystery—the Intellectual Power who harmonized mind, passion and goodness—the unity of all things. To the Frenchman he was either a natural force, or an aristocratic First person—precise, distinguished and remote, clad not in clouds but in dogma."[12]

These broad distinctions, based on a much wider survey of Elizabethan and Pléiade writers than this essay has attempted, may be said very generally to hold true for Ronsard

---

[9] "The Pléiade and the Elizabethans," *The Edinburgh Review or Critical Journal*, 205 (1907).
[10] *Ibid.*, p. 376.   [11] *Ibid.*, p. 377.   [12] *Ibid.*, pp. 377-378.

CONCLUSION

and for Spenser. But Du Bellay will not fit the pattern. His attitude toward love, more honorable than Ronsard's (though no more honest) falls short of the unified concept of chastity that Spenser achieved in the *Faerie Queene* and in the *Epithalamion*, a marriage on earth of all that is best in the spiritual and physical configuration of man and woman.[13]

But Du Bellay and Spenser are at one with each other in their consideration of mutability and their profound personal concern with it. Here there is no national or racial boundary, but a real concomitance of feeling: Du Bellay the Frenchman is a "gloomy idealist." In religion also he is "heavier-hearted and more strenuous." He is a Christian humanist *manqué*, and this is probably a partial source of his bitter pessimism. Had he lived in an English atmosphere instead of in the corruptions of Rome; or had he grown to maturity amid the arguments of Episcopalianism and Puritanism at Cambridge, instead of amid the irresponsible enthusiasms of the Brigade, his bitterness might have sweetened from pessimism into melancholy. But poetry would have lost a note that has never since been duplicated.

The primary concern of all Du Bellay's verse was personal and interior; he writes about himself, as did Montaigne. Indeed, Pierre Villey makes an interesting parallel between the development of Du Bellay and of Montaigne, from servility to Latin, and then to Italian literature, to the idea of imitation, and thence to mature work "tout à fait personelle,"[14] in Du Bellay's case, his *Regrets*. One cannot say, however, as Villey seems to imply, that Du Bellay found

---

[13] See W. L. Renwick's *Edmund Spenser:* "Heavenly Love and Earthly are not eternal antagonists, but complements one of the other, and so the story of Chastity is a love-story ... for chastity is nothing other than truth and honour in the question of sex, sanctified by the spirit of God, Who is Love, and serving the world as His agent" (p. 167).

[14] Pierre Villey, *Les Sources & L'Evolution des Essais de Montaigne* (Paris, 1933), p. 545.

CONCLUSION

himself at last in the *Regrets* as Montaigne found himself in the "Third Book" of his *Essais*. Du Bellay, in spite of the technical achievement represented by the variety of his work, in spite of his return to more comfortable circumstances in Paris after his last Roman stay, never truly found himself in either his life or his work. He remained until the end essentially *dépaysé*, a nostalgic wanderer in another land than his own:

> Heureux qui, comme Ulysse, a fait un beau voyage,
>   Ou comme cestuy là qui conquit la toison,
>   Et puis est retourné, plein d'usage & raison,
>   Vivre entre ses parents le reste de son aage!
> Quand revoiray-je, helas, de mon petit village
>   Fumer la cheminee, & en quelle saison
>   Revoiray-je le clos de ma pauvre maison,
>   Qui m'est une province, & beaucoup d'avantage?
> Plus me plaist le sejour qu'ont basty mes ayeux,
>   Que des palais romains le front audacieux,
>   Plus que le marbre dur me plaist l'ardoise fine,
> Plus mon Loyre gaulois que le Tybre latin,
>   Plus mon petit Lyré que le mont Palatin,
>   Et plus que l'air marin la doulceur angevine.[15]

Du Bellay could never forget that the handwriting was on the wall. His childhood must have been lonely, orphaned as he was at the age of nine, but nevertheless the land of his forebears, his "petit Lyré," haunted his maturity. He sought an Anjou that he could never find because it was not in this world; and the "doulceur Angevine" for which he longed was the bitter-sweet memory of an irrecoverable past. The timeless poignancy of Du Bellay's poetry does not depend on the geographical location of Rome or of Anjou, or on a record of his journeys, but on the gulf that exists between human desires and human attainments. Du Bellay

[15] Joachim du Bellay, *Les Regrets*, ed. E. Droz (Lille and Genève, 1947), "Sonnet XXXI," p. 56.

CONCLUSION

could never go home again, and from this terrible fact he made great poetry.

Like Du Bellay, and yet in contrast to him, Ronsard in all his work was primarily concerned with himself. His concern, however, is external, not inward. Ronsard is the center of his own world. He conquered this world very early, and he continued to reign over it until the very last moment. His perpetual self-confidence, his enduring *joie de vivre*, is spoiled only by isolated and intermittent outbursts of anger, or hurt pride, or, as he grows older, of protest against a physical body which had served him long and well because in spite of his excesses he had cherished its health and vigor. On the whole, Ronsard's life and his work approximate a classically serene acceptance of life. He lived as he taught; his life and his poetry are full of sunlight. For thirty-five short years he both lived and wrote at fever pitch, producing a body of verse unparalleled in French literature for richness, energy, and variety until Victor Hugo wrote many years later in the nineteenth century.

Ronsard is the love poet *par excellence*: not only love of woman, but love of the natural world and love of men, if not of mankind. He is the spiritual brother of all who from the beginning of time have awakened with a feeling of exuberance on a cool summer morning, with the scent of earth and flowers and the songs of birds in the air; awakened to the certain knowledge that life is good and true and beautiful, and that nothing else is of any importance whatever. He writes in "La Salade," from *Le Premier Livre des Poemes*, a book dedicated to Mary Queen of Scots, whom he loved, and who gave him a portrait of herself:

> Lave ta main, qu'elle soit belle et nette,
> Resveille toy, apporte une serviette;
> Une salade amasson, et faison
> Part à nos ans des fruicts de la saison.

CONCLUSION

> Là, recoursant jusqu'au coude nos bras,
> Nous laverons nos herbes à main pleine
> Au cours sacré de ma belle fontaine;
> La blanchirons de sel en mainte part,
> L'arrouserons de vinaigre rosart,
> L'engresserons de l'huile de Provence:
> L'huile qui vient aux oliviers de France
> Rompt l'estomac, et ne vaut du tout rien.[16]

Similarly, in *Le Quatriesme Livre des Odes*, "Ode XXI" he revels gaily and gloriously in nature:

> Dieu vous gard, messagers fidelles
> Du printemps, vistes arondelles,
> Huppes, cocus, rossignolets,
> Tourtres, et vous oiseaux sauvages
> Qui de cent sortes de ramages
> Animez les bois verdelets.
>
> Dieu vous gard, belles paquerettes,
> Belles roses, belles fleurettes,
> Et vous, boutons jadis cognus
> Du sang d'Ajax et de Narcisse;
> Et vous, thym, anis et melisse,
> Vous soyez les bien revenus.
>
> Dieu vous gard, troupe diaprée
> Des papillons, qui par la prée
> Les douces herbes suçotez;
> Et vous, nouvel essain d'abeilles,
> Qui les fleurs jaunes et vermeilles
> De vostre bouche baisotez.
>
> Cent mille fois je re-salue
> Vostre belle et douce venue.
> O que j'aime ceste saison
> Et ce doux caquet des rivages,

---

[16] *Oeuvres*, ed. Cohen, II, 347-348

CONCLUSION

> Au prix des vents et des orages
> Qui m'enfermoyent en la maison![17]

Even when he was shut up indoors, Ronsard was nourished by field and stream, by the very bosom of nature herself. One accords him glady, indeed with gratitude, that, nourished at a thousand miscellaneous breasts, natural and metaphorical, he transmuted this nourishment into a multitude of fine poems, all as truly inspired as he himself said they were.

Spenser now, who has been our chief subject, maintained in his maturity an equilibrium between the external and the inward that neither Ronsard nor Du Bellay could achieve. Spenser was concerned with himself, but always with humility or with a just self-esteem. He avoided excess; excess of melancholy, which possessed Du Bellay, excess of prideful exuberance, which sometimes made a fool of Ronsard. He lived the ancient Greek principle of $\mu\eta\delta\epsilon\nu\ \mathring{\alpha}\gamma\alpha\nu$, keeping the letter of the pagan principle but imbuing it with a Christian meaning, as Milton later did through Raphael in *Paradise Lost*. Spenser achieved in both his life and in his work an harmoniousness that was truly classical, combined with a tension that was truly Christian. That he is alleged to have died in poverty,[18] and that his great long poem remained unfinished, surely does not diminish the magnitude of his achievement, or make him less worthy of the final peace for which he earnestly hoped and, if any man may ever deserve it, so richly earned.

Although Spenser, perhaps significantly, never mentions Ronsard, he wrote a poem to Du Bellay. In "L'Envoy" of the *Rvines of Rome: by Bellay*, he writes:

> *Bellay*, first garland of free Poësie
> That *France* brought forth, though fruitfull of braue wits,

[17] *Ibid.*, I, 559-560.
[18] For a significant denial of this traditional rumor, see Josephine W. Bennett, "Did Spenser Starve?" *MLN* 52 (1937), pp. 400-401.

CONCLUSION

> Well worthie thou of immortalitie,
> That long hast traueld by thy learned writs,
>   Olde *Rome* out of her ashes to reuiue,
> And giue a second life to dead decayes:
> Needes must he all eternitie suruiue,
> That can to other giue eternall dayes.
>   Thy dayes therefore are endless, and thy prayse
> Excelling all, that euer went before . . .

Spenser was generous, as any English writer of the Renaissance should be. One cannot count his debt to Du Bellay, who was probably one of the first poets in any vernacular to rouse in Spenser a youthful enthusiasm for poetry that was never to wane throughout his lifetime, in spite of the distractions of public affairs and the perpetual discouragement of slow preferment. And far more than Du Bellay excelled all French poets that ever went before him, so Spenser excelled his own masters, except only the first, Chaucer.

Without Ronsard and Du Bellay on the Continent, neither Spenser nor English poetry in the latter half of the sixteenth century could have become what we know it to be. Critical theory of poetry, and the classic concept of the poet as seer, as *vates*, came from Italy, and from Rome and Greece as well as from France. But this magnificent burst of vernacular melody that issued from the Pléiade was perhaps more inspiring than anything else to the young Elizabethans. Emulation is never as actively excited by theory as it is by successful practice, and if Spenser sought to overgo Ariosto and Tasso in his epic, he as surely had Ronsard and Du Bellay in his mind when he tried the great variety of lyric genres into which they, and only they, had penetrated in a vernacular language. The woods that answer and the echo that rings in Spenser's lyric verse are intimately related to the forest of Gastine and the echoing caves along both Loire

CONCLUSION

and Loir. But Spenser's poetry is much more than an echo of these Frenchmen, and of many other poets. His own immortality rests upon the loveliness and the chaste purity of his own verse, running soft and sweet as his own "Themmes," an important part of the mainstream of English poetry.

Poetry, like the Renaissance itself, divided during the seventeenth century, although the lines of division were not parallel. The Pléiade and Spenser fell into neglect, each in its own land. The caves and fields and streams and even the soul of man came into the care of geologists, agronomists, hydrodynamists, and psychologists. Only in the nineteenth century did poetry recover and, recovering, recognize once more Spenser and Ronsard and Du Bellay. One may hope with Spenser that each may now enjoy eternal rest, not so much in the new security of his worldly reputation as in the bosom of the great Sabbaoth; hope with Ronsard that each may live again in the recurrent cycle, to give new joy to a new age; and hope with Du Bellay that the least futile of terrestrial monuments may be that divine gift, Poetry.

APPENDIX I

Up to the present time it has been assumed that Edmund Spenser translated all fifteen sonnets of the section entitled "Sonets" in Van der Noot's *A Theatre for Worldlings* (1569). I wish to suggest strongly that while there seems to be little doubt that Spenser translated the first eleven of these sonnets (from originals by Joachim du Bellay), he did not translate the last four, the so-called "sonets" from the Apocalypse, the originals of which were presumably written by Van der Noot himself.

Even a casual reading of the fifteen sonnets reveals that whereas the first eleven sometimes, in short passages, read quite well and rarely very badly, the last four are jerky because of a super-abundance of end-stops; the lines are rarely enjambed; and the meaning is often obscure. This distinction is to some extent present in the French originals, but the discrepancy between the French of Du Bellay and that of Van der Noot is substantially less than that between the English acknowledged to be by Spenser and that of the last four sonnets upon which I seek to cast a reasoned suspicion.

Statistical analysis of language and punctuation is the only procedure available in view of the complete lack of external evidence. I shall compare the translations of the sonnets from Du Bellay, and the "sonets" from the Apocalypse, in terms of (1) the ratio of stops in the French text to stops in the English text (2) the ratio of deviation from strict line-for-line translation in the first eleven sonnets and in the last four, and, finally (3), the ratio of mistranslations in the first eleven sonnets and in the last four.

Among stops I include full stops, colons, question marks, and exclamation marks. The following analysis should demonstrate the striking discrepancy between the translations of the two groups of poems.

The total number of stops in the *Le Theatre* (1568) text

of Du Bellay's sonnets is forty, whereas the total stops in Spenser's text of A *Theatre* is fifty-six. This makes the average number of stops per sonnet in the *Le Theatre* text 3.6, and the average number in A *Theatre* 5.0. The percentage increase of stops in Spenser's text over that of Du Bellay is thus 38.9.

Next, the total number of stops in the *Le Theatre* text of the Apocalypse sonnets is twenty-one, whereas the total number in the English text is thirty-seven. This in turn makes the average number of stops per sonnet in the *Le Theatre* text of the Apocalypse sonnets 5.2 and the average in the translation 9.2. Thus the percentage of increase of stops in the English translation is 76.9. This last percentage is remarkably higher than that of 38.9 in the translations acknowledged to be by Spenser.

There is an additional factor in the analysis of stops that gives more weight to the above discrepancy. In the sonnets translated by Spenser there is only one case of three *terminal* stops in sequence (in "Sonet" 4), and in the other ten sonnets there are never more than two in sequence. In the translation of the Van der Noot Apocalypse text, on the other hand, there are six terminal stops in sequence in the first sonnet, five in sequence in the second sonnet, three in sequence in the third, and four in sequence in the fourth. Such a plethora of pauses of course destroys the fluency of the verse, and since the English text of the "sonets" from the Apocalypse has in the case of every sonnet except one a substantially greater number of stops than any of the translations of Du Bellay acknowledged to be by Spenser, this stilted and restrictive overpunctuation in the Apocalypse sonnets would seem to point to a translator other than Spenser.

Next, there is the question of comparative deviation from strict line-for-line translation, a method which is followed with considerable rigor by Spenser in the first eleven sonnets

APPENDICES

but which is relaxed to a suspicious extent in the next four. By a deviation from line-for-line translation I mean the displacement from the original French line of two or more words and their inclusion in either the antecedent or the subsequent line. An example of this occurs in the second sonnet translated from Du Bellay:

> Sur la croppe d'un mont je vis une fabrique,
> De cent brasses de hault, cent colŏnes d'un rond ...

which Spenser translates:

> On hill, a frame an hundred cubites hie
> I saw, an hundred pillers eke about ...

The only other case of deviation is the well-known example in the eighth sonnet from Du Bellay, in which Spenser not only shifts phrases from line to line but manufactures a whole line and a half to translate a half line by Du Bellay, and in addition transposes two lines from the French. The result is that this "Sonnet" has fifteen lines:

> Si sest Hydre nouveau, digne de cent Hercules,
> Foisonnant en sept chefs de vices monstrueux,
> Ne m'engendroit encor à ces bords tortueux,
> Tant de cruels Nerons, & tant de Caligules.

Spenser, in his only moment of real aberration in these eleven sonnets, translates this:

> But this new Hydra mete to be assailde
> Euen by an hundred such as Hercules,
> With seuen springing heds of monstrous crimes,
> So many Neroes and Caligulaes
> Must still bring forth to rule this croked shore.

This is a blatant example of the abandonment of the strict line-for-line method which, except in the instances cited, has been maintained throughout all the rest of the eleven sonnets from Du Bellay.

APPENDICES

In sum, the deviation from line-for-line translation in the first eleven sonnets amounts to only four lines out of a total of a hundred and fifty-four. This constitutes a deviation of 2.5 per cent. The total deviations of this kind in the four "Sonets" from the Apocalypse amount to nineteen lines in a total of fifty-six, making a percentage of 33.9, a truly remarkable departure, of which I shall cite the most glaring example, from the first sonnet from the Apocalypse:

> A celle d'un Lion, & le Dragon puissant
> Luy donna son pouuoir: Et je vy tout sanglant
> Une teste blessee à la veoir merueillable.
> Ce Dragon adoré, l'on crioyt haut & cler,
> Qui est sembleble à elle? & la poeult resister?

The following translation of these lines not only demonstrates the variation from line-for-line translation but also provides an example of the addition of terminal stops where they do not exist in the French text:

> Feete of a beare, a Lions throte she had.
> The mightie Dragon gaue to hir his power.
> One of hir heads yet there I did espie.
> Still freshly bleeding of a grieuous wounde.
> One cride aloud. What one is like (quod he)
> This honoured Dragon, or may him withstande?

These lines constitute a radical departure from the habits of translation observed in the eleven Du Bellay sonnets.[1] And as well as technical points already considered, they yield, as a sort of extra dividend, an excellent example of inexact translation: "a grieuous wounde" for the French "blessee à la veoir merueillable."

[1] A full reference list of deviations from line-for-line translation follows: in the sonnets from Du Bellay, Sonnet II, lines 1-2, and Sonnet VIII, lines 11-12. In the sonnets from the Apocalypse, Sonnet I, lines 2-3, 5-10, 12-14; Sonnet III, lines 1-2, 6-7; and in Sonnet IV, lines 1-2 and 9-10.

APPENDICES

The two conclusions above point to conspicuously different methods of work in the translation of the Du Bellay sonnets and those from the Apocalypse. The following differentiation will concern the incidence of mistranslations.

There are only three cases of mistranslation in the first eleven sonnets of Du Bellay, and even these may well proceed from causes other than ignorance of the French language. The first occurs in the fourth sonnet, and has been pointed out by Louis S. Friedland as a mistake:[2]

> A chaque face estoit proctraicte [sic] une victoire,
> Portant ailes au doz, auec habit Nymphal . . .

which Spenser translates:

> On eche side portraide was a victorie.
> With golden wings in habite of a Nymph.

It is an open question whether this was a mistake. The French says nothing about "golden" wings; it says that the wings were on the back, and it is hardly likely that Spenser read "doz" to mean "d'or." Perhaps he thought it unnecessary to mention that the wings were on the back, since wings are rarely anywhere else, and perhaps he thought it appropriate that the wings of a victory should be golden. But the important point is that this failure literally to translate "doz" may quite as well be due to the exigencies of the metre or to the creative instincts of the young poet as to carelessness or to ignorance of French.

In my own counting of mistranslations, I have restricted the count to exclude all instances, both in Spenser's translations from Du Bellay and in the translations from the "sonets" from the Apocalypse, that deviate from a literal rendering of the French for reasons that are clearly and distinctly literary. All dubious instances have been counted,

---

[2] "Spenser's Early Poems" (unpublished Ph.D. dissertation, New York University, 1912), p. 23/33.

259

APPENDICES

such as the one quoted above. In addition to that one, I have found only two others, one of which is probably the result of awkwardness rather than of ignorance, the other almost certainly a misprint rather than a mistranslation.[3] Thus there is not, in the translations from Du Bellay, the plenitude of inexact lines to which Friedland makes reference. His multiplicity of instances is probably intended to apply to the *Sonets* from the Apocalypse, which, as I shall now demonstrate, are rich in garbled lines.

The second *Sonet* from the Apocalypse contains in its first six lines three examples of mistranslations which are all more clearly mistakes than any in the first eleven sonnets from Du Bellay:

> Une femme en apres sur une beste assise
> Je vis deuant mes yeux, de migrainne couleur:
> De blaspheme la nom deffroy, aussi l'horreur
> Escorte luy faisoit: sept testes je rauise,
> Et dix cornes aussi pleine de mignardise:
> Ceste femme apparoit d'escarlate l'honneur . . .

The translation is as follows:

> I saw a Woman sitting on a beast
> Before mine eyes, of Orenge colour hew:
> Horrour and dreadfull name of blasphemie
> Filde hir with pride. And seuen heads I saw,
> Ten hornes also the stately beast did beare.
> She seemde with glorie of the scarlet faire.[4]

A close analysis of these lines reveals first that the words "en apres" in the French have been omitted in the English. In the second line, the word "migrainne" is translated

[3] The first example is line 3 of the seventh sonnet from Du Bellay; the second, and last, is line 3 of the tenth sonnet from Du Bellay. The latter is almost beyond doubt a misprint.

[4] It should be pointed out parenthetically that this sonnet in lines 5-11 has six terminal stops to match only one in the French text.

260

APPENDICES

"Orenge," which is a mistake proceeding from ignorance either of French or of English. The word "migrainne" means an off-red color and is clearly correlated in the French text with the word "escarlate" in the sixth line, which is correctly translated. The color red is essential to the symbolic meaning of the whole sonnet, dealing as it does with the Whore of Babylon who is drunk upon the blood of martyrs, who implies in turn the Church of Rome, with which a brilliant and bloody red was traditionally associated by Protestants. Thus the word "Orenge" fails to convey the implications of the French.[5]

Next, in the fourth line, "Escorte luy faisoit" is translated "Filde hir with pride," an obvious mistranslation. Furthermore, in the fifth line, the phrase "plaine de mignardise" is rendered by the word "stately," which has neither the literal meaning of "mignardise" nor any of its disagreeable associations.[6] And finally, the sixth line is a far freer rendering of the French than any line in the sonnets from Du Bellay translated by Spenser.

The above sonnet contains the largest single aggregate of mistranslations among the four "sonets" from the Apocalypse. There is in addition the mistake to which I have referred (p. 258), which occurs in the first sonnet. The third is remarkably clear of errors, standing among the four as the only one which achieves a degree of exactitude comparable to Spenser's translation of most of the first eleven. The fourth sonnet has two mistranslations, neither of which is

[5] The French word "migrainne" in this sense is related to the word "grenade," which means pomegranate. *The New English Dictionary* describes the pulp of the pomegranate as of a "reddish" color, and the flower as "usually scarlet."

[6] See the standard Spenser *Concordance* for examples of his use of the word "stately." From forty-three examples the overwhelming preponderance of evidence is that Spenser did not normally use the word to imply pompous pride and that the word does not, of itself, convey a pejorative meaning. (*A Concordance of the Poems of Edmund Spenser*, compiled and edited by Charles Grosvenor Osgood [Washington, 1915], p. 184.)

APPENDICES

as striking as those discussed at length above.[7] Thus there are seven errors of translation in the Apocalypse sonnets, an average of 1.75 per sonnet, as against three errors, each of smaller magnitude and of more dubious quality, in the eleven sonnets from Du Bellay, an average of .27 per sonnet.

A tabular form will clarify my conclusions:

Increase in stops in translation assumed to be Spenser's	Increase in stops in suspicious translation
38.9%	76.9%
Deviation from strict line-for-line translation in Spenser's text	Similar deviation in suspicious translation
2.5%	33.9%
Mistranslations in Spenser, average per sonnet	Mistranslations in suspicious text, average per sonnet
.27	1.75

This information, statistical or mathematical as it is and based as it is on internal evidence, is itself suspect; it is of necessity subject to the same limitations that govern all pseudo-scientific investigations in which the methods of science are applied to a field in which scientific truth may and often does differ from the real truth. The above table is based on opinion, on judgment, not on objective fact.

But how much more subjective and how much more suspicious is the critical opinion that bases the ascription of these poor poems to Spenser on "human probability,"[8] or on a vague reluctance to face the possibility that Van der Noot may have employed another poet inferior to the young Spenser,[9] or on a weak theory that Spenser revised a putative English version by Van der Noot.[10]

Mine are conjectures, however, and something more than conjecture is needed to exonerate Spenser positively from

[7] The first in the fourth sonnet occurs in line 11; the second in line 13.
[8] Harold Stein, *Studies in Spenser's Complaints* (New York, 1934), p. 118.
[9] C. S. Lewis, *English Literature in the Sixteenth Century* (Oxford, 1954), p. 359.
[10] W. J. B. Pienaar, "Edmund Spenser and Jonker van der Noot," *English Studies* 8 (1926), pp. 33-44.

APPENDICES

the responsibility for verse which on the whole is worse than anything else in the Spenser canon. The fruit of this analysis can amount to nothing more than a purely tentative indication that there are certain reasons for believing that Edmund Spenser was never so bad a poet as was the translator of the "sonets" from the Apocalypse.

APPENDIX II

It should be noted that there has been a recent interpretation of *The Ruines of Time* in conjunction with the *Antiquitez de Rome* that differs capitally from all previous readings. William R. Orwen in an article entitled "Spenser and the Serpent of Division"[1] takes both poems as examples primarily of political propaganda in verse. He believes that *The Ruines of Time* is part of a literary movement which grew out of the Elizabethan fear of civil strife consequent upon an uncertain succession.[2] While this anxiety may have something to do with the lament of Verlame in the first section of the poem, and with the elegies in the second section, it nevertheless seems hard to reconcile the long passages on poetic immortality and the terminal visions with such a narrow view. Orwen writes that Spenser's poem "expresses political hopes and anxieties by means of several literary devices."[3]

Such a totally nonliterary opinion seems to reverse the elements of a just estimate. Similarly, Orwen disposes of the *Antiquitez de Rome* as literature: "When Du Bellay's *Antiquitez* and *Songe* are set in the political background of the religious wars of the [sic] sixteenth century France they clearly seem propaganda against the civil disorder which broke out shortly after their publication in 1558."[4] This apparently means that a poem published in 1558, but written in the middle fifties of the century in Rome, and not unnaturally concerned with reflections on mutability and the vanity of earthly works, directly stimulated by the ruins of the Eternal City and the corruption of the Papal Curia and its entourage, is in fact a propagandistic poem intended to discourage or obviate the civil war of religion which broke out in France in the sixties.

[1] SP 38 (1941), pp. 198-210.
[2] *Ibid.*, p. 202.   [3] *Ibid.*, p. 198.   [4] *Ibid.*, p. 207.

APPENDICES

The association of concern for a shaky and uncertain royal succession, and fear of armed religious strife, on the common basis of civil war, is at best tenuous, and is tenuous *a fortiori* in view of the time-lag between the composition of Du Bellay's sonnets and the outbreak of armed conflict in France. Orwen's interpretation is specious in its affirmation of a connection between *The Ruines of Time* and the *Antiquitez de Rome* that is extraliterary, and in the simultaneous failure to take account of other and more striking connections: temperamental, literary, and philosophical.

APPENDIX III

IN THE dedication to the four poems, Spenser says that the first two hymns were written "in the greener times" of his youth. He says further of the earlier poems: "I resolued at least to amend, and by way of retraction to reforme them, making in stead of those two Hymnes of earthly and naturall love and beautie, two others of heauenly and celestiall."

These statements have been understood by Josephine W. Bennett to mean that the early poems were changed to eliminate the "naturall" and the "earthly" and conform to the "heauenly" and the "celestiall." This is indeed what Spenser says, quite literally. But in view of the texts of the early poems as we have them, full of an earthiness compared to the later hymns, which are far aloft in heavenliness, this would seem to be a time to suspect the poet's simple, literal statement.

Mrs. Bennett uses this phrase of Spenser's to argue that the hymns are not two pairs but instead are "a single, carefully constructed poem, in four parts."[1]

While I do not wish to involve this study in an argument so remote from its central subject, I nevertheless should point out that the preoccupation with the beloved and with the worldly situation in the first two hymns seems to substantiate Spenser's statement about "greener times" and seems further to lead one to believe that whatever corrections were made did not radically alter the earthbound orientation of the poems. These hymns seem not to have been as thoroughly purged as Mrs. Bennett's keen argument would lead one to believe.

[1] "The Theme of Spenser's Fowre Hymnes," SP 37 (1931), p. 48.

APPENDIX IV

R. V. MERRILL maintains that Héroët's *La Parfaicte Amy* is "the best example of . . . true Platonism which appears in French before Joachim's time."[1] He states further that an understanding of this poem is of capital importance to any insight into Du Bellay's final concept of neo-Platonism. I quote his summary of the poem: "The poem is an analysis and justification, supposed to be given by a lady of gentle breeding, of her love for her 'ami.' Far from being inspired by any physical attraction or by consideration or worldly advantage, this love is directed purely and solely to the spiritual qualities of the beloved person; it does away with all thoughts of uncertainty, coquetry or jealousy. Even separation through death could never cause the lady to swerve from her content and the adoration of ther [sic] lover, for whose sake she would perfect herself in philosophical studies until finally her soul should return to be united with his own amid the eternal beauty of heaven."[2]

Merrill links this poem very closely with Du Bellay's "Elegie" in the second edition (1553) of the *Recueil de Poesie* (1552). Such a joining seems to be entirely justified on certain grounds, as an examination of Du Bellay's poem will indicate. It is true, furthermore, that this "Elegie" of Du Bellay's is the last poem he wrote that could be called neo-Platonic in some sense. Merrill represents it, however, as the culmination of Du Bellay's Platonism, a lofty point from which he progressed no further, as a consequence of his disruptive journey to Rome—a lofty point indeed which he was never again to reach at all. I believe that such a statement constitutes a misreading of Du Bellay's development.

The "Elegie" is a monologue of 114 lines, spoken by a

[1] *The Platonism of Joachim du Bellay*, p. 126.
[2] *Ibid.*, pp. 124-125.

lady to a gentleman with whom she has long been in love. She reminds him that he had often urged her to marry; why he could not marry her himself is not indicated. The poem is an announcement of her forthcoming marriage to a third person, and an explanation of her understanding of the triangular situation that will be created. She explains:

> Ce n'est un joug qui captive mon ame
> Soubz le lyen d'une impudique flamme:
> Ce n'est un joug qui dompte mon desir
> Soubz l'aiguillon d'un follastre plaisir:
> Mais c'est un joug d'amitié conjugale,
> Qui d'une foy honnestement egale
> Separe en deux celle chaste amitié
> Dont vous avez la premiere moitié.[3]

These are lines with a moral emphasis; they are in the manner of Spenser rather than in the ecstatic manner of the neo-Platonists. The lady sets her new love above the level of the lewd and lustful, the "impudique"; she characterizes it as an "amitié conjugale"; she says that "honnestement" it divides a friendship that has been "chaste." The stress that is put on the decency of both relationships is very like Spenser; it is very like the theory of true love in the earthly hymns, very like some of the intersexual relationships in the *Faerie Queene*, such as that of Britomart to Sir Arthegall on the one hand and to her male comrades-in-arms on the other. In this poem woman is on a par with man; she is not far above him, as in the courtly Provençal-Petrarchan tradition, nor far below as she is in the more common and less attenuated mediaeval tradition: she is equal, as she is in Spenser. This is a triple union whose propriety is ideal in the sense that this ideal can and should be realized in this world.

Du Bellay's lady goes on to assure her old friend that she

[3] *Oeuvres*, ed. Chamard, IV, 217.

APPENDICES

will love his "vertu" no less for her marriage. She urges him not to fear:

> ... que d'un coeur honnestement lié
> L'honneste amour soit jamais oublié.[4]

And, near the end of the poem, she sums up:

> O doncq' heureux, heureux double lyen,
> Qui deux espris unis avecq' le mien,
> Double lyen, qui d'une double force
> Plus fermement que la corde retorse
> N'estreinct le faiz, enschaines dedans moy
> Troys coeurs unis d'une eternelle foy ...[5]

She points out in conclusion that virtuous loves are not mutually exclusive:

> Le feu ne peult habiter nullement
> Avecques l'eau, son contraire element·
> Les animaux de diverse nature
> Ne prennent point ensemble nourriture.
> Mais un amour saigement entrepris,
> Qui sur vertu son fondement ha pris,
> Ne crainct jamais l'amour qui lui ressemble,
> Car la vertu à la vertu s'assemble.[6]

These long quotations should indicate beyond any reasonable doubt that this poem is concerned emphatically with the honesty and virtuousness of this triple love. The resemblance of the poem to Héroët's *La Parfaicte Amy* summarized above seems to be rather superficial: that both poems are spoken by a lady, that both analyze and justify some kind of love. There is nothing in the "Elegie" that hints at anything such as separation through death, or the transcendence of love over death through the pursuit of

[4] *Ibid.*, p. 218. [5] *Ibid.*, p. 219.
[6] *Ibid.*

APPENDICES

philosophical studies which will lead to a perfection that is prerequisite to postmortal union in a heaven of souls.

Héroët was dealing in neo-Platonic fashion with a moral idealism that is very much of this world. The connection of the morality of Du Bellay's elegy with neo-Platonism is very tenuous, but its connection with the morality that Spenser expresses in the first two of his *Fowre Hymnes*, in *The Teares of the Muses* and in *The Ruines of Time*, is strikingly close. It may be said without exaggeration that the moral tenor of the "Elegie" is far closer to Spenser after Du Bellay than to Héroët before him. If to some extent Du Bellay reflects Héroët, to a greater extent in this poem his moral view foreshadows Spenser's. And it is unlikely that Spenser, who had so much admiration for his French senior and precursor, was ignorant of this poem.

R. V. Merrill makes two categorical statements about the "Elegie" that seem on the one hand to assert its Platonism and on the other hand to narrow the definition of the word to such an extent as to make the statements almost meaningless. He says first that this poem is "the fullest expression in his [Du Bellay's] history of a love which is Platonic in the social sense of the term."[7] What "social sense" means is somewhat obscure, for surely Plato's theory of love was concerned with the individual, and not with society. Indeed, it is open to some question whether the discourse of Pietro Bembo in Castiglione's *Courtier*—social courtesy book that it is—is a "social" discourse.

Merrill's second assertion is that Du Bellay, in this "Elegie" in which his Platonism reaches "its peak . . . holds fast to the fundamentally Platonic principle: that love of a human being must be exalted by the vision of an object transcending that being itself. . . ."[8] The transcendent object in this case is apparently "honneste amour"; and Merrill

[7] *Platonism*, p. 142.
[8] *Ibid.*, p. 147.

goes on to say that during the seven years of life that remained to Du Bellay after the writing of this poem, his conception of "honneste amour" gradually expanded to become "honneur" and "vertu."[9]

One is initially struck by the fact that while honesty (in the French sense of uprightness) in love, and virtuousness, and honor, do indeed transcend the individual in this world, they are not transcendent in the Platonic sense; they are not like τὸ καλόν in the *Symposium*. They are ideals in the modern meaning of the word, not ideas in the Platonic meaning. They are neither truly ultimate, nor are they fully transcendent. They are terrestrial goals attainable in this life, and the "Elegie" is the poetic image of their attainment.

Not only has the unsatisfied yearning of the Petrarchans been abandoned in this poem; the poem abandons also the yearning of the neo-Platonists. The poem represents the highest possible type of sublunary perfection; it pushes mutability as far back as it can, but it does not eliminate it because it cannot. A truly neo-Platonic poem would entirely escape the sublunary world, ascending beyond it to an ecstatic union with the perfectly immutable. This Du Bellay does not do, either in this poem or elsewhere.

It seems to me highly probable that the cause of Du Bellay's failure to mount the conventional neo-Platonic ladder to union with the absolute lies in the poet's fundamentally simple belief in Christianity, and in a growing embarrassment or sense of guilt for connecting paganism in any form with Christian thought. Du Bellay's view of the ultimate reality is more closely associated with the view Spenser expresses in the final unfinished Canto at the end of the *Faerie Queene*; it is a purely Christian view, to be reached through Christian faith, and not through Plato, Diotima, or Socrates.

[9] *Ibid.*, p. 148.

APPENDIX V

It deserves to be noted for its symbolic significance that Du Bellay loved cats as much as Ronsard hated them. See his poem of 202 lines, "Epitaphe D'Un Chat."[1] This long mock-epic epitaph indicates by its affectionate references to the beauty and prowess of Belaud, Du Bellay's Roman mouser, that he loved cats for straightforward reasons, as more recently T. S. Eliot has demonstrated a similar affection in similar terms. Du Bellay was not concerned either with the occult qualities of contemporary cats or with their deification by the Egyptians; he was not superstitious, perhaps because he was more of a city-man than Ronsard, who was always close to his land, and according to Lebègue picked up his superstitions from local peasants.[2]

This divergent attitude toward cats may perhaps be considered significant of the whole relationship between the two poets. Du Bellay writes this epitaph in the light style of Ronsard, with the use of many rhyming diminutives to produce a lilting sound. He has written and will write many expressions of love for Ronsard, calling him among other things, half of his soul, or the greater part of the Pléiade.[3] Ronsard, on the other hand, accords only formal praise to Du Bellay during his lifetime,[4] and returns no warmth. After Du Bellay's death he uses Du Bellay as an example of a poet who deserved more patronage than he got, in a poem addressed to the King's mother, Catherine de Medicis.[5] Here he is clearly more interested in himself than in the deceased poet.

But the longest and most extraordinary reference to Du Bellay is in the "Discours a Loys des Masures" (1562), in

[1] *Oeuvres*, ed. Chamard, v, 103-111.
[2] *Ronsard*, p. 15.
[3] *Oeuvres*, v, 360; *Les Regrets*, viii.
[4] *Oeuvres*, ed., Cohen, ii, 314-315.
[5] *Ibid.*, i, 866.

APPENDICES

which Ronsard has a vision of his dead friend in an advanced and fully described state of decomposition.[6] Here Du Bellay bids Ronsard fear God above all things, and Ronsard admits what he had never acknowledged during Du Bellay's lifetime, that his fellow poet had preceded him in the initiation of new genres.[7]

It is as if the superstitious Ronsard had been a prey to dreams of guilt, which he sought to exorcise in verse.

[6] *Ibid.*, II, 570-573.
[7] See Cohen's note, II, 1100.

INDEX

Academie de Musique et de Poësie, 42, 43
Addison, Joseph, 90
Adonis, 149, 195
Aeschylus, 14
Aesop, 115
Alberti, Leon Battista, 40
Aquinas, Thomas, 5, 82
Arcueil, 16
"Areopagus," 53
Ariosto, Lodovico, 240, 252
Aristotle, 5, 37, 88, 182, 204
Ascham, Roger, 20, 52, 56
Augé-Chiquet, Mathieu, 40, 42, 43
Augustine, St., 5, 7, 134n, 160
Autels, Guillaume des, 9n

Bacon, Francis, 126n, 242, 243
Baïf, Jean-Antoine de, 9n, 13, 15, 16-17, 18, 39-62
Baïf, Lazare de, 12, 13, 14
Bartas, Salluste du, 238
Bayle, Pierre, 243
Bellay, Cardinal Jean du, 13, 184, 202
Bellay, Guillaume du, 13, 14
BELLAY, JOACHIM DU (c. 1522-1560): character of verse, 20, 21, 27-28, 32-34, 41-42, 46, 47, 51, 95, 97, 111, 112, 116-117, 121-123, 171, 178, 179, 182, 199, 210, 211, 213, 219, 247, 248-249, 255-263, 272; classical influence, 17, 44, 47, 71, 88, 97, 100, 111, 175; deafness, 50n, 122, 212; debt to French poets, 15, 17-18, 44, 45, 133-134, 173-174, 182, humanism, 7, 8, 13, 241-247; immortality of poetry, 98-104; milieu, 3, 13-14, 16-17, 21, 98, 102, 110, 111, 134, 173, 201, 247-249, 264-265; paganism, 16-17, 103-104, 199, 203, 210, 271; Platonic influence, 133-135, 170, 171-200, 214, 267-271; relation to Renaissance, viii-ix, 7-9, 13, 124, 129, 239, 241; religious orientation, 8, 16-17, 30-31, 102, 104, 118, 119, 135-136, 174-185, 199, 201-272; rivalry with Ronsard, 51, 224-225, 272-273; temperament, 17-18, 27, 47, 70-73, 107, 112, 114-123, 130-132, 176, 210-216, 288; theory of poetry, 32, 33, 37, 38-39, 41, 44-46, 130, 85n, 102, 133, 172-183, 210, 247, 267-271; view of nature, 18, 218; view of society, 200; view of time and mutability, 97, 98, 99, 102, 104, 112, 120, 122n, 125, 239, 247, 264, 270

WORKS

Antiquitez de Rome, viii, 20, 26-36, 51, 93-98, 111-112, 116-122, 264-265; *Le Songe*, viii, 20, 25-36, 51, 54, 93-95, 114-123, 209-210, 255-263
Autres Oeuvres Poétiques: "A Salmon Macrin," 100; "Contre les envieux poëtes" (Ronsard), 99
Deffence, 20-21, 28, 33, 34, 38n, 45, 51, 52, 69, 72, 73, 80, 87, 98, 199
Discours au Roy sur la poësie, 38n, 98
"Énéide" de Vergile, 183-184, 217
Inventions de l'autheur: Complainte du desesperé, 122n, 214, *Hymne Chrestien* (1552), 184, 214-219; *Monomachie*, 184, 217; *Lyre Chrestienne*, 102, 174, 184, 203, 214, 217-218; *L'Honneste Amour*, 102, 174-184, 199, 203; *Adieux aux Muses*, 74-75
Jeux Rustiques, 210; "XIX, À Olivier de Magni," 38n, 74; "Contre les Pétrarquistes," 38n; "Epitaphe d'un chat," 272; "À Bertran Bergier," 38n
Musagnoeomachie, 68-73, 79
L'Olive, 28, 46n, 51, 100, 102,

275

INDEX

171, 175-177, 184, 199, 211-214, 219, 221
  Poemata, 47
  Poésies Diverses, 210; "xix, À Pierre de Ronsard," 38n, 272; "xxx, Hymne Chrestien," 218-221
  Poëte courtisan, 68-69, 71, 72, 73, 79
  Recueil de Poësie, 51; Premier édition, 1552 (*see Inventions*), 172-175, 184; Second édition, 1553, "Elegie xix, La Mort de Palinure," 172, 175, 183, 184, 267-271
  Regrets, 28, 29, 51, 96, 120, 122, 182, 210, 217, 247-248; Sonnets VIII (Ronsard), 272; XXI, 248; XLIII, 73; LXXVII, 122; LXXXIV, 85n; XCIV, 85n; XCVII (À Remy Doulcin), 85n; CXLVII (Ronsard), 38n; CLIV (Baïf), 73; CXC (François Ier), 73
  Vers Lyriques, "Ode XII" (to brother-in-law), 122n
Bellay, René du, 14
Belleau, Remy, 9n
Bembo, Pietro, 133, 146, 173, 187, 200
Benivieni, Girolamo, 134, 152, 174
Bennett, Josephine W., 266
Bèze, Théodore de, 5, 129
Bhattacherje, Mohinimohan, 158, 206n
Bible, 7, 157, 206, 208, 218, 219; see New Testament, Old Testament, Scriptures, etc.
Binet, Claude, 15, 232, 234, 235
Blank verse, 31, 32, 33-34, 35, 46, 47, 54, 176
Boccaccio, Giovanni, 240
Book of Common Prayer, 7, 157, 158, 206
Bosch, Hieronymus, 182, 222
Breughel the Elder, Pieter, 222
Briçonnet, Guillaume, Bishop of Meaux, 5, 240
Brigade, The, 16, 45, 47, 71, 188, 199, 238, 247; see Pléiade
Bruno, Giordano, 134, 152

Brunschvicg, Léon, 4
Budé, Guillaume, 40
Burckhardt, Jacob, 3
Burghley, Lord (William Cecil), 116
Bush, Douglas, 8, 209

Callimachus, 14
Calvin, John, 5, 128
Cambridge University, 21, 170, 202, 247
Campion, Thomas, 56, 57-58, 64n
Castiglione, Conte Baldassare, 20, 81n, 134, 146, 164, 173, 187, 200, 270
Catholic Church, 5, 6, 115-116, 118, 134n, 143-144, 169-170, 201, 218, 226n, 227, 261
Catullus, 84, 210
Chamard, Henri, 18, 26, 27, 28, 45, 46, 76, 176, 177, 178, 179, 182, 215, 219, 221
Chancellor, Richard, 19
Chapman, George, 126n
Charles IX, 42, 43, 79
Chaucer, Geoffrey, 8, 207, 252
Cheke, Sir John, 20
Christianity, 4, 6, 7, 14, 133, 143, 158, 160-161, 169; see also Catholic Church, Christian humanism, Protestantism
Cicero, 15
Classical metres, viii, 36-65
Clements, Robert, 172n, 174, 186n
Cohen, Gustave, 24, 107, 196
Colet, John, 5, 6, 7, 8, 240
Collège de Coqueret, 13-18, 45, 134n, 223
Colligny, Cardinal Odet de, 225-226
Copernicus, Nicolaus, 241
Corneille, Pierre, 49
Council of Trent, 7
Counterreformation, 6
Courtly love, 42, 183, 193, 268, 270; see also Provençal tradition
Courville, Thibault de, 42
Cranmer, Thomas 7
Crashaw, Richard, 207

276

INDEX

Daniel, Samuel, 56, 57
Daniello, Bernardino, 176-177
Dante, 5, 7, 142-143, 154n, 162, 168, 182, 193, 195, 204, 208
Dati, Leonardo, 40
Davis, B. E. C., 205
Demosthenes, 15
Descartes, René, 9, 242-243
Desportes, Philippe de, 10, 190, 232, 238
Diotima, 136-137, 140, 158-159, 163, 200, 271; see also Plato, *Symposium*
Dodge, R. E. Neil, 9, 68
Donne, John, 207, 211, 213
Dorat, Jean, 9n, 13-19, 23-24, 57, 77n, 111, 134n, 175, 187, 223
Drant, Thomas, 52-58, 61
Dryden, John, 90
Dudleys, 93, 99
Dyer, Edward, 53, 56, 57, 59

Ecclesiastes, 125
Edinburgh author, 11, 246
E. K. (Edward King?), 78, 99n, 178
Eliot, T. S., 8, 272
Elizabeth, Queen of England, 79, 82, 240
Elizabethan drama, 85-91
Elizabethan poetry, 31, 252; English devotional verse, 207-208
ἐνθουσιασμός, 22, 78
Epicurus, 131
Erasmus, Desiderius, 5
Eros (Cupid), 137, 139, 140, 141, 145
Étaples, Lefèvre d', 240

Ficino, Marsilio, 130, 133, 134n, 146, 173, 187
Fletcher, Jefferson B., 9, 31-32, 78, 152
Fontenelle, Bernard le Bovier de, 243
Foxe, John, 19
François II (Dauphin, later King of France), 46n
Fraunce, Abraham, 55, 56

French sixteenth-century drama, 85-91
French sixteenth-century poetry, 51, 195n
Friedland, Louis S., 9, 39, 94, 97, 114, 117n, 259-260

Galilei, Galileo, 241, 242
Gammer Gurtons Needle, 89
Garnier, Robert, 90
Gascoigne, George, 50n, 58-59, 63
Gorboduc, 89
Grévin, Jacques, 86, 87
Grocyn, William, 240

Harvey, Gabriel, 21, 52-62, 126n, 178
Henri II, France, 73, 74, 104
Henri III, France, 38n, 43n, 78
Henry VIII, England, 5
Herbert, George, 207, 208, 213
Herodotus, 121n
Héroët, Antoine, 173, 187, 267-271
Hesiod, 14, 137
Homer, 14, 15, 97, 98, 107, 137, 245; *Iliad*, 198, 200, 217; *Odyssey*, 52, 222
Hooker, Richard, 4
Horace, 15, 37, 73, 88, 244
hubris, 3, 76, 125; see also outrecuidance, surquedry
Hughes, Merritt, 9
Huguenots, 16; see also Protestantism
Humanism, 4-9, 13, 19-21, 50, 57, 74, 76, 84, 239, 241-247; Christian humanism, 4-9, 170, 238, 240-243

Jansenism, 7
Jodelle, Étienne, 9n, 87, 88, 89, 90
Johnson, Samuel, 8

Keats, John, 117
Keble, John, 208

La Haye, Robert de, 125
Langland, William, 207
Laumonier, Paul, 186, 188, 221, 238

277

INDEX

Lebègue, Raymond, 84, 129, 135, 187, 272
Lee, Sidney, 9
Leo the Jew, 174
Lewis, C. S., 68
Linacre, Thomas, 240
Linguistic theory, 20, 38-66, 130
Luther, Martin, 5
Lycophron, 14
Lydgate, John, 117

McElderry, Bruce Robert, 33
McKerrow, R. B., 53, 55
Machiavelli, Niccolò, 240-245
Marguerite of Navarre, 172, 240
Marlowe, Christopher, 90, 126n, 243
Mary, Queen of England, 249
Mary, Queen of Scots, 19
Massacre of St. Bartholomew's Eve, 44, 110, 130n
Maynadier, Howard, 53
Medici, Catherine de, 190, 272
Medici, Lorenzo de, 169
Menander, 87
Merchant Taylor's School, 19-21
Merrill, R. V., 172, 173, 174, 175, 176, 177, 178, 184, 214, 215, 217, 267-271
Milton, John, 8, 16, 64, 82, 117, 129, 159, 217, 218, 241, 242, 243, 251
Minturno, 63
Mirandola, Pico della, 133-134, 174
Montaigne, Michel de, 4, 9, 20, 23, 231, 239, 241, 247, 248
More, Sir Thomas, 5, 7, 129, 207, 240
Mulcaster, Richard, 19-22, 26, 33, 111
Musaeus, 14
Muses, viii, 22, 66-91, 101-107, 111
Music, 41-42, 43-44, 49-50, 63-64

Nashe, Thomas, 126n
Neale, John Mason, 208
Nerval, Gerard de, 120
New Testament, 6, 205-206, 225, 226; *see also* Bible
Newton, Sir Isaac, 243

nonchalance de salut, 4, 241; *see also* skepticism

Occultism, 130, 221-222, 229-230, 272
Old Testament, 6, 141, 216, 217, 219, 225, 226; *see also* Bible
Orléans, Charles d', 12
Orpheus, 14
Orwen, William R., 264-265
outrecuidance, 49, 76, 125; *see also* hubris, surquedry

Padelford, F. M., 134, 164
Palace Academy, 43n
Papal court, 184, 219, 264
Pascal, Blaise, 4, 8
Paul, St., 6, 7, 162
Paulet, Sir Amias, 56
Peletier, Jacques, 9, 12, 13, 14
Péruse, Jean de la, 9n, 105, 272
Petrarch, Francesco, 10, 25-26, 27, 114, 116, 138n, 139-147
Pindar, 14, 51, 75, 200
Piranesi, Giovanni Battista, 117
Plato, 5, 21, 37, 133, 172, 174, 180, 181, 182, 189, 190, 192, 196, 200, 204, 233, 272; *Apology*, 186n; *Ion*, 22, 77, 175, 186, 187; *Laws*, 133; *Meno*, 182; *Phaedo*, 77, 133, 136; *Phaedrus*, 133, 136, 152, 176, 178, 181, 187; *Republic*, 137, 158, 162, 186n, 187, 191, 192; *Symposium*, 133, 136-138, 140, 141, 158, 163, 164, 187, 271; *Timaeus*, 133, 187; *see also* Diotima
Platonic Academy, Florence, 134n
Platonism, viii, 22, 78, 133-170, 171-200, 267-271
Platonism, Neo-, viii, 133-170, 171-200, 206, 207, 267-271
Pléiade, The, 9n, 10, 14, 16-17, 18, 20-21, 26n, 35n, 36, 37, 38n, 43, 50n, 53, 66-88, 93, 97, 107, 113, 123, 134n, 178, 187, 188, 202, 238, 246, 252, 253, 272; *see also* Brigade
Plotinus, 233
Prometheus, 182

INDEX

Protestantism, 5, 7, 115, 116, 123, 126, 127, 128, 129, 134n, 157, 160, 169, 170, 199, 201-202, 206, 209, 210, 218, 227, 228, 241, 247; *see also* Puritanism, Reformation

Provençal tradition, 183, 268; *see also* courtly love

Puritanism, 19, 110, 202, 210, 223, 243-244, 247; *see also* Protestantism

Puttenham, George, 55, 57

quantitative verse, viii, 36, 38-39, 40, 41, 44, 52-65; *see also* classical metres, *vers mesurés*

Rabelais, François, 9, 13, 84, 124, 170

Racine, Jean Baptiste, 8, 49, 64, 90, 91

Reformation, 3, 5, 6-7, 118, 169, 205, 241, 243; *see also* Protestantism

Renaissance, vii-viii, 3-11, 19-20, 37, 39, 40, 56-57, 66, 95, 97-99, 137, 140-141, 169, 174, 239, 240, 241-246, 253

Renaissance, English, vii-viii, 3-11, 37, 39, 40, 56-57, 66, 95, 97-99, 126, 240

Renaissance, French, vii, 7-11, 37, 39, 40, 69, 97-98, 124, 126, 169, 239, 240

Renaissance, Italian, 7, 15, 37, 39, 40, 126, 169, 240, 241, 244, 245, 247, 252

Renwick, W. L., 9-10, 20, 39, 62-63, 64, 68, 76, 78, 90, 94, 95, 98, 104, 113, 139, 143, 168, 203

Roister Doister, 89

RONSARD, PIERRE DE (1524-1585): character of verse, 17, 20, 41-42, 47-51, 63-64, 111, 128, 130-131, 134-135, 147, 171, 185-186, 188, 192, 224-232; classical influence, 13-18, 23-24, 44, 47, 51, 65, 71, 84, 88, 125, 130, 131, 149, 186-188, 194, 200, 225, 233, 235-236, 244-245, 249;

deafness, 12, 50n, 63, 110, 111, 132; debt to predecessors, 15, 44, 125, 187-188; humanism, 7-8, 9, 50, 76, 241-245; immortality of poetry, 98, 103-110; milieu, 3, 12-13, 15-17, 21, 79, 103-107, 134, 188, 201; moral emphasis, 82, 83, 84, 123, 124, 129, 130, 131, 194; paganism, 14-17, 23-24, 170, 188, 200, 203, 222-227; Platonic influence, 77, 125, 130, 133-135, 149, 150, 171-200, 226-228, 233; relation to Renaissance, viii-ix, 124, 126, 239, 241-243, 249; religious orientation, 9, 12, 16-17, 83, 126-130, 135-136, 170n, 191, 194, 200, 201-271; rivalry with Du Bellay, 51, 224-225, 272-273; temperament, 18, 24, 47, 65, 78, 84, 104, 107-108, 111, 124-132, 210, 221-222, 231-232, 238-239, 242, 246-247, 249; theory of poetry, 38n, 39, 41, 49-50, 111; view of love, 83, 84, 133, 185-198, 247, 249; view of nature, 18, 128, 131-132, 188, 218, 227-230, 242, 249, 250-251; view of society, 127, 187, 190, 200, 238, 272; view of time and mutability, 103-104, 108-109, 124, 127-128, 131, 196, 232-239, 253

WORKS

Amours de Cassandre (1552), 171, 186; Sonnets XLV, 83; XLVI, 83; LXXXI, 188-189; CXV, 83-84; *Amours de Marie* (1555), "Amourette," 84; *Amours de Marie* (1578), Sonnet IV, 131; *see also Pièces Retranchées*

Bocage Royal, *Première partie*, "À Henry III," 38n; "Dialogue entre les Muses deslogées et Ronsard," 66, 69, 78-83; "Au Roy Charles IX," 38n; "Discours à Seigneur de Montmorenci," 191-192; *Seconde partie*, "À Catherine de Medicis," 272

Discours des Misères, 128-129; *Continuation du Discours*, 128-

279

INDEX

129; *Response aux injures et calomnies*, 38n, 128-129; *Discours à Loys des Masures*, 238; *Remonstrance*, 201n

Elegies, 111; "Discours I," 111, 193-194; "Adonis," 195; "Elegie xv" (À de la Haye), 124-126; "Elegie xx" (À Genèvre), 194; "Elegie xxv en forme d'invective," 38n

Épitaphes, "À Luy-mesme," 127n; "Le Tombeau de Marguerite de France," 130

Folastries, 84; see *Gayetez* and *Pièces Retranchées*

Françiade, 49, 50

Gayetez; Livret des Folastries, 84, 103n; "Blasons," 234

Hynnes, 48, 130, 135; *Premier Livre*, "Les Daimons," 221-223; *Second Livre*, "Hercule Chrestien," 223-227; "Hynnes" to the Seasons, 28, 38n, 128; "Hynne de la Mort," 127n, 196; see also *Pièces Retranchées*, and *Pièces Posthumes*

Lettres; Lettre VII, "À M. de Sainte-Marthe," 79n

Odes, 48, 51, 88, 234; *Premier Livre*, "Ode X, À Michel de L'Hospital," 38n, 69, 75-79; "Ode XII, À Bouju," 69; "Ode XVII, À Sa Maistresse," 131; *Second Livre*, "Ode II, À Calliope," 106; "Ode XXVI" (À Du Bellay), 38n; *Troisiesme Livre*, "Ode I, Au Roy Henry II," 104-105; "Ode XII, sur la naissance de François, Dauphin de France," 46n; "Ode XIX, À Charles de Pisseleu," 128; *Quatriesme Livre*, "Ode XXI," 250; "Ode XXXVIII," 132; *Cinquiesme Livre*, "Ode XIX," 107; "Ode XXXII," 109; "XXXIV, Ode Sapphique" and "XXXV, Vers Sapphiques," 47-48, 60; see also *Pièces Retranchées*

Oeuvres en Prose: "Avertissement au Lecteur," 49; "Épistre au Lecteur," 128-129; *Abbregé de l'Art Poétique*, 38n, 49, 50

Pièces Hors Recueils: Elegie (from Théâtre of Jacques Grévin), 38n, 86-88

Pièces Posthumes, 222-223, 232, 234-238; *Derniers Vers* (1586), 232, 234-238; "Stances," 236; "Sonet III," 236; "Sonet V," 234-236; "Sonet VI," 236-237; "Pour Son Tombeau," 236; "À Son Ame," 236; *Oeuvres* (1587), 222, 232; "Encores au Lecteur," 38n; "Elegie II" (À Desportes), 232-233; "Les Hynnes," 222-223; "Hynne XII" (S. Blaise), 233-234; Ronsard's last poem, 234, 237-238; *Oeuvres* (1609), "Caprice," 105-106

Pièces Retranchées: *Odes* (1550), "À Jan Dorat," 23-24; "Au Seigneur de Langues," 189; *Continuation des Amours* (1555), Sonnet on reading Homer, 245; *Nouvelle Continuation* (1556), "Sonet," 107-108; *Hynnes* (1556), "Hynne des Astres," 196n; "Épistre à Charles, Cardinal de Lorraine," 38n; *Sonets pour Helene* (1578), "Sonet," 190

Poëmes, 50, 130, 135; *Premier Livre*, 51; "À Jean de la Péruse," 105n, 272; "La Lyre," 38n; "Le Chat," 227-231; "La Salade," 234, 249-250; "Discours d'un amoureux desesperé" (Scévole), 196-199; "Discours de l'alteration et change," 126-127, 170; *Second Livre*, "Discours Contre Fortune," 38n; "Discours à Jean Morel," 38n

Sonnets pour Helene, 84, 190-193; *Premier Livre*, "Sonnet L," 190-191; *Second Livre*, "Sonnet I," 192-193; "Sonnet XLIII," 108-109; see also *Pièces Retranchées*

Rubel, Veré, 32, 96

Russells, 93

Sackville, Charles, Earl of Dorset, Lord Buckhurst, 117

280

INDEX

Sainte-Beuve, Charles Augustin de, 51-52
Sainte-Marthe, Scévole de, 79n, 196-197, 198, 199
Saulnier, V.-L., 29, 185, 210
Scève, Maurice, 173, 187
Scriptures, 169, 170; *see* Bible
Secundus, Johannes, 125
Shakespeare, William, 90, 243
Shelley, Percy Bysshe, 117, 138
Sidney, Sir Philip, 40, 52-53, 55, 56, 59, 60, 62n, 69n, 86, 89, 90, 93, 101, 175, 186n
Skepticism, 4, 7, 169, 241-242, 244; *see also nonchalance de salut*
Smith, G. Gregory, 59
Socrates, 136-137, 152, 166, 272
Sophocles, 15, 87, 88
SPENSER, EDMUND (c. 1552-1599): character of verse, 20, 30-36, 39, 59-64, 67, 93-98, 111-123, 134-138, 141-142, 144, 153-168, 206-207, 245-246, 252-253, 255-263; classical influence, 21, 65, 71, 77, 99-100, 109-110, 111, 121, 155, 157, 175, 245, 251-252; debt to French poets, vii, 9-11, 20-21, 27-28, 33-34, 36-39, 67-75, 91, 93-94, 98-99, 111-112, 113, 116, 118, 202-203, 251-253, 270; humanism, 9, 19-21, 84, 241-245; immortality of poetry, 98-112; milieu, 18 22, 79, 98, 103-105, 110-111, 153, 201, 264-265; moral emphasis, 10, 82-83, 85, 113-130, 142-143, 150, 167-168, 195, 204-212, 243, 247, 270; paganism, 101, 103, 202-203, 251; Platonic influence, 22, 133-171, 176, 192-193, 199, 203-204; relation to Renaissance, vii-ix, 3, 7, 37-38, 81, 126, 239, 241-243; religious orientation, 8, 19, 30-31, 83, 103-104, 110, 115-116, 118, 135-140, 149, 156-170, 201-271; temperament, 22, 24, 27, 65, 67, 91 92, 104-105, 107-109, 113-123, 130-132, 208, 238, 246-247, 251, 265; theory of poetry, vii, 22, 37, 38n, 63, 66, 91, 130; view of love, 83, 85, 133-147, 151-155, 195, 197-199, 247; view of nature, 193, 218; view of society, 115, 119-120, 121; view of time and mutability, 27, 30, 35-36, 93, 98-101, 106-107, 109-121, 132, 138, 209, 233, 239, 247, 264

WORKS

Amoretti, 10, 134n
Colin Clout, 38n
Comedies, 90
Complaints, 113; *Ruines of Time*, 38n, 92, 93-106, 109, 111-112, 114, 117, 251-252 ("L'Envoy"), 264-265, 270; *Teares of the Muses*, 38n, 66-80, 142, 270; *Visions of the World's Vanitie*, 92, 113-132, *passim*, 205; *Visions of Petrarch and Du Bellay*, 25, 28, 35
  Daphnaïda, 134n, 143n
  "The English Poete," 37, 90
  Epithalamion, 85, 145-146, 151, 195, 209, 247
  Faerie Queene, 10, 22, 30, 36, 38n, 85, 117, 134, 138, 144, 149, 154, 193, 195, 208-209, 221, 233, 247, 272
  Fowre Hymnes, 7, 38n, 133-138, 145, 158, 161, 167-169, 173, 195, 199, 221, 228, 231, 266; *Hymne in Honour of Love*, 136, 138-146, 150, 152, 266, 270; *Hymne in Honour of Beautie*, 136, 138, 139, 140, 146-155, 161, 165, 266, 270; *Hymne of Heavenly Love*, 135-136, 138 319, 145-146, 151, 156-167, 177n, 183, 202-208, 211, 266; *Hymne of Heavenly Beautie*, 136, 138, 140, 147-148, 160-168, 176, 181, 266
  Mutabilitie Cantos, 233
  Shepheardes Calender, 22, 24, 31-33, 37, 38n, 54n, 57, 99n
  Spenser-Harvey Correspondence, 44, 52, 53, 54, 59, 60, 61

281

INDEX

Theatre (Van der Noot), viii, 20, 25-36, 54, 209, 255-263
Speroni, Sperone, 45
Spingarn, Joel Elias, 40
Stanyhurst, Richard, 55
Stein, Harold, 31-32, 66-67
Surgères, Hélène, 84, 108-109, 190-193
surquedry, 3, 22, 76, 125; see also *hubris*, *outrecuidance*
Swift, Jonathan, 8

Taille, Jacques de la, 41, 43
Tasso, Torquato, 252
Taylor, A. E., 136-137
Tolomei, Claudio, 40
Tottel's Miscellany, 33
The Tragedie of Tancred and Gismund, 89
Tyard, Pontus de, 9, 173-182

Van der Noot (Noodt), 25, 26, 29, 54, 118, 123, 210, 255, 263
Variorum Edition of Spenser, 69, 76, 97, 133, 140, 165
Vaughan, Henry, 207
Venus, 139, 147, 149, 155, 163, 164, 165
Vernacular, 20-21, 22, 36, 37, 39, 45, 46, 52, 56, 61, 63, 64, 65, 252
vers mesurés, viii, 38-65; see also classical metres; quantitative verse
Viglione, Francesco, 115-119, 120
Villey, Pierre, 247
Virgil, 5, 15, 55, 118, 182, 183, 184, 217

Watkins, W. B. C., 138
Watson, Master (later Bishop), 52, 56
Webbe, William, 55, 56, 57
Winstanley, Lilian, 148, 150, 152, 153, 243